BETWEEN THE STATE AND THE EUCHARIST

Between the State and the Eucharist

Free Church Theology in Conversation with William T. Cavanaugh

edited by
JOEL HALLDORF *and*
FREDRIK WENELL

With a Foreword by Stanley Hauerwas

☙PICKWICK Publications • Eugene, Oregon

BETWEEN THE STATE AND THE EUCHARIST
Free Church Theology in Conversation with William T. Cavanaugh

Copyright © 2014 Wipf and Stock Publishers. All rights reserved. Except for brief quotations in critical publications or reviews, no part of this book may be reproduced in any manner without prior written permission from the publisher. Write: Permissions, Wipf and Stock Publishers, 199 W. 8th Ave., Suite 3, Eugene, OR 97401.

Pickwick Publications
An Imprint of Wipf and Stock Publishers
199 W. 8th Ave., Suite 3
Eugene, OR 97401

www.wipfandstock.com

ISBN 13: 978-1-62564-111-3

Cataloguing-in-Publication data:

Between the state and the eucharist : free church theology in conversation with William T. Cavanaugh / edited by Joel Halldorf and Fredrik Wenell; with a foreword by Stanley Hauerwas.

xiv + 184 pp. ; 23 cm. Includes bibliographical references.

ISBN 13: 978-1-62564-111-3

1. Church and state—Sweden. 2. Christianity and politics. 3. Church and the world. 4. Cavanaugh, William T. I. Halldorf, Joel. II. Wenell, Fredrik. III. Hauerwas, Stanley, 1940–. IV. Title.

BR115.W6 B48 2014

Manufactured in the U.S.A.   07/07/2014

Contents

List of Illustrations   vii
Contributors   ix
Foreword—Stanley Hauerwas   xi

Introduction—*Joel Halldorf and Fredrik Wenell*   1

Part One—Modern Discipline: The Free Churches in the Disciplinary Society

1. Statist Individualism: The Swedish Theory of Love and Its Lutheran Imprint—*Lars Trägårdh*   13

2. Scattered Conversion? Youth, Free Church, and the Swedish Welfare State—*Fredrik Wenell*   39

3. The Loss of Theological Visions: Free Church Ecclesiologies in Sweden from the Nineteenth Century to the Present —*Sune Fahlgren*   55

4. Evangelicals, Practices, and the Univocity of Being: Avoiding the Pitfall of Gnosticism —*Joel Halldorf*   68

Part Two—Catholicity: Being a Free Church in Late Modernity

5. The Real Thing? Practicing a Spirituality of Everyday Life— *Tone Stangeland Kaufman*   85

6. The Constantinianism of the Free Church Tradition and the Promise of a New Asceticism—*Patrik Hagman*   102

Contents

    7   Thinking With: The Need for Tradition in Free Church Theology—*Andreas Nordlander*   114

Part Three—Lutheran Responses

    8   We Are All Moderns: Swedish Free Church and Folk Church Ecclesiologies as Kindred Spirits —*Jan Eckerdal*   129

    9   What's So Great about Being Different? A Folk Church Response to Exceptionalism—*Jonas Ideström*   140

Part Four—"Love Your Neighbor"

    10   Eucharistic Identity in Modernity
           William T. Cavanaugh   155

           Bibliography   173

Illustrations

Figure 1: World Values Survey (WVS), Fourth Wave (1991–2001) 23

Figure 2: Generalized Trust—An International Comparison 26

Figure 3: Power Relations in the Modern Welfare State 29

Figure 4: Embedded and Intentional Spiritual Practices as Mutually Dependent Upon and Enriching Each Other 89

Figure 5: Four Approaches to Intentional Spiritual Practices 90

Contributors

WILLIAM T. CAVANAUGH, Professor of Catholic Studies at DePaul University, Chicago. His publications include *Torture and Eucharist* and *The Myth of Religious Violence*.

JAN ECKERDAL, PhD in Systematic Theology at Uppsala University. His publications include *Folkkyrkans kropp*.

SUNE FAHLGREN, Associate Professor of Practical Theology at the Stockholm School of Theology. His publications include *Predikantskap och församling* and *Shalom Inshallah*.

PATRIK HAGMAN, PhD in Systematic Theology at Åbo Academy. His publications include *Understanding Asceticism* and *Efter folkkyrkan*.

JOEL HALLDORF, Associate Professor of Historical Theology at the Stockholm School of Theology. His publications include *"Av denna världen?"* and "Lewi Pethrus and the Creation of a Christian Counterculture."

STANLEY HAUERWAS, Gilbert T. Rowe Professor Emeritus of Divinity and Law, Duke Divinity School.

JONAS IDESTRÖM, PhD in Ecclesioloy at Uppsala University and researcher at the Church of Sweden. His publications include *Lokal kyrklig identitet* and *For the Sake of the World*.

ANDREAS NORDLANDER, Associate Professor of Systematic Theology at Gothenburg University. His publications include *Figuring Flesh in Creation*.

TONE STANGELAND KAUFMAN, Associate Professor of Practical Theology at MF Norwegian School of Theology. Her publications include *A New Old Spirituality?*

Contributors

LARS TRÄGÅRDH, Professor of History at Ersta Sköndal University College, Stockholm. His publications include *State and Civil Society in Northern Europe*, "Pippi Longstocking: The Autonomous Child and the Moral Logic of the Swedish Welfare State," and "Rethinking the Nordic Welfare State through a Neo-Hegelian Theory of State and Civil Society."

FREDRIK WENELL, PhD candidate in Systematic Theology at Uppsala University and lecturer at the Örebro School of Theology. His publications include "Religion som politisk resurs."

Foreword

What am I doing writing a Foreword to a book about challenges facing the church in Sweden? I have been to Sweden but it was some years ago. I have been fortunate to be befriended by Arne Rasmusson and Joel Halldorf, who have tried to help me understand the role of Christianity in Sweden. They have been wonderful teachers, but I am acutely aware of how little I understand about what it means to be Swedish, or, even more complex, what it means to be a Christian in Sweden. So what can I possibly say in this "Foreword" that would be useful?

I can only dare to write because I have read this extremely interesting book. I have learned much about how to understand the Swedish welfare state as well as how that state is an expression of Lutheranism. That, of course, seems counterintuitive given the Lutheran strong distinction between the work of the state and the work of the church. But I have also learned that in many ways the challenges facing Christians in Sweden are not that different than the challenges facing Christians in what can in general be described as modernity.

I confess one of the reasons I enjoyed reading this book is that some of the essays confirmed an impression, or perhaps better put a judgment, I made after my visit to Sweden. My trip to Sweden was organized by Arne Rasmusson which meant I was primarily interacting with those in the Free Church tradition. I did, however, give lectures at Lund and Uppsala Universities so I also had some interaction with Lutheran academic theologians. I confess I found my exchanges in the universities less interesting than the discussions I had with those in the Free Church tradition. I came to the judgment that when theology has been made safe by the state you cannot expect theologians to take great intellectual risks. But that was not the primary impression with which I came away.

I had come to Sweden just prior to the disestablishment of the Lutheran Church by the state. I was told often that this would be a deep challenge to the Lutheran Church in Sweden. I have no reason to doubt that may well be the case, but I thought the disestablishment of the Lutheran Church would present a deeper and more lasting challenge to the Free Church. I thought that might be the case because the Free Church had positioned itself primarily as "not Lutheran." What do you do when you lose the primary identifying marker that makes you who you have been?

Reading the essays in this book, however, has helped me see that while that impression may not have been wholly wrong it was too simple. For many of these essays help me understand that the challenge is not the Lutheran Church itself, but the Swedish welfare state. The latter turns out to be the expression of a Lutheranism that makes difficult any strong distinction between church and state. It seems outside the welfare system in Sweden there is no salvation. Accordingly the Free churches of Sweden, at least as these essays suggest, are manifestations of the very modernity they may well think they are reacting against. Ironically, spontaneous prayer turns out to be a practice that insures the Free churches will lack the resources to understand, much less resist, the forces that threaten their life.

If that is right then I understand why it is not entirely inappropriate for me to write this "Foreword." For it turns out this is not a book only relevant to the Swedish context, but rather this is a case study of particular developments in Sweden that has implications for how modernity is to be negotiated in other contexts. That is why I think it was such an important decision to organize the book as a discussion with Bill Cavanaugh's work. I cannot resist, however, observing that it took someone completely outside the Swedish context to get the challenge right. By "outside" I do not mean that Cavanaugh is an American, but rather the very way he understands the political character of the Eucharist clearly reflects his Catholicism.

Cavanaugh's contention that the modernity that has shaped the Swedish welfare state, as well as the Lutheran and Free Church traditions in Sweden, is itself an outgrowth of Christendom I take to be the crucial insight that makes this such an interesting book. He quite rightly refuses to make the "state" "the enemy" because to so describe the state risks making the state a far too abstract entity. Rather in light of Cavanaugh's account of the development of the modern state we are confronted with an uncomfortable realization: Christians have met the enemy and it is us. That is why the challenge before the church, Lutheran or Free, is so difficult to locate and, consequently, why it is difficult to know how best to respond. Too often, as many of these essays make clear, the very strategies used to try and recover the mission of the church turn out to be carriers of the illness that made us sick in the first place.

I am honored to have been asked to write this "Foreword" to a book that I believe should be read not only by Swedes but by anyone who wants to understand what it means to be church in our age. We have much to learn from the challenge confronting the churches of Sweden. Christians, Swedish and non-Swedish, need all the help we can get if we are to reclaim the church from "statist individualism." This book is one of the ways such help comes.

Stanley Hauerwas
Gilbert T. Rowe Professor Emeritus of Divinity and Law,
Duke Divinity School

Introduction

Joel Halldorf and Fredrik Wenell

Freedom is a cherished ideal in Western modernity, particularly the freedom to express one's supposedly unique personality. We should all listen to that inner voice, take the road less travelled, and create the inimitable life we wish to lead. This imperative cannot be hindered by taboos or regulations; no one should tell anyone else what to do. Except, of course, that they should "follow their heart."

But despite this praise of freedom and diversity, there is an eerie feeling that things are becoming more and more the same. Cultures, subcultures, languages, and even religions seem to be merging. Sociologists tell us that teenagers today believe more or less the same things, whether they are evangelicals, Buddhists, or Mormons.[1] And any young urban westerner who believes herself to have a unique taste should read Christian Lander's *Stuff White People Like* for a reality check. It turns out that microbrews and authentic sushi are not signifiers of a unique and developed taste, but rather shared cultural markers.

Modernity, it seems, professes freedom and diversity, but practices homogenization.

This is in some sense the story of this book. It is a book about how the Free churches in Sweden failed in their attempt to uphold unique identities, separated from the surrounding "world." They made an admirable effort, but lacked adequate resources and were, in the long run, unable to withstand the pressure from the modern nation-state. In the end they succumbed to what Charles Taylor has called the disciplinary society, and thus lost their distinctiveness.

---

1. Smith and Lundquist Denton, *Soul Searching*.

The story involves global phenomena such as modernity, the modern nation-state, the Free Church tradition, and Evangelicalism. The stage, however, is limited to the Free churches in Sweden and their struggle in and sometimes against the nation-state and its national church—the Church of Sweden. Aspects of this study might be trying for non-Scandinavians: to read quotes from unknown bishops, hear arguments from provincial evangelical leaders, or follow a discourse analysis of an obscure evangelical magazine. But we are convinced that this is how global phenomena must be understood. Not in the abstract, but through concrete empirical material. And not only through the American experience, which in many ways differs from the experience in Europe and other parts of the world. Sweden's story differs as well. Ours is a country of social engineering, and the goal of the twentieth century was to modernize. This turned Sweden, according to some studies and estimates, into the most modern country in the world—a state-facilitated hypermodernity. We believe that the story of the Swedish Free churches and their struggles with modernity and the state helps us understand the bigger picture—not despite but thanks to this particularity.

THE ARGUMENT OF THE BOOK

This is an anthology held together by a person and an argument. The former is the theologian William T. Cavanaugh, whose work we engage, draw upon and sometimes challenge, as we try to understand the Swedish experience of modernity. The argument is the one outlined above: that the Swedish Free churches have been "tamed" by modernity and the nation-state with its welfare projects, and so lost their original distinctiveness. The book consists of four parts. It begins by looking at the Swedish welfare state and its disciplinary tendencies, and then goes on to show how this has affected the Free churches. The point made is that their vulnerability to modern discipline has much to do with a lack of concrete ecclesial practices. The second part is more constructive, suggesting practices that might revitalize the Free churches. This is followed first by responses from two Lutheran ministers in the Church of Sweden and finally by William Cavanaugh.

The bulk of the book is written by theologians from the Free Church tradition, but it begins and ends with contributions from sympathetic outsiders. First, historian Lars Trägårdh presents a reading of the Swedish welfare state as ultimately an individualistic project. Contrary to common perception it does not reflects a Marxist dream of collectivization. Rather it is a social contract designed to set people free from local ties and dependencies by offering them the strong state as sole protector and provider. While supporting Cavanaugh's reading of the modern state as an entity that severs local ties and weakens organic communities, Trägårdh challenges his understanding that this results in a cold and impersonal society. The fact that modern individualistic societies demonstrate a broader social trust than traditional religious and family-oriented cultures is, he claims, a clear sign of the opposite. Since theological narratives must be rooted in concrete historical and social realities, anyone agreeing with Cavanaugh's reading of Western modernity must pay attention when Trägårdh claims that he is "empirically speaking on shaky ground." Finally, Trägårdh accuses Cavanaugh of telling a story that is too American.

Theologian Fredrik Wenell continues the story and ties his analysis of the fate of the Swedish Free Church tradition to Trägårdh's concept of the Swedish "statist individualism," that is an individualism guaranteed by the strong state. He finds among the Free churches an example of tension between a Baptist and a revivalist ecclesiology. In the former, conversion incorporates the individual into a covenantal relationship, while in the latter conversion is an individual experience resulting in a "personal relationship with Jesus." The revivalist discourse became dominant, Wenell argues, because it was more adjustable to the individualizing tendencies of the Swedish welfare state.

This image of a Free Church tradition with an increasingly weaker identity is supported by ecclesiologist Sune Fahlgren. After painting the picture of a rich ecclesiological landscape in the nineteenth century, where each Free Church denomination was characterized by its own distinct ecclesiology, he notes that today this variety is replaced by uniformity. The Swedish Free churches are unaware of their ecclesiological heritage and suffering from a "spiritual dementia." The consequence, he argues, is an unintended "McDonaldization" of the Free Church tradition, where all denominations now serve more or less the same spiritual dish. He ends his article with a call for a return to embodied visions of the church, and emphasizes that these visions must be rooted in concrete ecclesial practices in order to be sustainable.

Church historian Joel Halldorf continues along these lines by focusing particularly on the theological neglect of ecclesial practices within the broader Evangelical movement to which the Swedish Free churches belong. He claims that the tendency to neglect practices within this tradition reflects ideals of simplicity and spontaneity, ideals that are rooted in a univocal understanding of being. According to this metaphysical understanding there is only one kind of being, which God and creation are thought to share. This means that God can no longer be thought of as present in and through created matter. Instead, God and created matter become competitors, which renders materiality and set practices problematic within the Evangelical movement, since it is thought to obstruct the divine. But neglecting a deeply formative element such as practices leads to cultural adaptability and, in the long run, inner secularization.

Here ends the first part of the book, the conclusion of which is that contrary to their ideals, the Free churches have conformed to the surrounding culture and done so largely due to their neglect of practices—in particular the lack of theological reflection over existing practices. The book's second part has a more constructive approach, suggesting ways in which the Free Church tradition can develop this neglected aspect of its identity. Catholicity is the central theme of this part: namely the suggestion that the Free churches develop their identities in dialogue with the great Christian tradition.

Norwegian theologian Tone Stangeland Kaufman begins by suggesting that discovering and appreciating the practices already in place might be a good starting point for this. In her study of the spirituality of priests in the Church of Norway, she noted a tendency to neglect simple practices such as table grace and evening prayer with children. In particular, priests from an evangelical background had difficulties appreciating these everyday habits. But it is, as Stangeland Kaufman suggests drawing on Dorothy C. Bass, our everyday practices that, woven together, form a way of life.

Following this is a chapter by Finnish theologian Patrik Hagman, who investigates the withering away of clear, bodily markers that set the members of the Free churches apart from the surrounding society. He argues that the lack of distinction is indicative of a new kind of Constantiniansm where Christians adapt to society—albeit not so much to the state, but to the market and commercial forces. Hagman then points to the necessity of practices to embody convictions. Here the asceticism of the early church is identified as a source of inspiration. As with Stangeland Kaufman, Hagman attempts to identify practices tied to "ordinary life" (for example the way we handle our smart phones) rather than highly intentional practices more suitable to a spiritual elite.

Joel Halldorf and Fredrik Wenell—*Introduction*

This second part ends with a chapter by philosopher and theologian Andreas Nordlander, who contributes with a sort metareflection on what this Free Church turn towards the practices of the great Christian tradition means. In dialogue with Alasdair MacIntyre, Nordlander probes the meaning of "thinking with" a tradition, of which he argues that Cavanaugh's work can be read as an example of. Nordlander's conclusion is that in the case of the Free Church tradition, "thinking with" must begin with both a recognition of being constituted by a wider and deeper history and an appreciation of the creative task facing Free Church theologians as they seek their own voice within that tradition.

The third part of the book is titled "Lutheran responses" and consists of two contributions by theologians and minsters in the Church of Sweden. These two texts also stand in an interesting intertextual relation to each other. Jan Eckerdal shows that while the Free Church and Folk Church ecclesiologies have understood themselves as opposites, they both spring from a shared demand for univocity. Either the church is a complete embodiment of the pure church (Free Church ecclesiology), or this is impossible and the church is not at all an embodiment (Folk Church ecclesiology). Against this Eckerdal argues for a sacramental understanding of the church as analogically the body of Christ, with the capacity to contain both similarities and differences in relationship to Christ.

Jonas Ideström instead points to resources within the Folk Church tradition in his contribution, "What's so Great about Being Different: A Folk Church Response to Exceptionalism." In an important and thought-provoking challenge to some of the ideals that carry this book, Ideström sees the accentuation of difference and uniqueness as a reflection of modern market thinking. In his empirical study of a local Church of Sweden congregation, he notes that the Folk Church identity is expressed through solidarity with the place and an ongoing sharing of a common life with the largely secular neighborhood. In this ecclesial self-understanding through commonality rather than difference he sees the potential of a true witness that is exceptional.

The last word goes to William T. Cavanaugh, who picks up a line from a Danish politician claiming that the idea of the welfare state is "the secularized idea of 'love your neighbor' in Christianity." Cavanaugh agrees, but is not convinced that this is a positive development. Still, Christians must recognize that the modern state is not something that "they" did to "us." Instead he argues that this part of modernity (too) has its roots in Christianity. Building on the works of Henri de Lubac, Charles Taylor and Ivan Illich he points to the increasingly spiritualized and individualized understanding of the Eucharist from the Middle Ages and onwards as something that changes the understanding of Christian communal life. The nation-state ties the individual to a new collective, but now in such a way as to ensure individualism. With the help of Trägårdh and his concept of statist individualism, Cavanaugh shows how this is particularly true in regard to the Swedish welfare state. Here love is institutionalized as disembodied governmental welfare, which can then rightly be characterized as a secularized version of "love your neighbor." And while Christians must always recognize feeding the hungry as a good, Cavanaugh asks us to also remember that programs of welfare are in fact a lesser good than that personal, embodied care to which Christ calls us. Life in the modern state promises us individual independence and an impersonal welfare bureaucracy. The Christian hope is something else: a Christian sociality that is an enactment of the Body of Christ here and now.

BRIEF BACKGROUND AND BASIC DEFINITIONS

The articles in this book provide the necessary background information for their analysis, but a brief sketch of Swedish religious history might provide a helpful overview for the unfamiliar reader.[2] The history of church and state in Sweden is largely a story of harmony and cooperation, with the Free churches appearing rather late on the scene. The Free churches in Sweden are those Protestant churches that are not a branch of the state. The freedom referenced is in other words first and foremost freedom from the state.[3] There are, to summarize, two main branches of the Free Church movement: One developed from revivalist movements within the Church of Sweden (Mission Covenant), and the other consisted of denominations that immigrated to Sweden during the nineteenth and twentieth centuries (Baptism, Methodism, etc.). Internationally, the concept "Believers' Church" is sometimes used for this tradition, based on their understanding of the church as a community in which all members profess a personal faith in Christ. The designation "non-creedal church" is another synonym.[4] Free churches

---

2. For a fuller account, see Ryman, *Nordic Folk Churches*.

3. Compare with Ellis, *Gathering*, 25–30.

4. The terms "Dissenter" and "Nonconformist" are dated and perhaps irrelevant. They were negative concepts, used in England for those who struggled for a "free church in a free state."

generally reject creeds as definitive statements of faith, even while agreeing with some creeds' substance. The designation "evangelical" includes a wider circle of churches than the Free churches, and has also influenced revival movements that remained within the Lutheran state church. But Evangelicalism has influenced most of the Free churches in Sweden, and some of the articles focus their analysis on Evangelicalism.

The Reformation was inaugurated in Sweden during the early sixteenth century, under the reign of Gustav Vasa. He became king in 1523 after defeating the Danish king Kristian II, who had been crowned king of Sweden by the archbishop Gustav Trolle. In the wake of this war, the new king faced two problems: he was in debt to the German merchants who had financed his army, and he had difficulties consolidating his power due to the remaining Danish loyalties of the archbishop. Moving into the Lutheran fold allowed him to solve both dilemmas. He could then confiscate the riches of churches and monasteries, and control the ecclesial hierarchy without interference from Rome. This political dimension gave the Reformation initial momentum and royal support, and over the course of the sixteenth century Sweden continued to move in a Lutheran direction theologically as well as liturgically. This process was confirmed by the Uppsala Synod of 1593, where Lutheranism, in the interpretation of the Augsburg Confession, was adopted as the only accepted confession in the country.[5]

During the seventeenth century, much effort was put into consolidating this religious unity on the grassroots level. The church and the royal state worked together to turn Sweden into a homogenous Lutheran country. Catholicism and Calvinism were equally forbidden, and when it appeared in the eighteenth century Pietism met the same fate. In 1726 the Conventicle ordinance forbade religious gatherings without the attendance of a Lutheran priest in an effort to quell Pietism and similar religious movements. The law was in place until 1858, when a growing religious pluralism and political liberalism made it impossible to uphold. The state, however, remained Lutheran and other churches were judicially named "foreign confessors." The rise of nationalism transformed the Church of Sweden from merely state church in a judicial sense, to the Church of the nation in an ideological sense as well.[6]

In the nineteenth century revival movements from within and without challenged the Church of Sweden. In the 1840s the so-called new

5. For a survey in English, see Grell, *Scandinavian Reformation*.
6. See Blückert, *The Church as Nation*.

evangelical revival emerged from the older Pietism, which had remained an undercurrent within the Church of Sweden. The initial ambition was reform from within, but in 1878 the movement split and the separatists left the Church of Sweden to form the Mission Covenant. Also in the 1840s, the first Free church appeared in Sweden when F. O. Nilsson introduced believer's baptism, and small congregations of Baptists were formed. The movement was perceived as a threat to religious unity and political stability, and the pioneers were arrested and ostracized.

Religious diversity continued to increase during the century, stimulated by a growing influence from the U.S. During the nineteenth century over a million Swedes immigrated to North America resulting in a strong cultural influx from America back to Sweden.[7] By the end of the nineteenth century the Baptists and the Mission Covenant were accompanied by among other denominations: Methodism, Adventism, the Salvation Army, and the Holiness Covenant. Shortly after the outburst of the Azusa Street Revival in 1906, the Pentecostal movement emerged in Sweden. This increased pluralism was however accompanied by a strong decline in church attendance, something that began already in the nineteenth century. The number of churches increased while the total of churchgoers fell dramatically. The state church system did ensure that most Swedes remained members of the Church of Sweden, even though many only went to church for baptisms, weddings, and funerals.

Sweden modernized relatively late. Important political reforms were launched around 1860, including the establishment of religious freedom. Industrialization and urbanization came with some force in the 1880s, but Sweden remained a predominantly rural and agrarian country for many decades still. After the democratic reforms in the 1920s, the Social Democrats emerged as the leading political party. They adopted the concept *"Folkhemmet"* ("the people's home") as an image of a nation characterized by unity, consensus, and equality. The ambitious welfare projects were made possible by massive economic growth during the 1950s and 60s, a result of the fact that Sweden was spared the grievances of World War II and had intact infrastructure and industries when most of Europe needed to be rebuilt.

Folkhemmet can be seen as a continuation of the homogenizing ambitions that have characterized the Swedish state since the Reformation. After some deliberation, the Social Democratic party decided to use the Church

---

7. See Gustafson, *Moody and the Swedes* for an example of this strong relationship in religious matters.

of Sweden as a tool in this process.⁸ The Church of Sweden was not only a state church in judicial terms, but also the church of the Swedish nation-state. Being a Swedish citizen meant belonging to the Church of Sweden, something the ostracizing of the religiously deviant during the years of the Conventicle ordinance shows. The Church of Sweden was an important ingredient in the national identity as the idea of the nation developed in the Post-Reformation era.⁹ Full religious freedom was established only in 1952, but even then the state regulated the organizational shape of the churches in Sweden.¹⁰ The Church of Sweden and the state did not go separate ways until the year 2000, and even after that the ties have remained strong both ideologically and judicially.

The Free churches were always the outsiders. They were part of modernity, but existed in the periphery of the modern Swedish nation-state and thus society. They challenged the laws, and when these were changed they challenged—and were challenged by—the homogenous identity of the Swedish nation-state project. Compared to other countries in Europe, including Scandinavia, the Swedish Free churches were relatively strong, but even counted together they were never more than five percent of the population, that is they were without question religious minorities. Today, with increased immigration and the establishment of Oriental, Orthodox, and neo-Pentecostal churches, the picture is more complex. From this perspective, the history of the Free churches in Sweden can serve as a historical case study of the country's ability to harbinger religious plurality.

WILLIAM T. CAVANAUGH AND SWEDEN

This book springs from a conference where William Cavanaugh was invited to join a number of Scandinavian theologians in reflecting on questions regarding church and modernity with the Swedish Free Church movement in particular focus. This was not the first time that Cavanaugh was invited to help Swedish theologians think about the identity of the church—*For the Sake of the World* (ed. Jonas Ideström) represents a similar project. His work has also been a source of inspiration for dissertations in various theological fields.¹¹ The appreciation of the scholarly work of Cavanaugh in

---

8. See Claesson, *Folkhemmets kyrka*.
9. Blückert, *The Church as Nation*.
10. For more on this, see Fahlgren in this volume.
11. See for example Ideström, *Lokal kyrklig identitet*; Fahlgren, *Predikantskap och församling*; Eckerdal, *Folkkyrkans kropp*.

Sweden is very much due to the ecclesiological method that he has developed, the focus of which is the concrete church. With analytical concepts such as theopolitical, practices, and embodiment he gives attention to the church as a social and historical reality that can be studied in relation to, for instance, the politics of the nation-state, the market, or globalization. As he himself has shown through his studies of the church in various contexts—Latin America, Europe, the U.S.—it is a method that can travel. It has, it seems, the ability to render interesting results and insights wherever it is implemented. This is surely true for Sweden. As a native you are likely to become blind to the particulars of your own context. With Cavanaugh's help, many of us have been made aware of the specific politics of the Swedish nation-state, as well as the theopolitics of the Free churches.

ACKNOWLEDGMENTS

Finally we would like to thank some people and institutions without which the volume would not have been possible. First C. E. Wikströms Foundation, which gave the crucial financial support for the conference. Then the castle Bjärka-Säby, which provided the space and gave us the opportunity to not only eat and talk, but also pray together. Finally the two Free Church seminars, Stockholm School of Theology and Örebro School of Theology, who hosted the event.

For the production of the book, we are grateful for the support by the generous people at Wipf and Stock who guided us through the process. Our native-language editors Jenny Arnerlöf and David Michael rescued us from many errors and helped us clarify our thoughts when these were obscure. A word of thanks should also go out to that army of people who at various stages have read different versions of the texts in the book—friends, colleagues, family members—the anonymous congregation that make scholarly work possible.

Part One

Modern Discipline

*The Free Churches in
the Disciplinary Society*

1

Statist Individualism

The Swedish Theory of Love and its Lutheran Imprint

Lars Trägårdh

To analyze the role of religion in the Nordic countries is not an easy matter. While these countries are among the most secularized in the world, this does not mean that the Lutheran legacy is without impact today, albeit in a secularized form, even if the church as a social institution is of less importance than in previous years. Thus it is often claimed that the Lutheran emphasis on a positive and dominant role of the state, on the one hand, and universal literacy on the other, have had long-term effects on social structure and political culture, fostering social trust, confidence in institutions, and an emphasis on the individual. Secular moral values associated with the modern welfare state, such as a stress on individual autonomy, equality, and social solidarity, are quite consistent with Lutheran dogma and morality. However, it is not always easy to separate out the influence of Lutheranism from either its secular successor ideologies, including Social Democracy, or other social and political legacies, such as early adoption of rule of law, the uniquely strong position of the peasantry, or a peculiar marriage pattern and family culture. Indeed, it may well be that these all interact and reinforce a social contract and a moral logic that favors social equality, individual autonomy, social trust, rule of law and a positive view of the state.

In this essay I will in a provisional manner engage these questions in the following way. I will begin by addressing William Cavanaugh's arresting analysis of the common good and the nation-state. Here I pay particular attention to his critique of the modern nation-state and the related trend towards individualization and, conversely, what he describes as the "atrophying" of the intermediate associations of civil society, not least the churches and "a truer Christian sociality that can be located in the Eucharist as the Christian social practice par excellence."[1] Next I will consider the Swedish social contract and the moral logic that underpins it, again by thinking through this logic theoretically in terms of the dynamic interplay between state, individual, family, and civil society. Finally, I will speculate on the historical roots of this social contract, paying particular attention to the possible influence of Lutheran theology and practice. I will argue that while the nation-state, and the individualism that appears to go with it, may well be conceived as antithetical to Catholic doctrine and practice, it looks quite different if we choose to view the interplay between modernization and religion through the lens of Lutheranism, especially in its Nordic instantiation. In this section I will also engage, head-on, the deeper issues concerning state and civil society—individual freedom and community—which Cavanaugh brings out. While the radical individualism of modern Sweden—and the assertive state that serves as the incubator for such individual autonomy—is sure to scandalize and threaten those for whom family values and the primacy of intermediate and "organic" community is dear, it is also clear that whatever the losses that one might want to lament, there are also gains from the point of view of the individual, not least for those who used to be locked up in unequal power-relations within patriarchal and hierarchical communal institutions.

Finally, in Sweden itself this tension between statist individualism and communitarianism can be located within the Christian community at large, pitting the legacy of the statist and individualist Lutheran state church against the ethos and practices of the "Free churches" with their far more communitarian thrust. Here, one might say, two freedom claims stand against one another. I will return briefly to this dimension, but a deeper analysis of this important matter deserves its own discussion which is outside the scope of this essay. Still, let me simply note that it is in this

---

1. Cavanaugh in this volume, 156.

context that a far more serious problem with the Swedish social contract emerges: its historical suspicion of religious diversity and the lack of a constitutionally embedded embrace of pluralism that allows for deep difference, including religious beliefs and practices, within civil society.

CAVANAUGH'S PROBLEM

In the essay "Killing for the Telephone Company: Why the Nation-state Is Not the Keeper of the Common Good," Cavanaugh has called attention to the need to more thoroughly analyze the origins and nature of the state and in particular to problematize the notion that it is the ultimate protector of the common good and that as such it deserves a degree of deference on the part of the churches, even the Catholic Church. Cavanaugh is primarily concerned with the Catholic Church and his essay is in general focused on the US, limitations that I will attempt to address by bringing in the rather different case of Sweden, a historically Lutheran state that has a very different tradition with respect to the view of the state and the role of civil society.[2]

Cavanaugh argues, with Tilly and others, that the state is of relatively recent origin and, secondly, that the chief agent of change that brought about its triumph against competing forms of political structures, such as more loosely organized secular or theocratic federations, trading networks, or feudal structures, was war and the centralized monarchical states' "superior ability to extract resources from the local population."[3] Here Cavanaugh's target is those political philosophers like Hobbes, Locke and Rousseau who in different ways argue that the modern state should be thought of as a social contract, suggesting a degree of voluntary approval on the part of the citizens, who give up their natural sovereignty in order to benefit from the protection of the state, viewed here as the guarantor of order, the freedom of the individual, and the keeper of the common good.

However, while the debunking of the notion of the state as the keeper of the common good is crucial to Cavanaugh's analysis, his main theme is the effect that the creation of the modern state has on society. Indeed, he stresses that "society," in the modern sense, is created by the state "by replacing the complex overlapping loyalties of medieval *societates* with one society, bounded by borders and ruled by one sovereign to whom allegiance

2. Cavanaugh, "Killing for the Telephone Company."
3. Ibid., 248.

is owed in a way that trumps all other allegiances."[4] This move from what he calls "complex space" to "simple space" entails a shift from a social order characterized by a multiplicity of communities to one rooted in a "duality of individual and state."[5]

How one is to normatively assess this historical shift is a major and recurrent concern of political philosophers. At the risk of greatly simplifying the matter, one can distinguish between those of a more liberal bent for whom this development, by and large, is good news and those for whom this new order is cause for great alarm.

Thus, when a thinker like John Locke imagines a political space with two poles—state and individual—he sees a world in which individual freedom and property rights can be secured to the great advantage of all. Similarly, if Locke can be thought of as the father of a modern *political* liberalism that over time will translate into a liberal democratic system based on the idea of one person, one vote, Adam Smith can be thought of as his twin in the realm of liberal *economic* thought. Indeed, as Cavanaugh notes, the society "that Locke's state enacts is coterminous with the market, to which individuals come to contract for certain goods, both material and political."[6]

This positive view of the modern order of things is not shared by all. Cavanaugh cites Conyers for whom Locke's conception of a political space defined at the one end by state sovereignty and at the other by individual rights is a "bipolar disorder," which transforms the older forms of communal life, "based on biology, locality, common blood, common tasks, or common calling" to the realm of privacy or "voluntary society."[7] What this in effect means, according to Cavanaugh, is that the modern liberal project at heart tends to diminish the space within which communal associations that stand between the state and the individual can develop and flourish: "The rise of the state is the history of the atrophying of such associations."[8] This is a controversial argument, and while Cavanaugh refers to "empirical studies," such data are not presented in the essay in any detail—though we may perhaps take Robert Putnam's influential work on the decline of

   4. Ibid., 251.
   5. Ibid.
   6. Ibid., 254.
   7. Ibid.
   8. Ibid., 256.

social capital as a major source for this position.⁹ But he does refer to an alternate reading, citing Murray, who argues that on the contrary liberalism is precisely a regime that "frees intermediate associations of civil society by limiting the state."¹⁰ I will return to this crucial matter below, after discussing the Swedish experience, which suggests that the decline of civil society and social trust cannot in general be theorized as a consequence of the growth of the modern welfare state since Sweden at the same time is characterized by a large welfare state (high taxes, big public sector), a vibrant civil society, and extremely high rates of social trust.

Cavanaugh then moves on to a discussion of the rise of the democratic nation-state, which, as he notes, represents a qualitative transformation of the modern state. This means that the vertical, up-down relations between a sovereign and absolute/authoritarian monarch/state and individual *subjects* are increasingly complemented by horizontal relationships between the newly minted *citizens*. This change involves both the spread of a sense of individuals being part of an (imagined) community and the development of democracy. The nation-state does not simply enforce its will upon its subjects, as did the absolutist state, but instead we see the emergence of a new duality at the individual level: the rise of the citizen-subject, empowered to make law as a citizen but also obligated to obey the law as a subject.¹¹ As Cavanaugh concludes: "Nationalism becomes a popular movement founded on consent."¹²

Tapping into the large literature on nations and nationalism, Cavanaugh stresses that in this process the power of the state plays a crucial role. Particularly through institutions like the school, the army, and popular media, a common language and national narratives and identities were promoted to great effect, making unitary nations where there were before a multiplicity of regions, dialects, and crisscrossing ethnic and religious communities. National identity became the dominant identity, trumping membership in competing collective categories such as gender, family, clan, or religious groups. This was true even for the great contender: class. Thus the "spirit of 1914" demonstrated to the chagrin of the leaders of the socialist Second International the falsity of Marx's prophecy that nations were headed for the dustbin of history. They expected the workers of the world

---

9. Putnam, *Bowling Alone*.
10. Cavanaugh, "Killing for the Telephone Company," 256.
11. Trägårdh, "Democratic Governance."
12. Cavanaugh, "Killing for the Telephone Company," 261.

to unite and join hands in revolution against capitalism and nationalism. Instead they marched to war, enthusiastically, under their various national banners.

The power of the idea of the democratic nation-state thus resides both in the promise of community and in the program to extend rights to the hitherto powerless and downtrodden. It becomes both a project of freedom and belonging. But the terms change. On the one hand the relative balance between individual freedom and communal constraint changes in favor of the former. On the other, the power of the community becomes more distant and formal as the nation replaces the family, clan and religious community. As Benedict Anderson's apt phrase for the nation—"the imagined community"—suggests, the nation is a community in which you personally know only a tiny fraction of the other members.[13] Together, the state, the market, and the nation become the key organizing principles for modern society, all three providing in different ways vastly increased autonomy for the individual: as a voter and citizen, as a producer and consumer, as a soldier and rights-bearing member of a national welfare state. In Cavanaugh's words: "The rise of rights language goes hand in hand with the rise of the nation-state, because political and civil rights name both the freeing of the individual from traditional types of community and the establishment of regular relations of power between the individual and the state."[14]

One might imagine that this development would reasonably be viewed as cause for celebration, but for Cavanaugh and other critics of the modern secular nation-state it is rather a story of decline, in which the weakening of smaller types of community and associations loom large: "The development of the nation-state in the nineteenth and twentieth centuries can be summed up as the completion of the contradictory process of alienation from local community and simultaneous parochialization of what is common to the borders of the nation-state. Neither movement facilitates the pursuit of a genuine common good."[15] Here Cavanaugh perceptively observes that globalization should be viewed as an extension—not simply a contradiction—of emergence of the nation-state. Globalization, he notes, is, in part, "the hyper-extension of the triumph of the universal over the local on which the nation-state is founded."[16]

13. Anderson, "Imagined Communities."
14. Cavanaugh, "Killing for the Telephone Company," 262.
15. Ibid., 264.
16. Ibid.

Cavanaugh's lament is based, then, on his conviction that the nation-state neither serves the common good nor constitutes a community. Or rather, he claims that it is somehow inauthentic and not "true": "The nation-state is neither community writ-large nor the protector of smaller communal spaces, but rather originates and grows over truly common forms of life."[17] As the title of his essay suggests, he is out to unmask this lack of authenticity of the nation-state. In invoking the notion of dying or killing for the "telephone company" he aims to debunk what so many feel, which is loyalty to the nation and membership in the nation.

Here Cavanaugh is empirically speaking on shaky ground. If there is one thing that nationalism has been successful in accomplishing, it is instilling in citizens the passions of loyalty that make them willing to die for the nation. And this is not a small matter or a side-issue either; the shift from armies made up by mercenaries to armies made up by citizens is often cited as crucial to the victories of the Revolutionary French armies with its loyal and enthusiastic citizen-soldiers pitted against the old regime powers that still had to rely on paid soldiers with dubious commitment to the cause. Cavanaugh is not unaware of this, of course, but he appears to argue in a neo-Marxist vein that people who think and feel in such a way suffer from "false consciousness." Thus the "urgent task of the Church, then, is to demystify the nation-state and to treat it like the telephone company."[18] That is, if people would only "get" that the modern nation-state does in fact not do what is claimed—providing a comfortable mix of freedom and community, of rights and duties—the odds would increase that the Church can re-complexify the social space and eke out a larger role for itself as the purveyor of an alternative moral authority as well as more humane social services and a promise of a Christian economic order that challenges the cold logic of the market.

In my view Cavanaugh fruitfully brings out the central tensions in the values that inform—must inform—all discussions of how we construct a good society. My own point of departure is the German philosopher Immanuel Kant who astutely observed that it is human nature to be caught between two major forces. On the one hand, there is the desire for individual freedom and sovereignty; on the other the absolute necessity to belong to a society. This he called man's "antisocial sociability."[19] I would contend

17. Ibid., 266.
18. Ibid.
19. Kant, *Werke VI*, 37–38.

that all societies at heart have to negotiate this fundamental tension or contradiction. What is not possible or at least not desirable is to err on one side or another. In the modern age this tension can be identified in different conceptions of human nature that are favored in religious and social thought, on the one hand, and in economic and political theory, on the other. Modern economics sees humans as basically selfish and profit-maximizing. This is also increasingly true for modern political science, with its preference for public choice theory and quantitative analyses that rely, like economics, on simplified assumptions of human nature in order to make mathematical equations workable. Meanwhile, many who promote religious ideals and communitarian social thought tend to over-emphasize man's social and altruistic inclinations. In my view both perspectives contain elements of truth but neither are helpful if taken to their extreme if the aim is a more balanced view of a human nature and society, one that engages the Kantian paradox head-on.

In the next section I will approach this matter by taking a closer look at Sweden, a society and a nation-state that in many ways exemplifies Cavanaugh's analysis. Indeed, one imagines that Sweden at least in a theoretical sense would be his worst nightmare: a modern market society, with both a large welfare state embedded in a sense of national community and rampant individualism. What the Swedish case will allow us to do is to nuance what Cavanaugh sees as a universal trend. Indeed, he tends to exaggerate both the statism and the individualism in the U.S. and conversely underestimate the enduring strength of the communitarian ethos and practices that in many ways characterize the U.S. On the other hand, the Swedish experience tends to undermine some of the alarmist claims that Cavanaugh is making in disparaging of the nation-state and the individualism that goes with its rise to dominance. Paradoxically, perhaps, many of the problems of the contemporary U.S.—the lack of trust, poverty, increasing inequality, decline in social mobility—are linked to too little state and a diminished sense of national community, not too much, and to the inability of civil society to tackle, in a meaningful way, these challenges. The divisions and conflicts that arise from both too much bonding social capital in the inward looking communities in U.S. civil society and too little bridging social capital that joins all citizens to the American national community at large, are currently manifesting themselves in the collapse of confidence in national institutions and the decline in generalized social trust.

THE SWEDISH MODEL REVISITED

What then, are the most outstanding characteristics of Swedish society and its underlying social contract? Traditionally, outside observers have put a strong emphasis on social solidarity—an ability to subordinate individual interest to collective rationality. Often, this stress on solidarity has been understood in opposition to the fundamental logic of the market: certain collective goods have been "decommodified" and effectively removed from the cold logic of the market society. Indeed, this was a perspective that Marquis Childs made famous as early as the 1930s, when he wrote *Sweden: The Middle Way*, suggesting that Sweden had found a way to a healthy balance between altruistic socialism and selfish capitalism, to use the crude binary of that period.[20]

But this is, at best, a half-truth. This emphasis on social solidarity hides the strong, not to say extreme, individualism that defines social relations and political institutions in Sweden. Indeed, it is precisely the fundamental harmony between the Swedish social contract and the basic principles of the market—that the basic unit of society is the individual and a central purpose of policy should be to maximize individual autonomy and social mobility—that is the key if we are to grasp that Sweden is not simply a kind of softly socialist country but home to particularly vibrant form of capitalism. In a European perspective, Swedes and other Nordics do not hold particularly strong leftist attitudes in terms of equality of classes versus individual freedom, equality of pay versus merit-based differentials or state versus private ownership of industries. Indeed, while recent studies underline the link between relative equality and a well-functioning economy typical of the Nordic societies, even more significant may be data that show higher rates of social mobility in the Nordic countries compared to, for example, the United States.

SWEDISH INDIVIDUALISM

While much has been written about the institutional aspects of the Swedish welfare state, few have paid much attention to its underlying moral logic.[21] Though the path hasn't always been straight, one can discern over

---

20. Childs, *Sweden: The Middle Way*.

21. Here I summarize arguments made at length in Trägårdh, "Statist Individualism"; Berggren and Trägårdh, *Är svensken människa?*; Berggren and Trägårdh, "Pippi Longstocking," and elsewhere.

the course of the twentieth century an overarching ambition in the Nordic countries not to socialize the economy but to liberate the individual citizen from all forms of subordination and dependency within the family and in civil society: the poor from charity, the workers from their employers, wives from their husbands, children from parents—and vice versa when the parents become elderly.

In practice, the primacy of individual autonomy has been institutionalized through a plethora of laws and policies affecting Swedes in matters minute and mundane as well as large and dramatic. Interdependency within the family has been minimized through individual taxation of spouses, family law reforms have revoked obligations to support elderly parents, more or less universal day care makes it possible for women to work, student loans which are blind in relation to the income of parents or spouse give young adults a large degree of autonomy in relation to their families, and children are given a more independent status through the abolition of corporal punishment and a strong emphasis on children's rights.

All in all this legislation has made Sweden into the least family-dependent and most individualized society on the face of the earth. To be sure, the family remains a central social institution in Sweden, but it too is infused with the same moral logic stressing autonomy and equality. The ideal family is made up of adults who work and are not financially dependent on each other, and children who are encouraged to be independent as early as possible. Rather than undermining "family values" this could be interpreted as a modernization of the family as a social institution. No longer dominated by a patriarch it has become a kind of "voluntary association." But while accepting the fact that long-term spousal commitment is no longer the norm, the "new Nordic family" takes parenthood seriously, both in a demographic sense (the Nordic countries have higher birth rates than more traditional family cultures in southern Europe) and in terms of the time that parents, married or not, spend with their children.

In quantitative terms, data from the World Values Survey (WVS) confirm this picture, indicating that the Nordic countries stand out as a cluster of societies in which people put a strong emphasis on the importance of individual self-realization and personal autonomy. In the language of WVS, the Nordics are characterized by their embrace of "emancipatory self-expression values" on the one hand, and "secular-rational values," on the other.

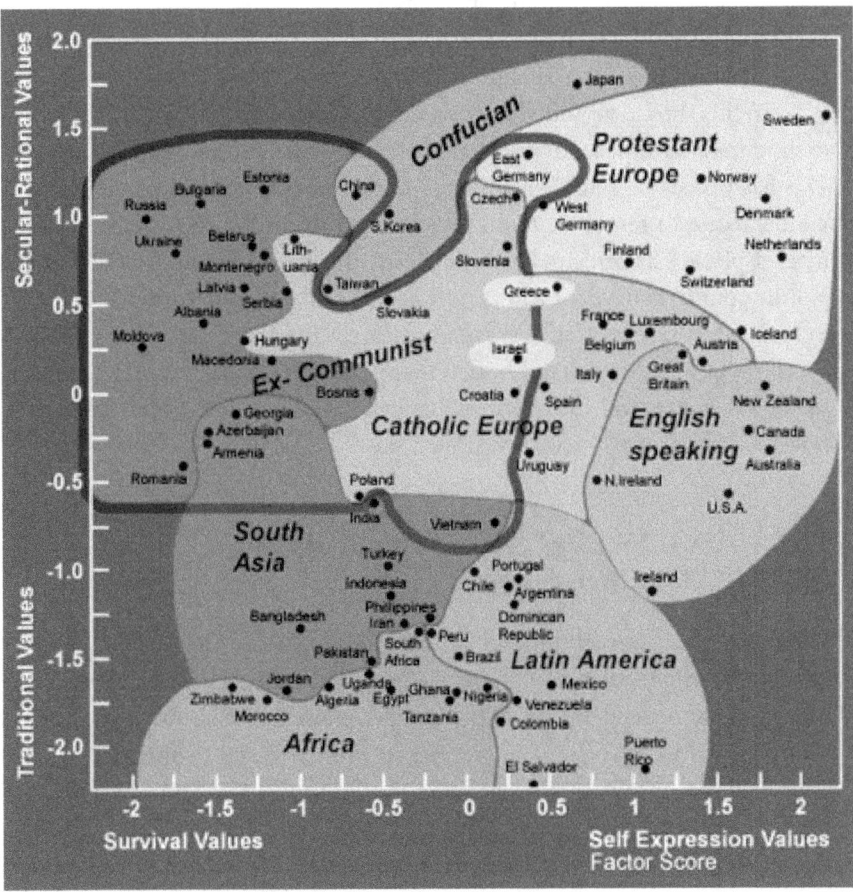

Figure 1: World Values Survey (WVS), Fourth Wave (1991–2001)[22]

One effect of this radical individualism is that, relatively speaking, people in the Nordic countries are more willing to accept the market economy both as consumers and producers. Less tied down by legal and moral obligations within the family, yet still protected from extreme risk by a universal safety net, they become more flexible on the labor market, while as individual consumers they have developed far-reaching needs of products and services that previously were satisfied within the traditional family. This market orientation is enforced in a number of ways in the Nordic countries, not least by a social insurance system based on the recipient's

22. World Values Survey (WVS), Fourth Wave (1991–2001). See also, Inglehart and Welzel, *Modernization, Cultural Change, and Democracy.*

level of earned income on the open labor market, thereby creating an incentive to work while at the same time providing adequate coverage for illness, unemployment and parental leave.

To this should be added the historical legacy emphasizing equal access to fundamental goods, not just healthcare and pensions, but also education. This has translated into a long history of investing in individuals and providing access to resources that allow them to maximize their value in the market place. Historically the countries with the highest rates of literacy, Nordic countries have for a long time scored at the very top when it comes to basic education and investment in research. For this reason, rather than speaking of a "welfare state," which many English speakers associate with social assistance and long-term dependency on the state, some scholars now prefer the term "social investment state."

THE "DUMB SWEDE" AND THE MAGIC OF SOCIAL TRUST

The image of a strongly individualized market society filled with solitary consumers might seem bleak and materialistic. Indeed, traditional social theory has associated the rise of the modern market with a shift from warm *Gemeinschaft* to cold *Gesellschaft*, leading with necessity to anomie, alienation and a breakdown of social trust. According to thinkers as varied as Marx, Durkheim, Simmel, Weber, and Tönnies modernity was characterized by selfish individualism, the freedom and anonymity of the big city, the loss of natural community, and the deadening life in the "iron cage" dominated by the bureaucratic state and the ruthless market.

The underlying assumption of these theories is that trust arises in small, closely-knit communities where there is large degree of interdependence. This nostalgic tradition has continued into our own time, from David Riesman's famous analysis found in *The Lonely Crowd* of American solitude and alienation in 1950's mass-society, through Christopher Lasch's book on "narcissistic individualism" in the 1970s, to Ulrich Beck's recent theories about the "risk society."[23]

A similar critique has been directed towards Sweden, linking the strong "colonizing" state to a "decline of the family," casting the Swedes as

---

23. Riesman, *The Lonely Crowd*; Lasch, *The Culture of Narcissism*; Beck, *The Risk Society*.

the "New Totalitarians."[24] In Sweden itself the so-called "civil society debate" of the early 1990s pitted the defenders of the welfare state against critics from both the left and the right who adopted a communitarian discourse in which "civil society" was a key polemical concept.[25]

Current research shows, however, that it is precisely the most modern and individualistic countries, most notably the Nordic countries, that are characterized by a broad social trust extended beyond the intimate sphere of family, clan, and friends to include other members of society.[26] This type of "cool" and broad social trust is linked to a transition from "the rule of blood" to "the rule of law," linked to modernization and the emancipation of the individual from the close-knit but also confining communities defined by family, clan, and kinship. In the traditional communities trust was "hotter" and more limited to family and clan. In the parlance of contemporary theories in trust, traditional communities are characterized by a "bonding" or "particularized" form of trust, as opposed to the "bridging" or "generalized" trust typical of the Nordic societies.

Again we find that the Nordic countries stand out in studies such as World Values Survey, European Social Survey, European Values Study and Eurobarometer. In addition to putting a strong emphasis on individual self-realization these countries are characterized by a high degree of social trust: well over 50 percent of respondents claim to trust other people, including strangers. This social trust furthermore co-varies with a high degree of trust or confidence in common institutions, such as the system of justice, public administration, and state institutions. Along these lines, current research also indicates that even an individualism that translates into living in single-person households is hardly synonymous with unhappiness. As Eric Klinenberg has argued in a recent book, singletons, far from being isolated and lonely, have more friends, are more involved in associational life, and are in general happier than others.[27] And the country with the most singletons is Sweden, with 47 percent of households consisting of one person (27 percent in the US), going as high as 60 percent in the city of Stockholm.[28]

---

24. Popenoe, *Disturbing the Nest*; Huntford, *The New Totalitarians*.
25. Trägårdh, "The 'Civil Society' Debate."
26. Trägårdh, "The Historical Incubators."
27. Klinenberg, *Going Solo*.
28. Ibid.

Part One—Modern Discipline

Furthermore, while particularly American researchers, such as Robert Wuthnow and Robert Putnam, claim that certain traditional values, most prominently religiosity, are correlated with a high degree of social trust, comparative data do not bear this conclusion out, at least not outside of the United States and certainly not in Sweden.[29] Instead it seems clear that religiosity correlates negatively with social trust, meaning that the more religious a person is, the less general trust does he/she display. Similarly, at the aggregate country level, a similar trend prevails, with some of the most secular countries—and most especially the Nordic ones—scoring highest when it comes to social trust. However, as I suggested above and will stress again later, this does not mean that the Lutheran tradition in its secular form does not have a continued impact in the Nordic countries in a more subtle and transformed way.

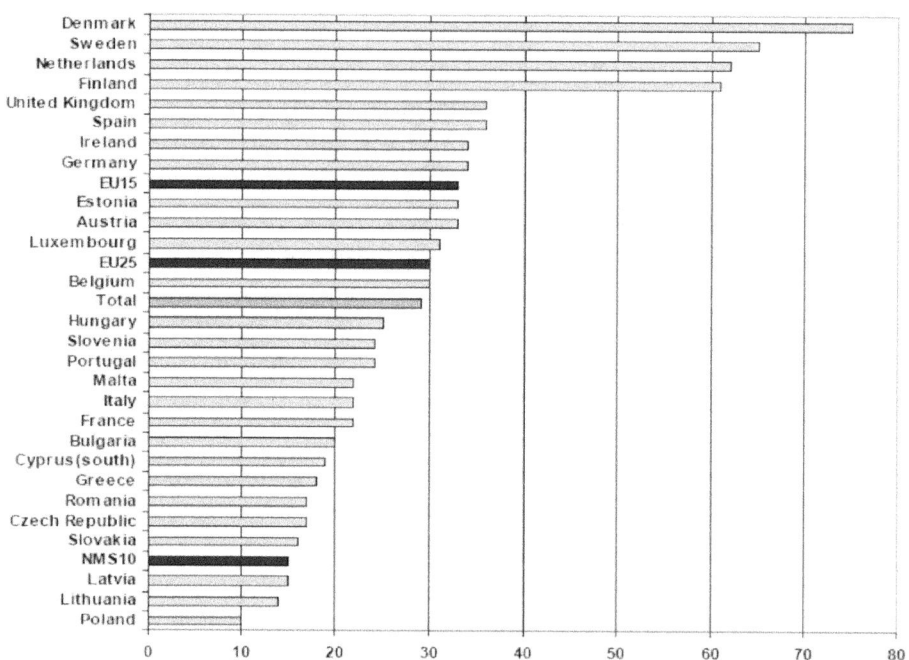

Figure 2: Generalized Trust—An International Comparison[30]

Social trust and adherence to the rule of law translate into a great systemic advantage, which economists call "low transaction costs." However,

---

29. Wallman Lundåsen and Trägårdh, "Social Trust and Religion."
30. The EuroBarometer 62.2 (2004). Data weighted.

this advantage is not limited to sheer direct economic transactions, lowering costs related to the need to resort to written contracts, legal protections, law-suits, and huge amounts of bureaucratic paperwork, but also includes social and political transaction costs that constitute burdens and inefficiencies in the political system and social life at large.

STATIST INDIVIDUALISM AND THE SWEDISH THEORY OF LOVE

The central axis around which the Swedish social contract is formed is the alliance between state and individual, what I have named "statist individualism."[31] Here an emphasis on individual autonomy coincides with a positive view of the state as an ally of not only weaker and more vulnerable citizens, but also the citizenry at large. This is coupled with a negative view of unequal power relations between individuals in general and hierarchical institutions in particular, such as the traditional patriarchal family and what is seen as demeaning charity organizations in civil society. In this regard the Nordic model differs in comparison with both its Anglo-American and continental European counterparts.

But to grasp how statist individualism was institutionalized in Sweden we must also consider the moral logic of this social contract from below, from a personal and existential perspective. This involves the ethical ideal I have called "a Swedish theory of love." In most countries mutual dependency is seen as intrinsic to love and intimacy—the ties that bind. From this point of view, we are always and unavoidably enmeshed in social relations that circumscribe and limit our sovereignty. Indeed, it is the very giving up of radical sovereignty that makes us human; as a fundamental social virtue, love is all about unmediated and absolute duty towards one's fellow man. In Sweden—and perhaps in the Nordic countries at large—on the other hand, the premise is the reverse. Rejecting the idea of love as constitutive of unequal and hierarchical social relations and basing instead the ethos of love on the principles of egalitarianism and voluntarism, the Swedish theory of love posits that all forms of dependency corrupt true love. Only mutual autonomy can guarantee authenticity and honesty in human relationships, turning them into free and voluntary associations.

One way to illuminate the peculiarity of Sweden's social policies is to make explicit comparisons with other countries. Though most welfare

31. Trägårdh, "Statist Individualism."

regimes share a number of characteristics and are all subject to the forces of modernization that Cavanaugh and I both describe, there is a marked difference between the welfare systems of the Nordic countries as compared with both their Anglo-American and continental European counterparts.

In *Germany* and other continental European states, a strong family is both a means and an end for social welfare policies. In line with the moral logic of the Catholic social principle of "subsidiarity" the state protects and supports the family, the churches and other institutions in civil society, so that they in turn can provide for the welfare of the individuals. In the *United States*, there is a general antipathy toward state intervention, both when it comes to the family and the individual. The individual citizen should, ideally, either provide for him- or herself on the level playing field of the market and through the purchase of insurance, or trust in the goodwill of the family or the community-based charity institutions. *Sweden* is, like Germany, characterized by much greater acceptance of state intervention, but in this case the key alliance is between state and individual, rather than family and state. The aim is to avoid subjecting individuals to the charity of others, and to make even relationships within the family as equal and voluntary as possible.

Below (Figure 3) I try to capture these different dynamics of power in modern welfare states graphically as a "triangle drama" by contrasting the position of state, family, and individual in the U.S., Germany, and Sweden. In the Nordic countries the state and the individual form the dominant alliance. In the U.S., individual (rights), family (values) and the autonomy of civil society trump the state (always seen as a threat to liberty). In Germany, finally, the central axis is the one connecting state and family and civil society, with a much smaller role of either U.S.-style individual rights or a Nordic emphasis on individual autonomy.

Power Relations in Modern Welfare States

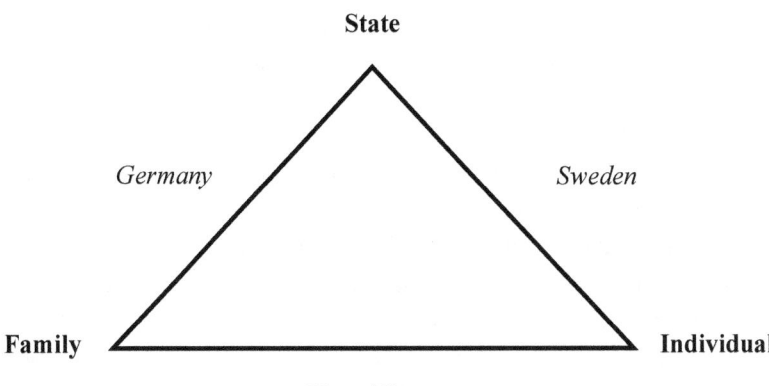

Figure 3: Power Relations in the Modern Welfare State[32]

THE MORAL LOGIC OF THE NORDIC SOCIAL CONTRACT AND CIVIL SOCIETY

However, it must be stressed that in emphasizing the centrality of individual autonomy as a key value this does not mean that the Nordic social contract is, somehow, hostile towards the family or civil society. The point is rather that the family and the associations in civil society are also informed and shaped by the same moral logic. As noted earlier, the ideal Swedish family is one where man and woman work, children have rights, and elderly parents do not depend on their children. Similarly, Swedish civil society is, in comparative perspective, typically characterized by associations whose structure and purpose express the same moral logic as the social contract at large.[33]

Comparing and contrasting the Nordic and the American state/civil society nexus illuminates a more general discussion of what is at stake in the civil society debate. One finding is that one can identify two major parts of civil society that for many reasons must be treated analytically and politically as separate and different. On the one hand there are those that

32. Berggren and Trägårdh, "Pippi Longstocking."
33. Trägårdh, "Rethinking the Position."

primarily have a political function of providing "voice" to groups in society, including interest groups and social movements. This is the part of civil society that has powered the on-going process of increased democratization, aiming to include and empower the historically disenfranchised and to provide a critical counterforce to the powers that be. One the other hand, there are the many charities, faith- and identity based institutions, and non-profit organizations that are engaged in providing relief, support, and social services to those in need, both at home and abroad (often in the form of NGOs active in the development industry).

It is clear that social and political movements devoted to making rights claims and charity and service-oriented organizations stand in tension with each other. Indeed, to some extent the classic social movements in Western Europe, and most especially in the Nordic countries, aimed to eradicate the need for charity and civil society and family-based social services by establishing state guaranteed social rights based on citizenship in the form of a universalist welfare state. To put it differently, the goal for *one part* of Swedish civil society (the social movements) was to liberate the individual from the ties of dependency in the family, the churches, and the charitable institutions of *the other part* of civil society. This should be contrasted with the (neo)liberal vision of civil society that centers on the idea that family- and civil society-based provision of social services though charities and local communities is preferable given the overarching aim to keep the state at arm's length.

Given these radically different normative views of the role of the state and civil society, it should come as no surprise that Nordic and American civil societies look rather different, as large comparative studies like the Johns Hopkins non-profit sector project show.[34] Nordic civil society is characterized by voice-bearing, membership-based, and democratically organized associations, often engaging in sports, culture, study circles, and adult education, while the U.S. counterpart is dominated by faith-based institutions, charities, and non-political, service-producing non-profit organizations. This is a difference that is continually supported through the structuring power of the state. In the U.S., for example, the state supports the charity and service providers of civil society while it attempts to discourage political organizations, particularly through the tax codes that privilege charities and punish political activists.[35] Furthermore, the relation

---

34. Anheier and Salamon, "The Nonprofit Sector."
35. Goss, "Civil Society"; Anheier and Salamon, "The Nonprofit Sector."

between state and civil society is normatively and institutionally configured quite differently. In the Nordic countries where the state is seen as a positive force, state and civil society are viewed as partners and linked in a myriad ways in a complex governance structure, while in America, with its deep anti-statist tradition, relations between the state and civil society are more fraught and the ideal, from the point of view of civil society, is to retain maximum autonomy in relation to the state.

The Historical Roots of Statist Individualism

Cavanaugh argues in his critique of the modern nation-state that one can identify general secular trends that are common to at least Western modernity. On the whole I am sympathetic to this perspective, even though I suspect he and I may differ on the normative implications of this development. Where I may spot "individual freedom rising" he may well see "the atrophy of civil society." But I also think that the broad-strokes-analysis tends to hide or at least underplay crucial differences between countries like the U.S. and Sweden, as suggested in my comparative analysis above. We face varieties of modernization just as we—post cold-war—are becoming aware of varieties of capitalism as we ponder the significant and fundamental differences that exist between market-societies as far apart as China, Russia, the U.S., Germany, or Sweden when it comes to economic, political, and social structures and the moral logics that inform these.

And these differences are rooted in history; the modern Swedish social contract is, like those of other nations, the outcome of both universal secular trends and specific local legacies. In this section I will therefore consider the historical roots of the modern Swedish social contract. This will involve the question of how we may want to assess the impact of Lutheranism in modern Sweden, thus returning to the question with which this essay began. But before we get back to Luther, let us consider a few other important contenders with respect to historical roots. Let me begin with the subject of rule of law.

Historically the Nordic region stands out as a "community of law"; indeed it was a community of law before the individual Nordic states were consolidated. Rule of law was central to the social contract that underpinned the emerging state, and adherence to the law by the King and his administration was crucial to the legitimacy of the state. As the Swedish saying went, *Land skall med lag byggas* (the country must be built through law).[36]

The trust in and reliability of institutions thus depends on the acceptance of rule of law, but even more important is the extent to which the values implicit in formal law are also internalized and embedded as social norms. Or differently put, the extent to which laws, rules, and institutions are viewed as legitimate, as the outcome of a democratic decision-making process, and are grounded in common values, will determine how well they work. The more accepted and internalized the laws are, the less prominent the specter of corruption and lawlessness, the less the need for policing and more draconian forms of state power.

The respect for law and the positive view of the state is linked historically to the relative freedom of the Swedish peasantry. The weakness, not to say absence, of feudal institutions corresponds with a history of peasant self-reliance, self-rule, land ownership, representation as an estate in the parliament, and the consequent willingness and an ability to participate in the political affairs of the country. There is, of course, a strong mythological aspect to this oft-claimed lack of feudal traditions in Sweden. The free Swedish yeomanry is in many ways an ideological construct much like the "free-born Englishman" or the "rugged individual" of the American frontier. But, on the other hand, it is no less grounded in actual history. The peasant in medieval Sweden, as the historian Michael Roberts has put it, "retained his social and political freedom to greater degree, played a greater part in the politics of the country, and was altogether a more considerable person, than in any other western European country."[37]

The consequence of the relative inclusion and empowerment of the Swedish peasantry was that their status as *subjects* was balanced by their position as *citizens*. As an estate in the parliament they played a part in passing laws, which in this way gained popular legitimacy. Furthermore, since the peasants and the King (at times joined by the Clergy) often were joined in a common struggle against their common adversary, the Nobility, many peasants came to view the State—in the figure of the King—as in some sense being "on their side." To be sure, in actuality political alliances shifted, some Kings were more powerful than others, and the Nobility was at times close to achieving the kind of subjugation of the peasantry that was the norm in most of the rest of Europe. But, all things told, the peasant

36. Trägårdh, "Democratic Governance."
37. Roberts, *Essays in Swedish History*, 4–5.

struggle to retain their legal, political, and property rights was remarkably successful, and by the time that democratic and liberal ideas found their way to Sweden from the Continent in the nineteenth century they were effectively fused with these politically strong yeoman traditions.

Aristocratic liberalism was not entirely absent, but there was no strong bourgeoisie with which it could ally itself with. When the great Swedish liberal poet and historian, Erik Gustaf Geijer, rewrote Swedish history in the early 1800s, he instead made the Swedish peasant into the prime mover of history, a free man who fiercely protected property but voluntarily would rally around the King if the nation was under attack. In poems as well as academic works he described the Swedish Viking and Yeoman as a citizen, who was characterized neither by bourgeois egoism nor by ancient republican virtue, but by a stubborn individual sovereignty. Freedom, said Geijer, meant not being subordinated to any other man, but to be without master like the Vikings of old. There were constraints: Geijer, a devout Christian, was not romancing about the Nietzschean Blond Beasts. Man was bound by the law, which "had been commonly agreed on, or inherited through the forefathers." But that was a safeguard of freedom, a precondition not a limitation. No individual man could be subjected to another, no one could impose authority arbitrarily; everybody was subject to the law. "I give to God and King what is their due," wrote Geijer in one of his most famous poems, but "that which is mine (...) I freely enjoy." Through Geijer and his followers this national narrative and associated values came to be expressed in literature and textbooks on Swedish national identity.[38]

Furthermore, as I have argued in more detail elsewhere, the historical peculiarities of Nordic family culture and marriage patterns are important.[39] These tended to emphasize, relatively and comparatively speaking, independence (of children), individualism, and (gender) equality. Sweden—and the other Nordic countries—fall very clearly on the one side of the fault line that John Hajnal drew in the 1960s, and which divides European family culture into very distinct traditions.[40] On the one side—in Northern and Western Europe—late marriages, nuclear families and children sent away to work outside the home. On the other—in eastern and Mediterranean Europe—early marriages, extended households and children mainly reared within these households.

38. Berggren och Trägårdh, *Är svensken människa?*.
39. Ibid.; Trägårdh, "The Historical Incubators."
40. Hajnal, "European Marriage Patterns."

Part One—Modern Discipline

According to Haynal and his followers the system in the Northwest—termed "the European marriage pattern"—was more conducive to individual autonomy and weakened traditional "honor culture" norms where women weren't allowed to move freely without supervision. According to the Austrian historian Michael Mitterrauer this mobility made the period of youth a time in which "the individual, the autonomous personality, was developed."[41] But even within the European marriage pattern Sweden stands out, according to family historians. In a comparative study David Bradley has shown how Scandinavian family legislation compares with its German and English equivalents during the first half of the twentieth century. Whereas German lawmakers were willing to intervene in the family to uphold patriarchal authority and English law was more neutral and respectful of the traditions of civil society, Scandinavian legislation combined state regulation with emancipatory individualistic ideals.[42] While in most European countries today's more liberal divorce laws, judicial equality between spouses, and legalization of homosexuality were put in place in the 1960s, in Scandinavia these reforms were carried through during the interwar years.

So, returning then to the question of the Lutheran impact and legacy, one might, for starters, speculate that both the positive view of the state and the emphasis on the individual is linked to Lutheranism, in which respect for state authority was one strain, and the centrality of the individual's personal relationship to God was another.

But it is also clear that the Lutheran instantiation in Sweden was equally shaped by the traditions discussed before. The claims regarding state authority were inflected by the emphasis on the rule of law; they did not simply become an argument for absolutist or authoritarian rule. Instead they were linked in a specific way to claims made by the peasants regarding their freedoms and rights. The notions of individual autonomy and social equality also received energy from Lutheran dogma but in Sweden such claims were successful whereas in the Lutheran German lands the emancipatory claims were defeated in the legendary Peasant's wars of 1524–25. Indeed, Luther himself was ambivalent but finally sided with the powers-that-be, launching his famous tirade "Against the Murderous, Thieving Hordes of Peasants," which appeared in May of 1525. Thus the crucial links between a strong but emancipatory state and the freedom and

41. Mitterrauer, *Ungdomstidens sociala historia*.
42. Bradely, "Family Laws."

the rights of the peasantry were strengthened in Sweden and destroyed in Germany, with huge and long-term consequences.

In this manner, the preservation of the civil and political rights of the peasantry laid the foundation for the state-friendly tradition of which the Swedish Lutheran state church was part. At the local level it functioned in many ways as a community-based, civil society organization, with the church and its calendar social-religious events at its center. But the local church was also linked to the state via both the hierarchical structure of the church itself and through the various duties and responsibilities that the state delegated to the church and which in actuality became local matters regarding social control and social welfare. Of crucial importance was the task of keeping track of all members of the community, keeping track of every single person, births, deaths, weddings, and so on.

Furthermore, at a somewhat mundane but also very important level, Lutheran dogma joined with state power also had enormous practical consequences. I refer to the insistence on the part of Lutheran pastors—in keeping with fundamental Lutheran doctrine—that each person must be able to read the Bible and, indeed, was tested on a regular basis to ensure that this was the case. This regulation, rooted in this curious mixture of religious dogma, the position of the state church, and the freedom of the peasants, played a significant role in laying the basis for a wide spread literacy that paved the way for a rapid economic development with a universal—and egalitarian—reach. Sweden and other Lutheran Nordic countries were thus in a position to benefit, as modernizing, secularizing market societies and nation-states, from ideas and practices that ultimately had roots in religion.

At the very minimum, then, many key elements of the modern, secular Swedish social contract were at the very least consistent with the Lutheran legacy: statism, individualism, universalism, and egalitarianism. At the same time, I would argue, the religious legacy must be understood and analyzed within the broader sociopolitical framework that I have tried to sketch out above. One must, in other words, temper the impulse to ascribe to modern, secular Sweden the status of a kind of Lutheranism in secular disguise even as one rightly points to the enduring importance of that legacy.

Part One—Modern Discipline

CONCLUSION

Building on this historical legacy, the twentieth century, and particularly the 1960s and 1970s, would see an even more radical transformation of Swedish society albeit one according to the same basic logic as the Social Democrats put their twist on this Lutheran-inflected alliance between nation-state and individual. Not in the direction of some kind of socialism in the sense of nationalizing properties, banks, and businesses, but toward a family and social policy that diminished the social and economic role of the traditional family and other institutions—paternalistic charities, churches, and companies—that stood between the state and the individual. Of especial importance was the removal of joint taxation, which is still in place in many countries. The combination of individual taxation and the lack of allowances for family deductions make the Scandinavian tax systems the most individualized in the world. Furthermore, day-care became next to universal, making it possible for women to work; corporal punishment of children was outlawed; children's rights were otherwise strengthened through the creation of a special ombudsman; and the responsibility for the elderly was moved from the adult children to the state.

It is this emphasis on egalitarianism, individual autonomy, gender equality, and children's rights that makes the communitarian ethos that Cavanaugh appears to embrace so problematic from the point of view of the "Swedish theory of love." Indeed, Cavanaugh himself is not blind to the problem. While obviously preferring the associations and communities of civil society—the family, the village, the church, the guild—that stand between and mediate between state and individual, he also notes that "such associations could, of course, be oppressive, and often were."[43] He continues by declaring that it is not his intention "to romanticize earlier historical eras."[44] He makes a similar point in the essay in this book, asking the crucial question: "What would an authentic Eucharist sociality look like in today's world?" Again he warns against any temptation to "turn back the clock," rejecting a "romanticism for the medieval period that was in fact riven with static social hierarchies." He concludes that "we can tell no simple Fall narrative of a Golden Age that was." Instead he calls for the building of "communities that offer the world a more personalized practice of social life."[45]

---

43. Cavanaugh, "Killing for the Telephone Company," 256.
44. Ibid.
45. Cavanaugh in this volume, 170–71.

It is hard not to feel sympathy with this plea. Indeed, there are voices in the Swedish debate over the future of the welfare state that say much the same. Yet others, myself included, point out that such an attempt to personalize care also risks throwing the object of care back into the position of being at the receiving end of charity. And what the champions of charity always seem to fail to consider is that while giving may provide the giver with a "feel-good experience," this is not always the case for the object of such good intentions. Paternalism always lurks in the shadows, along with paternalism's companions: a sense of superiority that borders on contempt.

Let us not forget that there was a reason why so many fought to reject charity and to replace it with social rights. In this venture the desire for individual freedom was joined to an ethical ideal that emphasized equality and solidarity. Freedom, equality, brotherhood—Swedish style—has rested on the ability of the state to guarantee individuals both the right to freely organize in civil society, and the right not to submit to communal constraints. This is the central paradox that communitarians often underplay; that the modern democratic nation-state is not hostile to civil society but rather is its incubator. Without a state protecting freedom of speech and the right to association, there would be no free associational life. This is true for Sweden as well, even while the state also guarantees, through its web of social rights, that membership in associations is voluntary; not necessary or obligatory, nor steeped in unequal, hierarchical and patriarchal relations of power.

On the other hand, what Cavanaugh may have emphasized more, had his concern been with Sweden, is the pluralist issue. In focusing on the negative effects of the nation-state, even in a relatively communitarian country like the U.S., he misses the point that the particular state/civil society configuration in the U.S. actually enables and promotes pluralism and religious diversity and freedom in a way that Sweden, with its one state, one church, one nation, Lutheran legacy has not. In the one case the virtue is freedom of communities and the allowance of deep difference, in the other the freedom and autonomy of the individual. In both instances we also register losses and unfreedoms: in Sweden that of communities that aspire to a more total immersion in subnational associations; in the US that of individuals who would like to benefit from the security and investments of the state to provide opportunity and autonomy.

If we turn back for a moment to the nineteenth century and the birth of a modern civil society in Sweden, the earliest and strongest movement was one that has many links to the American experience, what in Sweden is referred to as the "Free churches." At a time when the statist and bureaucratizing tendencies within the Lutheran state collided with the emerging, modern lust for freedom, the first revolt was in the religious sphere. Just as the Lutheran church began to lose its local and communitarian underpinnings, the Free churches spoke for such ideals. Modernization, in fact, was taking place both through the Lutheran legacy and against it. The individualistic struggle for freedom from community, inequality, and hierarchy was one side; the struggle to choose and freely join a community of one's own liking was the other.

Thus, in my opinion, the questions of whether the nation is a true or false community, or whether the state is emancipatory or oppressive, or whether the market is a project for or against freedom, are both empirical and normative. In so far as people claim to feel happy and free, that they trust each other, or have confidence in common institutions, whichever they are, we ought to take such testimony seriously. Of course, this does not mean that we cannot or should not differ in our normative positions on all these matters. It is quite possible to reject the Swedish Way as much as one may reject the American Way, to embrace statist individualism or prefer religious communitarianism, whatever the consequences and whatever the empirical data on happiness, trust, wealth, pluralism, or equality say.

2

Scattered Conversion?

Youth, Free Church, and the Swedish Welfare State

Fredrik Wenell

INTRODUCTION

The vision of the Swedish welfare state, *folkhemmet*, can be understood as a vision of independent individuals.[1] In this context emerged an understanding of conversion as an individual's datable experience which begin her personal relationship to Jesus, without a mediating congregation. This individualistic understanding of conversion scattered the Free churches as social bodies, and individuals were instead gathered under the notion of the welfare state. Their *telos* changed.[2] My thesis is that this theological change might, genealogically, be traced back to the struggle between understandings of the Church as a social body on its own, and the Church as an association of those who share a similar emotional and spiritual experience. To put it in another way, it is a struggle between different kinds

---

1. For more on this, see Trägårdh in this volume.
2. With *telos* I refer to the end towards which a human life is directed. A Christian *telos* would be the redeemed human being living in peace with God and fellow human beings, and not the autonomous human being.

of ecclesiologies, a Baptist and a revivalist ecclesiology. Both of these views presuppose a personal conversion, but they understand it differently. I will in this article analyze the genealogical relation between the political vision of the Swedish welfare state and the theological notion of personal conversion and Free Church ecclesiology.[3] My claim is not that there is no Baptist ecclesiology left in Sweden, but that this is no longer the dominant and most influential ecclesiology in Free churches.[4]

The Baptist theologian Stephen R. Holmes claims that it is foundational to Baptist theology that a personal conversion incorporates the individual believer in a new social body:

> God, through the Son and the Spirit, calls individual believers into covenanted relationship in the local church, and equips them to build up one another within the local church, and to hear and obey the ongoing missional call to make every other human person a believer.[5]

Incorporation in a "covenanted relationship" follows a personal conversion, but in a Swedish Free Church context this is not self-evident anymore. Conversion is not necessarily expected to mean participation in a local congregation. Nor is baptism necessarily related to church. A person can, for example, be baptized at a non-denominational Christian conference. It is common that conversion only becomes a matter of praying a salvation prayer, which should, of course, contain the right formulation: confession of sin, faith in Jesus and the individual's receiving of salvation. Conversion is thus understood as an individual experience with God; or as it is often framed, a personal relationship with Jesus. How is this detachment of conversion from church possible in a Swedish Free Church context, where the notion of the gathered community has been fundamental? The argument here is that conversion understood as a purely personal relation to Jesus has been made possible because one Free Church theological discourse of conversion has subsumed another: a revivalist theological discourse has subsumed a Baptist discourse. The discursive struggle between a Baptist and a revivalist ecclesiology is still ongoing.

---

3. Qvarsebo, "Swedish Progressive School," 217–35.

4. I use "theology" and "ecclesiology" as closely connected terms. A certain theological construction relates to an ecclesiology, and vice versa.

5. Holmes, *Baptist Theology*, 7

I use the terms "scatter" and "gather," from William T. Cavanaugh's book *Torture and Eucharist*, as analytical tools.[6] He applies these terms to the ways in which torture was used under the dictatorship of Gustavo Pinochet: "[T]orture was used as a social discipline to atomize and scatter social bodies which stand between the individual and the state."[7] Sweden, as we all know, is not a dictatorship, and torture is fortunately not used here, but there is certainly a strong state in Sweden. Associations within civil society are used to administer supposedly common values. This becomes especially visible through the Swedish concept of *"folkhemmet."* It is described as an idea of the welfare state, which is visualized as a perfect, just, and good society in which state and society become intertwined. I argue that this vision has made individuals in Sweden dependent on the Swedish nation-state as a social body and independent of other social bodies such as Free churches. A personal conversion relates to an individual's desire. But, as Cavanaugh has argued elsewhere, desire is not something that is "natural" but is disciplined in relation to different social bodies' ends or goals (*telos*).[8] Desires are constructed according to the ends of a vision.[9]

The example I use to highlight the process is a Baptist movement in Sweden, the Örebro Mission (*Örebromissionen*), and their struggle for Christian youth.[10] To be more specific, my material comes from their weekly newspaper, *Missionsbaneret* ("Missionary Banner").[11] Their rootedness in Baptist theology as well as their receptiveness to revivalist theology makes this movement suitable for the task of this article. The Örebro Mission started as a mission organization within the Baptist Union in 1892.[12]

6. Cavanaugh, *Torture and Eucharist*.

7. Ibid., 15.

8. Cavanaugh, *Being Consumed*, 9.

9. Ward, *The Politics of Discipleship*, Kindle loc. 2346; Bell, *Liberation Theology*.

10. There were in Sweden in the 1930s two Baptist denominations with slightliy different emphases of Baptist theology. They split in 1937, and the Örebro Mission became a denomination of its own. A very simplistic and superficial, but in some sense adequate, description is that the Swedish Baptist Union was more Lutheran. In the Örebro Mission there was a bit more influence from an Anabaptist heritage. There was for example repeated articles in *Missionsbaneret* that described perspectives from Mennonite Churches. Theses from their theological seminary that discussed Anabaptist theology were published in *Missionsbaneret*.

11. *Missionsbaneret* was the official weekly paper of the Örebro Mission during 1921–1993.

12. Literally—"The mission of Örebro." Örebro is a city situated approx. 200 km west from Stockholm. The Örebro Mission has subsequently merged with two other

The founder was a Baptist pastor, John Ongman, who returned from America.¹³ The revivalistic holiness movement had strongly influenced his local congregation, and as a result they had gone through a split. Ongman focused theologically on spiritual renewal and personal conversion. The Örebro Mission was later also influenced by the Pentecostal movement. These revival movements flavored the Örebro Mission theologically, with personal conversion as a foundation, but at the same time Ongman was also rooted in Baptist theology.

HISTORICAL AND THEOLOGICAL BACKGROUND

Swedish Free churches emerged from the so-called "new evangelical" *(nyevangelisk)* movement in the late eighteenth and early nineteenth century, which started as a pietistic revival within the Lutheran state church. Its focus was not a new theological definition of the church, but rather the true spiritual life of the individual.¹⁴ In this sense it was not unique, but shared affinities with the international Evangelical movement, especially the branch pioneered D. L. Moody.¹⁵ Joel Halldorf describes the movement's understanding of conversion as "a subjective experience through which salvation becomes internalized and personal."¹⁶ Initially the new evangelical movement did not create new denominations, but instead gathered "true believers" to informal meetings. The movement sought to work within the state church organization. Those associated with it gathered in separate associations meetings while still remaining within the Lutheran church. The basis for community within these associations was the common personal experience of conversion. This was a new way of being church, a gathering of those truly "born again" within the mixed body of the Swedish Lutheran state church. In that sense it represented a new ecclesiology, an *ecclesiola in ecclesia*.¹⁷

---

denominations (The Free Baptist Union and the Holiness Union) and has been renamed the Evangelical Free Church, although the official English name is Interact. Website in English: www.efk.se.

13. Janzon, *Den andra omvändelsen*, 81.
14. Bexell, *Sveriges kyrkohistoria*, 39
15. Halldorf, *Av denna världen?*, 74; Gustafsson, *Moody and the Swedes*.
16. Halldorf, *Av denna världen?*, 87.
17. For more on this, see Eckerdal in this volume.

The Baptist movement came to Sweden in the mid nineteenth century through the seaman F. O. Nilsson. He brought with him new ways of viewing Christian faith that were foreign to the Swedish Lutheran state church.[18] Sune Fahlgren has described the Baptist tradition as a "peculiar combination of Christian traditions."[19] The Baptist tradition represents a combination of a radical understanding of the priesthood of all believers, a cognitive emphasis on faith, and a specific understanding of power. Their view of power colors the relationships both within the congregations and to the official political power. Within the congregation we find a strong emphasis on the priesthood of all believers.[20] In relation to the official political power the Baptists claimed religious freedom. Fahlgren describes this as a new kind of organization in the Swedish public sphere.[21] He claims that the Baptist movement represented "first of all new ideas, new knowledge and not (. . .) new methods or sublime feelings."[22] The Baptist churches gathered as a result of a personal conversion that gave members another *telos*. Their *telos* was the gathered and redeemed congregation as something different from other associations in society. This was seen in the praxis of their congregations. The Baptists shared the new evangelicals' focus on personal conversion experience as the center of their theology, but they differed in their understanding of the consequences of this personal conversion. They did not organize themselves as associations within the Lutheran State Church, but rather gathered in believers' churches as new social bodies apart from the Lutheran State Church. Here personal conversion, though experienced individually, resulted in incorporation into a covenanted relationship in another social body.[23]

In Sweden, these two ecclesiologies have often been defined as *one* Free Church ecclesiology. This definition is mainly sociologically motivated, having to do with associations that were something different from the official state church, but the definition also has to do with the friendship these two movements shared regarding personal and heart-felt spirituality.[24] It seems to me, however, that this difference might better be understood

18. Westin, *Den kristna friförsamlingen*, 36–39.
19. Fahlgren, "Baptismens spiritualitet," 111.
20. Larsson, *De "Riktiga kristna."*
21. Fahlgren, *Predikantskap och församling*, 65–69; Hallingberg, *Läsarna*, 118–47.
22. Fahlgren, "Baptismens spiritualitet," 107.
23. Holmes, *Baptist Theology*, 7.
24. Hallingberg, *Läsarna*, 55–73.

as two different Free Church ecclesiologies. The new evangelicals gathered primarily because of a common spiritual experience of conversion, but then became associations within the Lutheran State Church. They became an *ecclesiola in ecclesia*. Through their creation of new and separate social bodies, the Baptists were something foreign to the homogenous Swedish society. The Baptists gathered as a consequence of another *telos* and can therefore be viewed as another social body. Baptist ecclesiology was consequently perceived as a theological and political threat against the united Swedish Lutheran nation.

An Ecclesiological Battle

The two different ecclesiologies described above have both been present in the Örebro Mission. This has created a tension within the denomination throughout its history. There was (and is) an ongoing struggle between them. It has been visible at different times when certain issues have been discussed. One striking example is an argument from 1972. Four years earlier the Swedish government had appointed a committee to examine the relation between state and church. The result was not, as some had expected, that the bond between the state and the state church was dissolved. Instead, the state chose to support other Christian denominations as well. The motivation for giving this financial support was "to increase the possibility for economically weak congregations to have halls and offer religious service such as worship, counseling and so forth."[25] In the 1970s the Christian faith was seen as a unifying factor and an important part of the construction of Swedish society. A discussion developed in *Missionsbaneret* about what "the principle of Free Church" had meant in the nineteenth century. The argument from the revivalists was that "free" meant freedom from constrained spirituality:

> When the revival forced its way during the nineteenth century, this revival was totally free from politics of any kind. The revival and the individuals' personal experience of salvation was primary. It wasn't the state church that was questioned as much as the spiritual constraint.[26]

---

25. Deminger, *Kejsarens pengar*. I have elsewhere argued that the financial support changed the way Örebro Mission interacted with the Swedish State, cf. Wenell, "Religion som politisk resurs."

26. Götestam, "Det integrerar oss inte i statsapparaten."

Constrained spirituality refers to a spirituality characterized set formulas and a given liturgical structure controlled by the priest.[27] This was seen as the opposite of a more personal spirituality—experiential and heartfelt. The Baptist side claimed that a personal conversion also had political implications, not as the primary concern but as a historical consequence. According to them, "free" meant not being dependent on any state or government whatsoever:

> It was of course not only spiritual constraint they wanted to break free from, when it comes to the nineteenth century revival in Sweden. The Conventicle ordinance, sheriffs, exile, and prison on bread and water, show clearly that they were brutally confronted with state engagement in religion.[28]

The revivalist side in the debate argued that the denomination should accept the financial support. Everything that could help the church to promote revival was welcomed. The Baptist side, on the other hand, saw problems with delivering "religious services" to society as a state-supported service. They feared that an acceptance of financial support would change their relationship to the state. They would no longer be separate social bodies, and in the long run this alliance with the state might threaten their religious freedom. The Örebro Mission decided first to renounce financial support, but one year later they entered into the arrangement of the Swedish state like every other Free Church denomination.

These two oppositional positions in the same movement can be understood as emerging from the two different ecclesiologies described above. It was the revivalist ecclesiology that came to dominate. I will now go on to argue that this can be understood as an effect of theological adjustments to the Baptist ecclesiology from the establishment of the Swedish idea of the welfare state, *folkhemmet*, during the 1920s–1940s.[29] A revivalist ecclesiology was easier to promote in modern Sweden than a Baptist ecclesiology.

---

27. For more on this, see Halldorf in this volume.

28. Deminger, "Sätt in statsbidraget." "Conventicle ordinance" was a law that forbade people to gather for religious purposes, such as to prayer meetings, without the attendance of a Lutheran priest.

29. It is beyond the scope of this article to analyze how the influence from the Pentecostal movement affected The Örebro Mission on this matter. For a closer look at the Pentecostal movement and its relation to society, see Carlsson, *Människan, samhället och Gud*.

Part One—Modern Discipline

THE WELFARE STATE AS THE VISION OF A GATHERED NATION

The notion of the welfare state can be viewed as a way to gather the Swedish nation. It was the conservative politician Rudolf Kjellén (1864–1922) who in 1912 launched the idea of the welfare state, *folkhemmet*, as a political goal.[30] He saw the nation as a gathered entity that carried the history of a specific race throughout history. He wanted to renew and gather the nation under the notion of the welfare state, *folkhemmet*. But it was the Social Democrats, led by Prime Minister Per-Albin Hansson (1885–1946), who filled the concept with the content that became dominant.[31] *Folkhemmet* was for him a vision of a new modern society founded on democracy and purged from the old conservative class society.[32] Democracy presupposed that every citizen was seen as an autonomous individual, and this autonomy should be guaranteed by the state.[33] Democracy became a set of values, an ideology.

Folkhemmet was characterized by social engineering, social-welfare and equal opportunities. A good society was supposed to emerge from efficient organization. Everything could be subject to public organization, for example population patterns *(befolkningsfrågan)*, housewives' movement patterns in the kitchen, childcare, and young people's spare time. Values and norms should be built on science, and these norms were expected to lead to the construction of a good society. The results of these investigations were for example: public advice on how to use the kitchen, laws that taxed spouses separately, financial support to associations for the purpose of disciplining teenagers' drunkenness, and regulations on how people's houses should be built. These norms should be grounded on scientific research.[34]

This has taken different directions throughout the twentieth century, but the foundational relation has been between the state and the autonomous individual. It is the obligation of the Swedish state to take care of its citizens, and in return the citizen is guaranteed autonomy by the state.

30. Dahlqvist. "Folkhemsbegreppet."

31. Ibid.; Rothstein, "Att administrera välfärdsstaten," 68. Per-Albin Hansson was prime minister between 1932–1946, but the first time he mentioned *folkhemmet* was in a debate 1928.

32. Ibid., 464

33. For more on this, see Trägårdh in this volume.

34. Sweden was at this time one of the worlds foremost proponents of racial biology. Frykman, *Modärna tider*, 35–41.

Consequently historians Henrik Berggren and Lars Trägårdh describe the Swedish ideology as "statist individualism."[35] The strong state exists not as a community, but in order to provide the individual with a security that frees him or her from local dependency of neighbors or family: "Sweden is not first and foremost a warm *Gemeinschaft* composed of altruists who are exceptionally caring or loving, but rather a hyper modern *Gesellschaft* of self-realizing individuals who believe that a strong state *and* stable social norms will keep their neighbor out of both their lives and their backyards."[36] This has led to the paradoxical combination of a strong state and a radical individualism in Sweden: "[an] active interventionism on the part of the state to promote egalitarian conditions is not a threat to individual autonomy but rather the obverse: a necessary prerequisite to free the citizens from demeaning and humbling dependence on one another."[37] This ideology is closely connected to the welfare state and the notion of *folkhemmet*. Democracy is seen as the foundation of the welfare state, and the state guarantees the autonomy of the individual that the democracy presupposes. It has therefore seemed reasonable that the state should promote certain values to guarantee both democracy and decent behavior.

Voluntary associations in the Swedish civil society have been used as agents in this construction. They have been used to promote and discipline what have been understood as the common and stable values that the welfare state needed. Political scientist Hans-Erik Olson has described this in terms of *disciplining as ideology*, in contrast to *ideology as disciplining*.[38] The first means "disciplining to prevent bad habits and abandonment, or to build community in general."[39] The second is first of all interested in promoting an ideology, where the presumed good consequences are seen as secondary.

> It was not the ideology of the associations that got financial support from the state. The associations were instead engaged as agents to discipline the youth, who were not active in any association, and instill within them common civic and respectable values.

---

35. Berggren och Trägårdh, *Är svensken människa?*, 33–55; Trägårdh, "Rethinking the Nordic Welfare State," 234. For more on this, see Trägårdh in this volume.
36. Trägårdh och Berggren, "Pippi Longstocking," 16. Italic original.
37. Ibid.
38. Olson, *Staten och ungdomens fritid*.
39. Ibid., 58.

> This was what the state wanted from the associations; for this they could receive financial support from the state.[40]

Associations within civil society were engaged by the state as agents not because of, but in spite of, their ideologies. They should promote the supposed common ideals, but had to put their religious or political ideologies aside if they wanted to receive financial support.[41]

The associations, including the Baptist churches, were engaged to promote the norms of the welfare state, *folkhemmet*. It was an idea and ideology that related the autonomous individuals in Swedish society directly to the state without any mediation. *Folkhemmet* became the unifying ideology. It created individuals that were released from bindings to other people, but who were united under the Swedish nation-state. I claim that *folkhemmet* was an ideology where Baptist ecclesiology, with its new knowledge and ideas, was something foreign and appeared as a competing idea. Revivalist ecclesiology was easier to adjust to the notion of *folkhemmet* since it primarily gathered around an *individual* spiritual experience and not around competing ideas.

To summarize: Since the early days of the the Örebro Mission, there has been a tension between a Baptist and a revivalist ecclesiology. These were intertwined in the denomination: a Baptist understanding of themselves as separate social bodies constituted by a specific *telos*, and a revivalistic vision of the church as a gathering of believers sharing a certain experience. In the twentieth century, the pressure from the Welfare state and the individualization thus promoted benefited the latter. The Free churches were incorporated into *folkhemmet* as allies, and given the task to promote ideals that the state and the churches were thought to share. I will now go on to show how the Baptist ecclesiology was subsumed into a revivalist ecclesiology in relation to the work with youth. Church was primarily understood as a place to promote a conversion experience for the individual, and not a redeemed community.

THE STRUGGLE OVER THE YOUTH

The Örebro Mission was a movement focused on personal conversion. This personal conversion was in the 1930s–1940s primarily understood as a

---

40. Ibid., 194.
41. SOU 1946:68, *Det fria och frivilliga folkbildningsarbetet del I*, 114.

matter of an emotional experience. Church was therefore seen as constituted of individuals who had experienced a personal conversion. It consisted of people who had "experienced the grace of reconciliation and had received the Holy Spirit."[42] Ecclesiologically, Church was seen as a community that should promote a personal emotional experience called "conversion,"—what I in this article have termed a "revivalist ecclesiology." Sanctification and the expectation of a "holy life" were then seen as consequences of conversion. Being a Christian youth was thus primarily described as an emotional experience, which was expected to result in a specific way of relating to society. This had implications for Christian youth, especially since they were exposed to popular culture. Popular culture was viewed primarily as different tools that affected the feelings of young people. This fear of popular culture was shared by the established society in general. Popular culture was at this time seen as a threat against the building of the modern Swedish welfare state, and was thus a threat against the gathered nation.

Conversion as an Emotional Transition

Conversion was first and foremost a matter of the soul. In the revivalist discourse, the soul was seen as the center or foundation of human beings and viewed as either spiritual or worldly.[43] The transfer of the soul from the worldly to the spiritual was what was understood as conversion.[44] Conversion was portrayed as an *ordo salutis* in emotional terms—from anguish to peace, from tears to rejoicing.[45] Church could then be understood as a place that should promote this emotional spiritual experience. The conversion experience was characterized as a much deeper experience than anything the world could offer. Thus the young people who had passed through a conversion experience were characterized as happier and more satisfied than the initiated young people of the world, as in this report from a Christian youth camp:

> They [Christian youth] had something that certainly separated them from the young people of the world. It was a happy, satisfied

42. Sollerman, "De ungas plats."
43. More like the biblical notion of "heart" as the center of the human life.
44. Red., "Ungdomsarbetet."
45. Magnusson, "Den troende ungdomen och de andliga livsfrågorna"; Sellerfors, "Några nyfrälsta"; En Jesu vän, "Till unga nyomvända"; Michelson, "Junior- och ungdomsläger"; Mauritz, "Juniorläger."

and sanctified horde. From their eyes shone purity, peace and thirst [after spiritual experiences]. They had already understood that life had a deeper meaning than cinema, dance and soccer.[46]

They were described as being different from other young people because of their emotional experience of conversion, a conversion that should be individual and datable.[47] This personal conversion was understood as a fundamental change, which by itself was expected to change their relation to popular culture.

Young people were seen as exposed to negative influences from popular culture outside church.[48] In the 1930s the threat from popular culture was a surface matter, not a matter of content.[49] Popular culture was viewed as unsafe and threatening, mainly because it affected the emotions. It was the sounds, the pictures, the emotional drama and lights that were viewed as a threat. The spiritual struggle was thus primarily pictured as a battle between feelings shaped by the conversion experience, on one hand, and feelings created by popular culture, on the other hand. Popular culture alluded to the lower parts of the soul, which affected the feelings, and was therefore seen as baneful. It was described as different kinds of atmospheres. This was a discursive struggle between different and competing emotions.

In the magazine *Missionsbaneret* there was a paradigmatic article that accentuates this perspective. It is about a visit to the cinema by a young boy called Ingemar Eldh, and seems to be a a kind of prescriptive parable, telling the story of a boy who slowly loses his faith.[50] Ingemar, who has experienced a true personal conversion, was invited by two of his "Christian" friends to visit a cinema.[51] A struggle started inside of him, but finally he decided to join them. He felt uncomfortable when he was waiting in the line outside.

> The Bible talks about the desire and attraction of the world, and the truth was that it was that urge and force which that very evening had brought these "Christian youth" to the horde of swearing

46. Ericson, "Gud ledde denna vecka."
47. Halldorf, *Av denna världen?*, 73–74.
48. Sollerman, "Den andliga utvecklingen."
49. The first time an argument of content or quality is used to dismiss the possibility to visit cinemas is 1959. Red., "Är det synd?"
50. Sergo, "Biografbesöket." The name is interesting. His family name is literally "Fire" and the article tells a story about a boy who loses his "fire."
51. The article has quotation marks to question if they really could be converted, since they wanted to go to cinema.

and immoral men and women. Jesus was not at their side, and therefore the sensitive Ingemar was sad and worried.[52]

The story goes on, describing how the cinema "shined its elvish light" upon the queue. The line was "absorbed" by the cinema. The light was turned off and "alluring music started to play." It was not pictured as a struggle between different worldviews, but between feelings. This was the same discursive struggle that was found within society in general. It was not the *telos* that was different, but rather the superficial emotions of the cinema.

Personal Conversion and *Folkhemmet*

This emphasis on personal conversion as a matter of emotions can be interpreted in relation to the unifying ideology of the welfare state, *folkhemmet*. The state church has since the Reformation played an important role in the construction of the Swedish nation, especially as a provider of an ethic suitable for this task.[53] The stable social norms have long been built on what is called Christian values, and as a country shaped by a Lutheran worldview, it is not hard to see that this cultural milieu could easily be interpreted as Christian. In the argumentation of politicians, it is sometimes claimed that Sweden is a Christian country.

This also applies to the discourse concerning Christian youth in *Missionsbaneret*. The Free churches, understood as a "people's movement" (*folkrörelse*), became subsumed to the construction of *folkhemmet*. A large youth meeting in Stockholm in 1939 gathered under the motto "Strong youth—Christian youth."[54] It was the Christian faith that should build the strong youth that society needed for the future. Another example was a preacher who, at the final service at a camp meeting in 1945 arranged by the Örebro Mission, proclaimed that "the Swedish way is the Christian way."[55] These two examples show that Free churches also shared the idea of Sweden as a country built on Christian values. Further, the young people at the Örebro Mission's youth camps gathered every morning during this

---

52. Sergo, "Biografbesöket," Quotation mark original.
53. Cf. Blückert, "Att erövra folket."
54. C. Th. Lm., "En tanke från Gud."
55. Sollerman, "Trygghet i farornas värld."

period under the Swedish flag and sang the national anthem.[56] The idea of a connection between nation and church was, of course, created and reinforced by these practices. But it was not only these obvious attributes that connected Free churches with the idea of a gathered nation. There was also a mutual indignation in society over what was understood as an increasing immorality—an immorality that would be a threat against the construction of the welfare state. Youth were of course seen as forerunners in this decay. The Swedish government appointed at this time a committee that was to investigate these matters, in order to secure the future morality of the youth.[57] The moral decay was interpreted as a threat against a "good recruitment of citizens." The youth, then, must be disciplined.[58] Free churches shared this anxiety with a large part of society.[59] Popular culture was viewed as an alternative "folk high school"[60] which fostered a new generation characterized by idolatry, ease and amusement.[61] Some Free Church leaders complained that they were not invited to be a part of the state sponsored public investigation. The Free churches saw the battle for the same moral question as a matter of spiritual revival, and had the same goal as other groups in society: to secure and gather the Swedish society. They wanted to participate in the building of society and as such they took the side of conservative values, which of course at that time were understood to be the same thing as Christian values. Their solution was not democracy or conservatism, but a "people's revival" which affected the entire Swedish nation. This is

---

56. Ragné, "Östersundslägret"; Cf. F. G., "Ungdomshögtid"; Chilo, "ÖM:s 12:e riksläger"; Ragné, "Vadstenalägret."

57. Netz, "Med blicken mot framtiden." *Ungdomsvårdskommitténs betänkande I*; *Ungdomsvårdskommitténs betänkande II*; *Ungdomsvårdskommitténs betänkande III*.

58. C.f Ambjörnsson and Carrigan, *The Honest and Diligent Worker;* Ambjörnsson, *Den skötsamme arbetaren*. It is interesting to note that the same cultural arenas were seen as dangerous by the labor movement, the conservatives, and the Free churches. Different arguments were used in each of these groups, but they all argued within the context of what was best for the nation.

59. Boëthius, *När Nick Carter drevs på flykten*; Olson, *Staten och ungdomens fritid*. It was of course not only cinema which was seen as the new school, but also for example outdoor dance floors and sports.

60. "Folk high school" is a Scandinavian concept where young adults have the opportunity to spend a year or more in a different type of school than a traditional university. This school form is financed by the state. Subjects studied can for example be arts, painting, music or literature. This has been a large movement that has also been important in fostering young people on their path to becoming adults.

61. Red., "Domen över ungdomen."

similar to Michel Foucault's argument in *Discipline and Punish*. He argues that even communities that are not official institutions or organizations, for example churches, can appear as exponents for the dominating values in a society.[62] They become partners of the disciplining forces that determine what the acceptable values are in a given society.[63] The Free churches were a mirror of the surrounding culture and reinforced the common values in society through their revivalist ecclesiology. Personal conversion as an emotional experience became an instrument for reaching the same goal as society in general. Not even the Baptists, who upon their emergence in Sweden were founded on new ideas and knowledge, could resist the idea of *folkhemmet*.[64]

Conversion was understood as a matter of a datable and individual emotional experience. It was a description of a theology of conversion that emerges from what I have labeled a revivalist ecclesiology. One could argue that there is a genealogical relation between the individuality of *folkhemmet* and personal conversion understood in a revivalist sense. It is the individual's own emotional experience that is fundamental. Personal conversion was no longer incorporation into a new body with its peculiar ideas and knowledge that directed the individuals' desire towards another *telos* than the vision of the "people's home," *folkhemmet*. Conversion and the believers' incorporation into another social body have thus been separated. The goal of an emotional personal conversion becomes the same as being a good citizen in the Swedish welfare state. This, I argue, can be understood as a scattered conversion. Genealogically I claim that it is similar to the dictatorship of Chile's attempt to scatter the Catholic church, although obviously in a more peaceful way.

CONCLUSION

I therefore conclude that the revivalist ecclesiology became dominant because it was easier to adjust to a nation which created an autonomous individual, guaranteed by the ideology of statist individualism, a state that was also supposed to be built on stable Christian values. In the Swedish Free churches, conversion has therefore primarily become a matter of an

---

62. Cf. Foucault, *Discipline and Punish*, chapter 3, "Panopticism." He claims that this is seen in their focus on conversion and morality, economic help and politic

63. Kennerberg, *Innanför eller utanför*.

64. Blückert, *The Church as Nation*, 219, 312.

emotional experience, and does not entail another way of seeing and valuing the world. It is the depth of feelings that characterizes the revivalist conversion, not the *telos* or content. Church becomes a place to promote a sense of spiritual feelings, which in this construction of Christianity is called conversion. The church as a new social body, which was the expected result of conversion in Baptist ecclesiology, was scattered and subsumed to the revivalist ecclesiology which was more at home in a nation gathered under the idea of the welfare state, *folkhemmet*. This theology has then developed in a nation that has guaranteed the autonomy of the individual, and has resulted in the autonomous individual's own experience becoming the ultimate judge of whether a true conversion has occurred or not. Conversion and salvation have been released from any external authority and a person can be converted without a relation to a church. This revivalist version of conversion becomes the tool to reach the same goal as society in general, because it lacks the connection to another *telos* that Baptist ecclesiology accentuates.

But what happens when a majority no longer thinks that society should be built on Christian values? Can this conclusion shed some light on why an average Free church member conforms to the moral views of society? Or can it give perspective on why another group of Free church members fights to maintain Christian values as the foundation of Christian Sweden?

3

The Loss of Theological Visions

Free Church Ecclesiologies in Sweden from the Nineteenth Century to the Present

Sune Fahlgren

INTRODUCTION

In Sweden in particular and in the Nordic countries in general, the national Lutheran church was the all-exclusive church for several centuries. Eventually, under turmoil and tension other churches were established in the nineteenth century, but they were all defined by their marginal relation to the majority Church. The Baptist union, the Methodist church, the Salvation Army, and others were labeled "Free churches" and were regarded as side-movements to the Church of Sweden.

Historians have offered several explanations for this religious shift. Here I will display the theological convictions that were embedded in the "new" churches and their ecclesial practices, which made them progressive in the society. I will also discuss the fact that theological visions have more or less been lost in the Free churches of the present day. The consequence of this "spiritual dementia" is that clear distinctions and colorful differences have been replaced by uniformity. This unintended "McDonaldization" of

Part One—Modern Discipline

the Free Church traditions can now be seen in the liturgical manifestations, in which all denominations more or less serve the same spiritual dish.

THE TREASURE

The parable of the Hidden Treasure is a well-known parable of Jesus, which appears in Matthew 13:44. The brief parable is as follows:

> Again, the Kingdom of Heaven is like a treasure hidden in the field, which a man found, and hid. In his joy, he goes and sells all that he has, and buys that field.

This parable is generally interpreted as illustrating the great value of the Kingdom of God ("Heaven"), embodied in Jesus Christ, and thus has a theme similar to the parable of the pearl, which comes directly after. However, other interpretations of the parable exist, in which the treasure represents for example the Church (*ecclesia*).[1] Even if the Church and the Kingdom of God are not identical—the Kingdom is a wider biblical concept—the Church is closely related to the Kingdom as its sign and instrument. Here I will use the parable in this ecclesial sense to introduce the plot of this chapter.

The Church is for many Christians in Sweden today the hidden treasure. Even if they have experience of the church, they lack a theological vision of the nature and the mission of the Church. They don't recognize that they are in fact Christians due to the fact that the Church is witnessing about Christ and praying for the world.

The spiritual mothers and fathers in the Swedish Free churches discovered the theological treasures of the Church. This treasure shaped their communities of faith and the members' daily lives. In the Free Church traditions many also suffered for their convictions and visions of the Church. It cost them everything they had—time, money, prayers, actions, and reflections. But today many members of the Free churches have only a vague idea about this theological treasure. It has been lost in the field of history, forgotten, and other matters have become more important in a secularized society. The Church is for them a forgotten treasure.

The designation "Free Church" refers here to a Christian community that is intrinsically separated from government and committed

---

1. Lockyer, *All the Parables*, 197–200.

to freedom.² The historic Free churches take the congregational (rather than the episcopal) form. In Sweden there are two kinds of Free Church denominations. One group developed from revivalist movements within the Church of Sweden (new-evangelical revivalism), and the other kind is denominations that immigrated to Sweden during the nineteenth century and twentiethc entury (Baptism, Methodism, Pentecostalism, Holiness movement, Salvation Army). Instead of "Free Church" the concept "Believers' Church" is also widely used, understanding the church to be a community in which all its members profess a personal faith in Christ. Sometimes "non-creedal church" is used as a synonym. Free Church traditions genereally reject creeds as definitive statements of faith, even while agreeing with some creeds' substance.

After this tentative definition of the term Free Church we can return to the parable. The man who found the treasure can also be interpreted as Christ, the Head of the Church. And the treasure can be seen as the Church, his body. The New Testament testifies that the Son of God suffered and gave his life on the Cross "to reconcile all things to" God (Col 1:20). In God's eyes, humankind is the precious hidden treasure; His redeemed people, His beloved Family, and "each one of you" are unique members of the Body of Christ (1 Cor 12:27).

This Christological perspective was often the starting point for the Swedish Free Church visions of the Church: "Because Christ first found us, we found Him, and He became the Lord of our lives." The Christian community was seen as a precious gift, not a given, in the sense of what the world would call natural rights or social entitlements. They understood the Church as rooted and born in the divine community of the triune God (1 John 1:3). Like the Church in Pinochet's Chile, which William T. Cavanuagh has analyzed in his groundbreaking thesis *Torture and Eucharist* (1998), the liturgy, along with their other practices, made the Swedish Free churches moreover into political bodies with an alternative *theopolitical imagination*.³ Cavanaugh's point is that such ecclesial practices presuppose the Church.

Thus, the Church is a precious treasure for both God and man. Compared to the picture I will give in the following historical sketch, it is obvious that the Free churches in Sweden are suffering from the loss of theological

---

2. Here I do not follow Ernst Troeltsch in his more expansive account of the "Free Church." See *The Social Teaching*. 661–75.

3. Cf. Cavanaugh, *Theopolitical Imagination*.

visions. This loss can be seen as a collective spiritual *dementia*, a loss that affects memory, thinking, language, and behavior.

NOTHING BRAND NEW

Once upon a time the Free churches in Sweden were vibrant spiritual movements that challenged both individuals and society, including the Lutheran national church. Today many think that these movements were a result of purely Swedish developments, which exploded like an original force of nature at a grassroots level during the nineteenth century. But they were not. Ideas and practices came from the outside. In the eithteenth century Pietism came with returning soldiers from King Charles XII's army, and the Moravian revival via Denmark.[4] Although the Moravian Church was forbidden in Sweden, the theology and spirituality of the movement spread among priests and laymen and became the breeding ground for the popular revival of the nineteenth century. One of its most prominent leaders, Carl-Olof Rosenius (1816–1868), was influenced by the Moravians' "heart religion," inter-confessional community life, zeal for mission, and groundbreaking pedagogy.

Several characteristics of the Free churches in Sweden can be traced back to the first centuries of the Christian era—e.g. the discipline and ascetic standards among the Montanists—and lay movements during the medieval period, such as civil disobedience and the critique of corrupt church practice of Albigenses and Waldenses.[5] The Anabaptists, the radical wing of the Reformation, turned alterity (being/thinking differently) and freedom from governmental interference into an ecclesial virtue. Simultaneously, movements appeared in England that established independent congregations. Eventually, they became a part of the strong Puritan

---

4. For an overview of the Church History in Sweden in the nineteenth century, see Bexell, *Sveriges kyrkohistoria*. Pietism and Herrnhutism attracted also women from all social classes. It can be said that these movements gave women a forum and a voice. From a religious perspective, their experiences were just as valid as those of the men, but the scope of their contributions was more restricted. See Aurelius, "The Language of Desire."

5. The Church historian and Baptist Gunnar Westin (1890–1967) has written an exposé over the history of Free Church traditions in this perspective: *Den kristna friförsamlingen*. Even if the exposition is short of theory and methodology, it reveals dimensions in Church History that often get left in the shadows. But it is not a Landmarkists' belief that there has been an unbroken "succession" of Free churches since the time of the Apostles.

movement in the seventeenth-century. Due to persecution and oppression many Anabaptists and Puritans immigrated to America, where they grew in number. The American model was established and became a pattern for Swedes and many others: a system of Free churches in open competition.

During the eighteenth century Methodism was added to the Free Church branch of Protestantism in Sweden, and at the dawn of the twentieth century the Azusa Street Revival in Los Angeles led to another new form of ecclesial community. The Pentecostal theology of the baptism in the Holy Spirit, and the practices related to that experience, deeply influenced Swedish Free Church denominations.[6]

The founding of Swedish Free Church traditions took place between 1848, when the first Baptist congregation was formed, and 1878 when the Swedish Covenant Church was established. The first Free Churches came through migrant workers and Swedish seamen, but they were judicially and in other respects an anomaly. Sweden was a uniform society and the idea of other churches being parallel to the Church of Sweden was unthinkable. Church and state had a largely symbiotic relationship although the nationalistic discourse, especially in its rhetoric, had a somewhat parasitic relationship to Christian traditions. Nationalism was the super ideology.[7]

The immigrant Churches were already well established as legitimate Churches and denominations outside of Sweden. First came Methodism and Baptism. As is still true today, they practiced a voluntary membership, personal confession of faith, and "the priesthood of all believers" (strong laity participation in worship and mission). These imported churches were certainly strange birds in the Lutheran Sweden. But Baptism and Methodism expanded, and cracks began to appear in the uniform culture of Sweden.

Additionally, the domestic revivalist movements—the so-called New evangelical movement—were inspired by Free Church traditions from outside the country. In the middle of the nineteenth century important impulses came from Presbyterian Scotland, where one third of the members of the Church of Scotland (a national church) seceded in 1843 and founded

---

6. Jacobsen, *The World's Christians*.

7. Blückert, *Church as Nation*. The parable "church as nation" pictures what happened to a national church when a theocratic and dynastic society, with a homogeneous ethnicity, was dissolved and a supranational point of reference was missing. The nation, in all its aspects, became an ecclesial mark (a *nota ecclesiae*) in the Church of Sweden in order to restore an ideal unity in society, a unity that was expected to be incarnated in, or at least summoned up by, the church. For more on this, see Trägårdh in this volume.

Part One—Modern Discipline

The Free Church of Scotland. Swedish theologians and leaders of the revivalist movements visited the newly founded Free Church in Scotland and established contacts with its theological seminary in Aberdeen. The principal of the Seminary in Aberdeen, James Lumsden, visited Sweden in 1853 and was shocked by the Lutheran national church system, by the laws forbidding spiritual meetings without a priest in attendance, and by the harsh treatment of members defined as deviant or heretical.[8]

Lumsden became one of many overseas actors that translated English religious tracts to Swedish and circulated them by carriers called colporteurs. This literature bore the Free Church visions, but it had a more Calvinist approach. It is no wonder that the Swedish Lutheran priests did all they could to stop the distribution. New convictions and commitments were threatening to the national church and its Lutheran theology. A shift of paradigm was inaugurated in Sweden. The transition had begun from a uniform to a differentiated society, from an administrative pattern to a transformative one.

These examples of historical memory (*anamnesis*) are embedded in the identities of the Free churches, and a vital part of the Free Church ecclesiologies. A loss of history is a loss of theology and what William Cavanaugh calls theological imagination.[9] The opposite is also true: Awareness of history, and the way we write and use history, can also shape theology.

In the past, the historical dimensions of their origination were more actively remembered in the Swedish Free churches—by storytelling, in documenting, in celebrating anniversaries, and in daily considerations. The understanding of history was also different from today's understanding. It was like the biblical history: a story of continuity and fulfillment, struggle and victory. Not the modern narration of development and progress informed by instrumental rationality and capitalism. The Free churches in general had an organic view of history. Even if they reacted against the idea of the authority of post-apostolic tradition in the church (*sola scriptura*), in ecclesial practices they showed deep respect for the work of the Spirit in the history of the churches, which is another way of saying tradition.[10]

8. Lumsden, *Sweden, Its Religions State*.
9. Cavanaugh, *Theopolitical Imagination*.
10. This understanding of development of doctrine is related to the idea of illumination by the Spirit. Free Church theology recognizes the continuing ministry of the Spirit in the Church. Early Baptists like John Smyth and Thomas Helwys called it "further light." In this theology of illumination there is a need for corporate interpretation of scripture to take place in the conversation of congregations with each other.

Sune Fahlgren—*The Loss of Theological Visions*

For many Christians in Sweden today, Church history means experiences they have left behind, perceived as primitive modes of being that they have outgrown. They assume that they are now more enlightened and better equipped than the Christians that came before them. But actually, what the loss of history and an organic historiography have given is a continuous present—boring and without visions for the future. My impression is that contemporary Free churches are less enlightened and not as well equipped as earlier. They are not aware that the historical heritage is a vital part of the hidden treasure.

IT WAS IN PLURAL

The loss of history is one reason that the current public discourse about Free Church traditions is now in singular and definite form: "The Free Church" in Sweden. But historically and theologically they were not uniform, except, maybe, in contrast to the majority church—the Church of Sweden. There is a multitude of Free Church communities, with different ways of incarnating and shedding light on Christ. Gradually these churches and movements shaped a new spiritual landscape in Sweden. The different theologies and ecclesial practices made a difference. New religious bodies were constructed, and old ones split. Further the revivalist movement was divided when new theological visions were spread. I will give three historical examples. With the distance of a hundred years, we might admire these Free Churches, but at that time the differences were provocative and abstractive.

- In the late nineteenth century, the evangelicals around Dr. Paul Petter Waldenström (1838–1917) dreamed about a low threshold into the Kingdom of God. "Come as you are," sounded the message from the many simple chapels ("Mission houses"). Waldenström and his followers wanted to be an attractive fellowship for "all life of faith," an alternative to the "unbiblical" national church, often called state church. In the year 1878 they founded the Covenant Church on the basis of a personal confession of faith. Individually and as a denomination they strived to be decent and respectable in the society. Well-organized Mission houses, solemn organ music, and educated pastors were important. The vision of a "life of faith" led them to an extensive involvement in cultural and political work. Many Covenant Church

Part One—Modern Discipline

members have had political positions in the Swedish parliament and city councils.[11]

- Members of the Holiness movement in Sweden gathered every Midsummer for camp meetings at a manor called Torp outside the city of Örebro. Their visions differed from those of the Mission Covenant. They wanted to be the "pure people of God," ready for the second coming of the Lord. They believed that their purity would attract others to "a deeper life with God," a concept related to the theology of Christian perfection in Wesleyanism. Around the message of Christian liberty from "the Reign of the Flesh" they established an informal community of Christians from different traditions. The Swedish Holiness movement erected clear borders between church and society, but it can at the same time be understood as an expression of the emerging modernity.[12]

- The Baptists in Sweden are another example of Free churches of the past that viewed themselves as a counter cultural and were influential actors in their society—because they were different. The theological vision among the Swedish Baptists focused on "following Christ." This faithful discipleship was manifested in the believers' baptism and by a life among the community of the baptized, expressed, for instance, in the concern for matters of conscience. The Baptists were not afraid of civil disobedience. The so-called Free Baptists refused to do military service. In the nineteenth century the Baptists in Våmhus, in the region Dalecarlia, were not permitted to marry because they did not belong to the Church of Sweden. So they got married without having their unions confirmed by the state. Even when the Lutheran priest came with the police to baptize their children by force, they resisted. It was a basic question of obeying God more than man.[13]

These days the Free churches are focusing on what they share under the umbrella of "ecumenism." This modern concept for overcoming the denominationalism of the past is in general not controversial because the key visions in the different Free churches have been de-theologized or neutralized. Sociologists and theologians claim that the operative differences are no longer between the Free churches or between the Church of Sweden

11. Read more in Walan, *Församlingstanken i Svenska Missionsförbundet*.
12. Halldorf, *Av denna världen?*
13. See e.g., Fahlgren, *Predikantskap och församling*.

and the Free churches, but within them. It applies to both convictions and spirituality, e.g. views on the Scripture and charismas.

The loss of a spectrum of ecclesiologies, which once emanated from the various Free churches in Sweden, is a loss of theological visions. Instead we find more of the same practices and clichés that are already in the secular-liberal culture. An unexamined secular-liberal ecclesiology has replaced the primary place of the "visible" local church with a stage- and me-centered church. The Free Church understanding of the autonomy of the local church is logically becoming every member's rights and freedom. The central place of "covenant,"[14] in the teaching of what it means to be faithful to each other and to God, has been replaced by the concept of "project." The dissenting communities, once contributing to the shift of the homogenous Swedish society to something pluralistic, are in today's multi-cultural and multi-religious context standing out as very dull, monotonous and predictable.[15] From this point of view the colorful spectrum of ecclesiologies is the hidden treasure.

RELATIONS TO THE "CAESAR"

The separation of Church and State has been mapped as a common feature for Free churches in Sweden. The government of the church cannot be given to any power other than Christ. What is crucial in this position is to maintain the freedom of the church to be itself. "Free" in "Free church" means here free from any coercion from external human authorities.

Members of the Free churches quote the following words of Jesus: "Give to Caesar what is Caesar's and to God what is God's" (Mark 12:17). There is also a historiography in support of this position. The Baptist version of it goes something like this:

In the earliest years of the Christian history, the church suffered persecution from the Roman Caesars. In the fourth century, the Roman Empire decreed not only toleration but also a privileged position for the Christians. This led to a union of church and state, which became a union of the prevailing government with the dominant form of Christianity. The arrangements varied through the centuries, but one thing remained

---

14. Several Free Church denominations had "covenant" in their name, e.g. Missionsförbundet, Baptistförbundet, Helgelseförbundet.

15. On the homogenizing pressure of the nation-state on the churches, see Cavanaugh, "Killing for the Telephone Company," 243–74.

constant—all forms of religious expression except the "official" one were persecuted. People who believed in freedom of religion were regarded as traitors by the emperors, and as heretics by the state-supported churches. Using the power of the state to enforce religion zapped the spiritual vitality of the established state churches and added a host of nominal Christians to the churches. Furthermore, efforts by governments to protect the established religion of a country resulted in wars and civil strife that undermined the governments. Thus, the union of church and state was and is harmful to both.

In line with this story, the Free churches believed that the political meaning of the Christian communities becomes clearer if the Church is separated from the State. They aspired to the full freedom to govern themselves regarding doctrine, liturgy, the congregation, the fellowship of congregations, ordination, and economy. Radical Free Church theologians claim that the universal Church is suffering from a *defectus* ("a serious wound") with regard to the full meaning of Church.[16] This lack appeared in the 4th century, when the Church became an integrated part of the empire (*Corpus Christianum*), sometimes called Constantinianism. How, then, did then the Swedish Free churches understand and construct freedom from the State in practice?

The Baptist denominations in Sweden have been Free churches in this dissenting sense. In the 1970s, the Baptists gathered in the Örebro Mission made a critical analysis of the Swedish government's economic support to religious communities.[17] The board of the Örebro Mission decided then to forego the governmental support to its theological seminary. One of the objectives was to highlight the dangers of state influence over the Church. "We problematized the whole thing," said former principal Sigfrid Deminger in an interview. "And already the problematizing was perceived in the 1970s as a provocation."[18]

Before the new legislation in 2009 on same-sex marriage, the Baptist Union in Sweden declared that it would not automatically mean that they were going to heed it. They see themselves as sovereign in relation to the

16. Cf. Vatican II, which speaks of a *defectus* in the Protestant churches (*Unitatis Redintegratio*, "Decree on Ecumenism"), refers to the sacramental life of these churches. The full meaning of this term is twofold. In the Latin, the one term (from the verb *deficio*) connotes both a "revolt" and a "lack."

17. Deminger, *Kejsarens pengar och Guds?*

18. Ericson, "Varningsord om Kejsarens pengar och Guds," *Svenska Dagbladet*, February 9, 2004. For more on this, see Wenell in this volume.

State in matter of conscience. Another Baptist denomination—The Evangelical Free Church—decided to return the right to perform legal marriage to the government as a mark of their Free Church theology and practices regarding marriage.

Aside from the Baptist churches, this distinctive form of dissenting is not particularly prominent in the Free Church denominations of Sweden. There can be several causes for this. One might be that the majority still understands the role of the state in light of the Lutheran two kingdoms doctrine, even among the Free Churches.[19] This doctrine is an echo of Martin Luther´s distinction between the worldly and the spiritual, and emphasizes that God rules in two ways. Ultimately this distinction developed the idea of a neutral secular sphere (the public sector) based on "common sense." It gradually came to be regarded as more fundamental than the spiritual, because it had God-given rationality as its basis. As a result, churches hesitate to perform in public if they do not behave in line with the secular-rational status quo. Religion has thus become limited to the sphere of the private individual.[20]

The theopolitical imagination of the Church is the hidden treasure.

RELIGIOUS FREEDOM WITH SECULAR CONDITIONS

It can be seen that the Free churches in Sweden have been proponents of toleration, and they pushed for a law that would give legal guarantees for religious freedom. In 1951 religious freedom was finally granted to Swedish citizens as a legal right.[21] But did it give freedom? The Church of Sweden retained its unique status because the Religious Freedom Act did not separate the Lutheran Church from the State. In that sense, the law was a half-measure; the State was still not free. The next change came in the year 2000, when the relationship between the Church of Sweden and the State

---

19. For more on this, see Trägårdh in this volume.

20. Cf. Cavanaugh, *Theopolitical Imagination;* See also Cavanaugh, *Migrations.*

21. Until 1860 it was illegal for Lutheran Swedes to convert to another confession or religion. From that point, until 1951, it was legal to leave the Church of Sweden for the purpose of becoming a member of another officially recognised religious denomination. In 1951 it became legal to leave the church, without giving a reason. From 1951 until 1977 religious communities (i.e. abbeys, priories, convents and such) were not to be established without the permission of the Lutheran Crown, but that clause was abolished in 1977.

was altered, but the National-State still defines the internal structure of the Church of Sweden.

That the Act of 1951 also infringed upon the Free churches' internal structures is less known. With the new law, all "religious denominations" (*trossamfund*) were granted legal status as associations, while the Church of Sweden retained its legal status as a church.

Thus, the tolerance required the Free churches to organize themselves as secular associations. The Baptists, who were organized as "the Church in the New Testament" with a pastor, deacons, church meetings, etc., had for a hundred years solved the legal issues by having a foundation (*stiftelse*) that met once a year. The new law turned the local and the trans-local Baptist Church into an association.

We can imagine the 1951 Act as a Trojan horse. For a long time, the Free Church communities demanded religious freedom in Sweden—for themselves and others. When it finally was granted, they did not recognize that by giving them "freedom" the State incorporated them, making them a part of the secular liberal project. The myth of private religion became the accepted standard. Liberty became the freedom of the (strong) individual, who could now also be completely free from any religious identity. Democracy was encoded into an established popular movement model—the association. The Free churches were tamed along the lines of the modern nation-state.

Instead of developing a typology for new ways of being Free churches in relation to the state—e.g: "we are a different social body with a different policy: we have a theological vision for engagement with the social and political environment"—Free churches were reduced to being an opposition to the national Lutheran church (Church of Sweden). The younger Free churches have pushed the pejorative even further: "We are not bound as the state church, we are free." This freedom has been interpreted literally by many: "They have their forms (liturgy), we are free (from forms)."[22] But it is the ecclesial practices that form a way of life, which make it possible for the Church to be another kind of *polis* (society).

The practices of the church (e.g., liturgy and church meetings) are the hidden treasure.

---

22. This passé and over-polarized opposition must be ended. We need a theological vision for mission in the post-secular Sweden, which embraces the inclusive model of the Church of Sweden and the gathered Church model of the Free churches. We have the momentum for an ecclesiological cross-fertilization. For more on this, see Halldorf in this volume.

REMEMBERING THE PAST TO IMAGINE THE FUTURE

Let me conclude by saying that we can read history in different ways. If you do not view history as a necessity but as a series of choices we made and visions we sought to realize, historical cases (as the ones above) can provide the basis for self-examination and give birth to new visions.

In retrospect, we have seen that the Free churches in Sweden paved the way for the differentiation, rationalization and pluralization of the homogenous Swedish society through their remarkable diversity. They became themselves varieties of modernity. How are the Free churches encountering an increasingly multi-cultural and multi-religious society? Here I have highlighted tendencies toward what can be called "McDonaldization" such as uniformity, predictability, and a thin faith consciousness. But there are also other tendencies.

One feature that unites the historical cases (*anamnesis*) is the loss of theological visions. Visions mean something we don't currently have and therefore are striving for. Visions are the mind-set of a Church *in via*.

The challenge is to have theological visions that make Christians less at home in this world. Only then will they be able to interpret their continuing task ("God's mission") based on their unique identity as members of Christ's Body, the Church. These visions must be made rooted in practices, so as to create concrete communities. Without concrete communities of faith, we have no idea what it actually means to follow Jesus Christ in this world. We are suffering from a spiritual dementia.

The medicine is theological visions. This is the hidden treasure, costly to get. The man in the parable sold all he had. What are we ready to do to make the treasure our own?

4

Evangelicals, Practices, and the Univocity of Being

Avoiding the Pitfall of Gnosticism

Joel Halldorf

INTRODUCTION

The argument of this chapter is that the evangelical ideals of simplicity and spontaneity are rooted in a univocal understanding of being. If there is only one kind of being, which God and creation are imagined to share, then God cannot be thought of as present in and through created matter but rather instead of it. Thus the tendency in the Free churches and Evangelicalism in general to perceive complex practices and materiality as competing with God's presence, as well as to favor simplicity and spontaneity. But the reluctance towards practices has resulted in an inability to withstand the cultural pressures of modernity. As a consequence Evangelicalism has turned into a mirror image of secular modernity. Furthermore, skepticism towards the material and a preference for authenticity is theologically problematic since it is, as this chapter will demonstrate, akin to a Gnostic worldview.

DEFINITIONS: SIMPLICITY, SPONTANEITY, AND PRACTICE

In this article I argue that simplicity and spontaneity are prominent features of the evangelical spirituality which characterized the Free churches, and that they are rooted in a univocal understanding of being.[1] Simplicity is used in a colloquial sense as denoting something plain and uncomplicated, while the spontaneous is defined as that which springs forth without external cause.[2] A spirituality characterized by simplicity and spontaneity will want to avoid set practices, external means, and material objects in worship since they restrain spontaneity and contradict simplicity by inscribing certain patterns on devotion. A spirituality centered on practices and material objects assumes that the divine is mediated through external means, while a spirituality of simplicity and spontaneity emphasizes the direct and personal relationship between God and man's soul. The preference of simplicity leads to a desire to clear the religious universe from what are seen as unnecessary or even contra-productive institutions, structures, and practices. These are perceived as potential obstacles to the presence of God. In a "simple" religious universe there is only Jesus and the individual believer—no means or middle-men.

A practice is, as Alasdair MacIntyre has put it, a "socially established" activity.[3] The fact that it is done according to a set and agreed upon pattern puts it in opposition to spontaneity. This is what creates the ambivalence towards practices within Evangelicalism, where simplicity and spontaneity are favored. But practices are vital to create and sustain the identity of any individual or group. A religious identity cannot be sustained by theological opinions and religious experiences alone. If a religious group in modernity neglects to develop and connect their identity to practices they will not

---

1. On spontaneity as a prominent feature in evangelical/pietistic spirituality, see Kaufman and Wenell in this volume.

2. Simplicity is a concept with wide connotations in philosophy and theology. Classical theists such as Augustine and Thomas Aquinas have described God as characterized by "divine simplicity" (*simplicitas Dei*), that is free from complexity or composition in terms of matter/form, potency/act, or existence/essence. This is a way of underlining the fundamental otherness of God. In relation to political theology, John Milbank has contrasted "simple space" and "complex space" with regards to the organization of society. See Milbank, *The Word Made Strange*, 268–92.

3. MacIntyre, *After Virtue*, 187. For a more thorough discussion on practices, see also Kaufman in this volume.

be able to withstand modern culture. The alternative imagination must be rooted in praxis in order to be realized.

EVANGELICAL SPIRITUALITY

Evangelicalism can be defined by history, principle, and methodology. The movement is genealogically connected to seventeenth-century Pietism, it emphasizes the need for personal conversion, and it has developed certain methods aimed at fostering such an experience.[4] Evangelicalism thus includes, but is not limited to, Methodism, Baptism, the Holiness movement, and Pentecostalism. These movements are united by certain shared historical roots, theological emphases, and methodology. The connection might at times seem loose, but it is there. Simply put: if someone asks you if you have been born again, you know that she is an evangelical—but you don't know if she is a Baptist or a Pentecostal.[5] Many evangelical movements formed separate denominations—Free churches—but there are also evangelicals within the state churches such as the Swedish Lutheran Church and the Anglican Church. According to the definition I work with here, the Free churches are evangelical, but not all evangelicals belong to a Free church.[6]

Evangelicalism is a broad category, but I argue that simplicity and spontaneity are crucial common denominators within this movement.[7] Simplicity is the cardinal virtue of Evangelicalism. Evangelicals want to be uncomplicated and down-to-earth. They gather in simple churches with little architectural embellishment, they sing simple choruses to Jesus, and they listen to preachers who preach the gospel straightforwardly in a plain and popular idiom. Evangelicals are generally not fond of liturgy, sacraments, or religious icons but cherish most of all a personal relationship with Jesus. In his liturgical study of the Free Church tradition, Christopher

---

4. Halldorf, *Av denna världen?*, 32–36. The latter part of the definition, the reference to revivalist practices, is inspired by Sweeney, *An American Evangelical Story*, 23–25.

5. Or in the words of W. R. Ward: "Evangelicals, in the Anglo-Saxon sense of the word, seem generally to have found it easier to recognise each other than others have found it to categorise them." Ward, *Early Evangelicalism*, 6.

6. The reason why I chose to work with "Evangelicalism" as a category rather than "Free church" is that much of my empirical material comes from representatives who belong to the latter category: evangelicals who don't belong to a Free church.

7. Halldorf, *Av denna världen?*, 219–21, 279–84. Cf. Ellis, *Gathering*, 27, 50, 67–68, 75 for the importance of simplicity and freedom from set structures in what he calls "the Free Church tradition."

J. Ellis comments that "there is a concern for *simplicity* and freedom [in worship]. This simplicity is evident in the lack of ceremonial activity and in the valuing of *spontaneity*."[8]

It is true that some evangelical denominations have more elaborate liturgies or refined church buildings, but this is generally a result of later developments, reflecting institutionalization and a strive for middle-class respectability. Accordingly, scholars tend to interpret evangelical institutionalization as a movement away from the original impulse.[9] Within the movement itself developments of this kind provide the background for the recurring call to go "back to basics": To leave theological quarrels behind, to disassemble organization and complicated structures, and to center the Christian life on Jesus and Jesus only.

REJECTION OF PRACTICES AND CULTURAL ADAPTABILITY

This evangelical quest for the simple and spontaneous is mirrored by skepticism towards structure and practices. Evangelicals have generally viewed creeds, hierarchies, tradition, and liturgy with suspicion.[10] The movement's ability to be contextualized in different cultural settings is connected to this skepticism—Evangelicalism is popular and pliable because of its suspicion towards elaborate fixed patterns. As a body without bone structure it has a remarkable cultural adaptability.[11] The downside of this flexibility is that it is unable to withstand the pressures of the surrounding world—modernity—and to preserve and develop a distinct identity.[12] This is something of a paradox. In its own perception, Evangelicalism is at odds with society,

---

8. Ellis, *Gathering*, 68. Italics mine.

9. Dayton, *Discovering an Evangelical Heritage*.

10. Bebbington, *Dominance of Evangelicalism*, 154–58. See also the works of D. H. Williams, which addresses the question of creeds and tradition from an evangelical perspective. For example Williams, *Retrieving the Tradition* and Williams, *Evangelicals and Tradition*.

11. See Balmer, *The Making of Evangelicalism*, 3 for a similar argument: "One of the reasons evangelicalism is so pliable is that, unlike other religious traditions, it is not (for the most part) bound by ecclesiastical hierarchies, creedal formulas, or liturgical rubrics." Cf. Noll, *The Rise of Evangelicalism*, 20–21.

12. In his classical study *Evangelicalism in Modern Britain* Bebbington shows that the evangelical movement has tended to mirror the dominant cultural mood of its time, be it Enlightenment rationality or Romantic sentimentality.

which it generally designates "the world." Evangelicals decry the drinking, dancing, and gambling of "the world," they sing songs with lyrics like "This world is not my home, I'm just a passing through," and they fight to keep their congregations free from any worldly influence. But on a more fundamental level Evangelicalism is very much in harmony with modernity. The focus on experience and the requirement of a personal conversion narrative mirrors individualism.[13] Emphasis on growth and numbers reveal an instrumental rationality and reflect a capitalist mood.[14] The "new measures" of Charles G. Finney's (1792–1875) revivalism gave Evangelicalism a scientific methodology of its own.[15] On the surface, Evangelicalism might reject "the world," but it is still as much a part of modernity as the Enlightenment, Romanticism or any other modern movement.[16]

A CASE: FREE PRAYER

A clarifying example of the evangelical rejection of practices in favor of the simple and spontaneous is its relationship to written or set prayers. The ideal of free prayers emerged among sixteenth century Puritans; Luther wanted to reform liturgy, but the more radical Puritans rejected liturgy altogether. Spontaneity came to be seen as a more sincere and authentic expression of spirituality, and was thus favored.[17] The same attitude permeates Evangelicalism.[18] Written prayers are perceived as dangerous since they might encourage a superficial rambling not grounded within, and if the heart is left out the prayers spoken do not count. John Wesley (1703–1791) allows set prayers, while adding: "But the sooner you break through this backwardness the better. Ask of God, and he will soon open your mouth."[19]

---

13. Brauer, "Conversion," 234; Hindmarsh, *Evangelical Conversion Narrative*, 337–40; Halldorf, *Av denna världen?*, 67–95.

14. Halldorf, *Av denna världen?*, 115–26.

15. Finney, *Lectures*, 248–62; Cross, *The Burned-over District*, 173–84; Robertson, *The Chicago Revival*, 43–62.

16. This assessment differs from that of David Bebbington, who sees Evangelicalism as a child of the Enlightenment. In my view, the Enlightenment and Evangelicalism are both children of modernity—they are siblings, in other words, rather than parent and child. Cf. Bebbington, *Evangelicalism in Modern Britain*, 42–74.

17. Branch, *Rituals of Spontaneity*, particularly pp. 35–62. This is of course related to Charles Taylor's description of modernity as an "age of authenticity." More on this below.

18. For an overview, see Randall, *What a Friend*, 76–85; Ellis, *Gathering*, 103–24.

19. Quoted in Randall, *What a Friend*, 77.

Charles H. Spurgeon (1834–1892) would not include written prayers in his daily devotional, claiming that his "conscience will not allow me to do so (. . .) To some persons the use of forms of prayer appears to be lawful; but as I cannot coincide with that opinion, it would be the height of hypocrisy for me to compose prayers for the use of others."[20] Even an Anglican bishop of evangelical stripe felt the need to warn of written prayers. In his tract *A Call to Prayer* bishop John Charles Ryle (1816–1900) writes: "Words said without heart are as utterly useless to our souls as the drum-beating of the poor heathens before their idols. Where there is no heart, there may be lip-work and tongue-work, but there is nothing that God listens to; there is no prayer."[21]

This is not a feature exclusive to the Anglo-American branch of Evangelicalism. The Swedish Holiness evangelist Emil Gustafson (1862–1900) emphasizes that attitude is more important than words in prayer, and claims that preparation, complex syntax, and complicated words threaten the simple innocence that ought to characterize prayer.[22] About the same time, representatives of the Swedish Mission Covenant discuss and reject written prayers as part of the communion services in their newly formed denomination.[23] According to one of the preachers, a read prayer should not even be counted as a prayer.[24] Lewi Pethrus (1884–1974), the leader of the Swedish Pentecostal Movement, echoes the same sentiment when he claims that "Many people read along in the prayer of confession, and in The Lord's Prayer, but they have never prayed a real prayer, never."[25]

This pattern of seeing set forms and concrete objects as obstacles to the divine can be found in other areas as well. An evangelical preacher should preferably preach without notes, since a written manuscript was perceived as a "denial of the help of the Holy Spirit in delivery."[26] When Henry Ward Beecher (1813–1887) placed a vase of flowers in the front in his church in Brooklyn, he was denounced by Evangelicals who saw this item as a

---

20. Ibid., 80.
21. Ryle, *A Call to Prayer*, 14. Italics in the original.
22. Gustafson, *Bref,* 25; Halldorf, *Av denna världen?,* 279–84.
23. Ahrén, *Nattvardsgudstjänsten,* 69–71.
24. Ibid., 69, n. 24.
25. Pethrus, *Samlade skrifter vol. 5,* 208. For Pethrus' significance for Swedish Pentecostalism and the Free churches in Sweden, see Halldorf, "Lewi Pethrus."
26. Bebbington, *Dominance of Evangelicalism,* 92; Wacker, *Heaven Below,* 114.

distraction from the spiritual.[27] Lewi Pethrus warned about the dangers of educated ministers, claiming that human knowledge was a threat to the preacher's "dependence on God."[28] Since the nineteenth century radical Holiness and Pentecostal preachers have told the faithful that they have to choose between taking "the Lord as healer" in an act of faith, or turning to professional doctors.[29] In all these instances the choice between God and the concrete, man-made form—between the divine and the created—is presented in terms of either-or.

So within Evangelicalism, spontaneity tends to trump set practices. Christian faith centered on practices has been described as "dead religion," and the practices themselves given names such as "dead ceremonies," "vain repetitions," or merely "superstitions."[30] The concrete and material, be it a written prayer or a vase of flowers, is perceived as something hindering the presence of God. This mirrors an inner–outer dualism, where the concrete is seen as creating a complexity that obstructs either the authentic spontaneous expression of the inner, or a direct dependence on the divine.[31] According to this logic, set practices are thought to stand in the way of a true relationship with Jesus. They are merely crutches for people of little faith—in the words of Holiness preacher Emil Gustafson: "For those who are not content with the outer structure of Christianity, our personal Saviour is precious. He is their life. (. . .) He wants to live by faith in our hearts."[32] Or again Lewi Pethrus, criticizing the vested clergy of the Catholic and Orthodox churches: "We have no need for these outer shrouds. The shrouds of the Old Testaments prefigured spiritual things. And the fact that many have returned to the outer things prove that they lack the ability to see the inner [spiritual things]."[33] Objects, structures, and set practices are for those who lack either insight in the spiritual or a personal relation to Jesus.

---

27. Bebbington, *Dominance of Evangelicalism*, 90–91.

28. Pethrus, *Samlade skrifter vol. 6*, 58.

29. Dayton, *Theological Roots of Pentecostalism*, 128–32; Curtis, *Faith in the Great Physician*, 154–63.

30. Branch, *Rituals of Spontaneity*, 37. See for example the publication of the German branch of the Evangelical Alliance from 1859, Steane, *The Religious Condition*, 224.

31. Ellis, *Gathering*, 75.

32. Emil Gustafson quoted in "Helgelseförbundets kvartalsmöte," 127. See also Gustafson, *Jag fann honom icke*, 16–18.

33. Pethrus, *Samlade skrifter vol. 6*, 123.

GENEALOGY: THE LEGACY OF NOMINALISM

How, then, can this perceived dichotomy of heartfelt, spontaneous spirituality on the one hand, and the cold routine of repeated practice on the other be explained? Why do evangelicals see means and material objects as a threat to authentic spirituality? In her investigation of the rise of spontaneous prayer Lori Branch points to the "crisis of representation" in the early modern West as a background to the opposition against written prayers.[34] This crisis led to an uncertainty as to whether words, signs, and symbols are really able to represent and communicate the divine. In a similar manner Charles Taylor has characterized modernity as an "age of authenticity," arguing that the modern disenchantment of the world resulted in a relocation of truth and divine presence from "out there"—nature and the social order, including ritual—to man's soul. Truth becomes internalized and subjectivized, and authenticity the cherished ideal: the natural, unconstrained expression of internalized truth.[35] The ancient words of an old, written prayer are now seen as an obstacle to rather than a vehicle of grace. Fixed practices obstruct the desired authenticity, and become problematic.

The early modern crisis of representation is related to late medieval nominalism; the philosophical school aptly named *via moderna*. This movement forwarded a new ontology, the importance of which has been highlighted recently by Brad S. Gregory.[36] According to the traditional Christian view, God's transcendence meant that God was distinct from the created order. According to this, God is not the most supreme creature in the universe, but radically other and distinct from the universe.[37] This ontological distinction ensures that God can be present in the world without having to eject the being already present in that created thing where God becomes present. Since God's being is radically distinct from created

---

34. Branch, *Rituals of Spontaneity*, 37; see also Ellis, *Gathering*. Ellis underlines the concrete historical circumstances behind the preference of simplicity, for example by pointing out that "Secret worship [of the seventeenth century Puritans] inevitably meant that only those elements regarded as essential were usually undertaken." Ellis, *Gathering*, 32.

35. Taylor, *Ethics of Authenticity*, 2–4, 25–29; see also Taylor, *Sources of the Self*, 143–58. Andrew Louth argues that the move away from tradition and the community of the church in modernity is a result of a tendency to ground authority in "some kind of inward experience of authenticity." Louth, *The Origins*, 211.

36. The narration below is primarily based on Gregory, *The Unintended Reformation*, 29–47.

37. Ibid., 29–30.

being these two do not compete. The fact that God is not spatial means that God neither threatens the integrity of the created thing, nor can he be obstructed by the created order. God is present *in* and *through* created things, not instead of them. This view of being is the foundation of Christian sacramental theology, of the view of salvation as the transformation of nature (divinization, or *theosis*), and last but not least it forms the basis for the doctrine that Christ is both fully God and fully man.

In the late Middle Ages the works of the so-called nominalists John Duns Scotus (c. 1266–1308) and William of Occam (c. 1285–1348) undermined this view.[38] They understood being as conceptually prior to God and creation, wherefore God is not radically distinct from the created order in terms of being, but instead share being with the creation.[39] The nominalists emphasized that God was radically distinct in other categories, such as power, freedom, and morals. But in terms of being, since it is univocal, God exists in the same manner as the created order.

The result of this is the domestication of God's transcendence—God is seen as the highest being in the universe, but still as part of the universe. This in turn leads to the end of divine immanence.[40] These two are connected since immanence—the presence in and not instead of—is based on God's otherness, that is, God's transcendence. The traditional emphasis on God's otherness in terms of being implies that God is not spatial and thus does not compete spatially with created matter. But if being is univocal and God shares being with created matter, then God is seen as spatial, or crypto-spatial, and competes spatially with created matter. The consequence of a univocal conception of being is that the divine is present instead of the created, and no longer in or through it. A loaf of bread cannot simultaneously be real bread and the real body of the divine Christ. We are faced with a troubling either–or: something is either divine/spiritual/supernatural or

---

38. Ibid., 37–39. There is a scholarly debate regarding the interpretation of this aspect of the theology of Duns Scotus and Willam of Occam, and the significance of it. The so-called Radical Orthodoxy theologians tend to put a great emphasis on the metaphysical univocity in the theology of Soctus and Occam. In doing so they are partly inspired by postmodern philosophers such as Heidegger and Deleuze. The historical accuracy of this interpretation has been questioned by amongst others Richard Cross, who claims that Scotus's claims are semantic, not metaphysical. See Cross, "'Where Angels Fear to Tread,'" 7–41. Cathrine Pickstock responds to this critique in an article where she also outlines the importance of and debates regarding Duns Scotus in contemporary theology and philosophy, see Pickstock, "Duns Scotus," 570–71, n. 4.

39. Gregory, *The Unintended Reformation*, 37.

40. Ibid., 37–38, 43.

created/material/natural. They cannot be both, which is to say that God cannot be truly immanent.

SECULAR AND RELIGIOUS MODERNITIES

This is modernity at its philosophical core. Modernity is not, as is often thought, first and foremost characterized by secularization. Rather its deepest philosophical identity is this choice between God and creation, natural and supernatural. On this basis, modernity can be constructed as secular or religious. In secular modernities God is excluded in favor of science, rationality, and/or human freedom. But there are also religious modernities. Here God is at the center, but in opposition to nature. When religious phenomena are explained, they are done so in a "strictly religious" manner—that is, with no reference to the "natural." Accordingly, religious moderns might want to emphasize that God's revelation stands in opposition to human rationality, that the Bible is God's word and not a product of historical circumstances, or that life exists because God created it and not due to evolution. These are articles of faith present in much of modern Evangelicalism, a movement which can be understood as a theocentric and religious—rather than anthropocentric and secular—modernity.[41]

Brad S. Gregory has argued that this nominalist univocity of being and Occam's razor are the seeds of the Weberian disenchantment of the world.[42] The univocity of being sets up a choice between natural or supernatural, and Occam's razor encourages the elimination of multiple entities in favor of simplicity. According to this logic, when a natural explanation of a phenomenon is found it means that there is no room for God. If the sun rises as a consequence of planetary movements, it cannot also be raised above the horizon by the finger of God. God becomes, in the words of Pierre-Simon Laplace (1749–1827), an unnecessary hypothesis.

Here Gregory finds the basis of the Protestant critique of the Catholic teachings of the real presence of Christ in the Eucharistic elements.[43] But the nominalist position might easily—perhaps necessarily—lead to a rejection of sacramentality all together. Since God is no longer present in or through the created order, the created order must stand in the way of God. The methodology of Occam's razor can be used in religious life as well: use

41. Halldorf, *Av denna världen?*, 237–39, 313–16.
42. Gregory, *The Unintended Reformation*, 25–73.
43. Ibid., 41–43.

as few entities as possible—always strive for simplicity. Do not use written prayers but pray the words that pour forth in your heart. Preach without notes. Do not follow liturgy but be lead by the Spirit. The product of these priorities is a spirituality that favors the simple and spontaneous. Complex practices and material concreteness is a problem in evangelical spirituality, since this spirituality is a manifestation of the nominalist, univocal either-or of created and divine.

PRACTICES AND IDENTITY IN MODERNITY

The view of practices as obstructions of the divine rather than of vehicles of grace has been detrimental to evangelical identity in modernity. There are certainly evangelical practices, but in the name of simplicity evangelicals have neglected to develop a theology of practices, and to use practices in a conscious way to construct a stable identity. Evangelicals are aware that "the world" constantly threatens to corrupt the saints, even the congregation, and they recognize that some kind of resistance is necessary. But the basis of the evangelical opposition has too seldom been corporeal and socially grounded. The ideal has rather, in romantic fashion, been the heroic individual who "swims against the tide." Independence and individual self-discipline are the cherished virtues.[44]

Modernity is not merely an idea or a philosophy, but also a way of life. We experience the world through practices, and accordingly they shape the way we see it. This is why convictions, affections, and arguments are not enough to create and preserve an identity.[45] The alternate vision must be rooted in and expressed through a way of life in order to become an imagination. A practice can be described as imagination rooted in space and time.[46] By being social and concrete the practice provides the imagination

---

44. Wacker, *Heaven Below*, 29–30.

45. It is not clear if Taylor himself sees different, co-existing social imaginaries within a society as at all possible. Even if he discusses tensions within Western modernity, and uncovers a variation of sources, part of his project is to show that despite these variations, modernity exists as a coherent and shared cultural outlook. Cf. Taylor, *Sources of the Self*, 495–521.

46. This definition is inspired by William T. Cavanaugh, although I have not found the relation between imagination and practices expressed in these very terms in his works. But see for instance Cavanaugh, *Migrations*, 5: "In this book I point to church practices that resist the colonization of the Christian imagination by a nation-state that wants to subordinate all other attachments to itself. It is necessary, in doing so, to

with a social base and therefore a greater stability.[47] A network of practices form a social imaginary—a culture, or sub-culture.

Evangelicalism has not lacked practices so much as a theological appreciation of their practices. To the extent that evangelicals have been able to preserve an identity distinct from the culture surrounding them it is due to practices, and not to affections, convictions, or self-discipline. Revival meetings, class meetings, and prayer meetings have done more for evangelical identity than holy affections and religious convictions.[48]

THEOLOGICAL ANALYSIS: NOMINALISM AS GNOSTICISM

As stated above, the rejection of set practices and material objects in worship reflects an either-or with regards to God and creation. God cannot be truly immanent, but instead created objects are thought to stand in the way of divine presence. The problematic nature of this evangelical rejection of immanence becomes evident if we turn to the perception of salvation within the movement. In justification as well as holiness, God's presence in man is understood as "pure grace"—anything else would indicate an unacceptable "righteousness by works." Man can open the door to God, but can't in any way contribute or cooperate in his own salvation.[49]

With regards to holiness, many preachers and theologians within the evangelical movement has emphasized that while a morally upright life might on the surface seem to demand some measure of self-discipline, even this is at its core God's work in man.[50] The progress in holiness is typically described in terms of "dying to self," and the growth of God in man is directly related to the diminishing of the self.[51] There is a general tendency in much evangelical theology to understand salvation as the termination rather than

---

complexify political space: to create forms of local and translocal community that disperse and resist the powers invested in the state and corporation." See also Cavanaugh, *Theopolitical Imagination*, 4–5; Cavanaugh, *Migrations*, 121–22.

47. Cf. Cavanaugh, *Torture and Eucharist*, 264–73.

48. On practices as a basis for an alternative identity in modernity, see Bass, *Practicing Our Faith*, 7–10; Cavanaugh, *Migrations*, 24–41.

49. In the words of Dwight L. Moody: "When a man tries to better himself, that is reform. Regeneration is letting God do it all." Quoted in Gundry, *Love Them In*, 127

50. Cf. Maddox, *Responsible Grace*, 83–92; Edwards, *Religious Affections*, 424–26; Gustafson, *En konungs brud*, 43; Randall, *What a Friend*, 111–28.

51. Åberg, *Individualitet*, 78–95.

transformation of natural man. Sanctification becomes a zero-sum game where the growing presence of God in man is dependent on the diminishment of man. This reflects the nominalist univocity of being: since God and creation compete, they cannot simultaneously occupy the same space. God is present instead of created matter, not in and through it. Prominent Holiness evangelist Andrew Murray (1828–1917) makes this clear:

> There is nothing that has such an attraction for God, that has such affinity with holiness, as a contrite and humble spirit. The reason is evident. There is no law in the natural and spiritual world more simple, than that two bodies cannot at the same moment occupy the same space. Only so much as the new occupant can expel of what the space was filled with can it really possess. In man, self has possession, and self-will the mastery, and there is no room for God.[52]

Here God is described as competing spatially with man's nature, and the two cannot occupy the same space. Salvation is therefore understood as the extinction of nature rather than its transformation.[53] The nominalist upheaval of the distinction between God and creation changes the terms for interaction between the divine and the created in a way that undermines both sacramental theology and the vision of salvation as the transformation of nature. The presence of the divine is no longer thought to transform created being according to its nature but instead replaces it. In the nominalist framework created and divine are not distinct but opposites. Therefore, grace does not complete nature, it crushes it. This is a dualistic worldview, where nature cannot be restored as nature, but either remains in a fallen state or is replaced by God. Created matter cannot become sacrament, and man cannot be properly divinized. This view of the created order as ultimately fallen and un-restorable represents the deeper theological disenchantment of the modern world.

Consequently salvation is viewed as a purely spiritual process in Evangelicalism. Matter is excluded from the order of salvation. This is reflected

---

52. Murray, *Holy in Christ*, 119.

53. One could of course object that the reference here is to the "ego," flesh, or sinfulness of man, and not to "natural man." But in the evangelical discourse it generally emphasized that man in himself is nothing but sinfullness, as Murray himself states earlier in his book: "We know not how unholy, how abominable, sin and the sinful nature are in God's sight." Ibid., 41. Moody expresses the same sentiment: "We are wicked by nature; there is nothing good in us, the Bible teaches us that all the way through." Quoted in Gundry, *Love Them In*, 92.

in the limited place given to the body. Asceticism is not embraced as a road to salvation, and appreciation of the divinized body of the saint through the veneration of relics is vehemently rejected.[54] Instead salvation is internalized and thought of in spiritual categories: God resides in the heart or soul of man, not in his body.

This combination of dualism between God and creation and an individualistic internalization of the divine is structurally akin to a Gnostic cosmology and anthropology. Hans Jonas has given the following characterization of the gnostic mindset: "The cardinal feature of Gnostic thought is the radical dualism that governs the relation of God and world, and correspondingly that of man and world." The gnostics saw spirituality as connected to man's soul or spirit rather than his body. Deep within man there is a "portion of the divine substance from beyond."[55] Dualism with regards to spirit and matter, and a spiritualized internalization of the divine, in other words. The same characteristics that have been recognized in that nominalist type of religiosity which Evangelicalism represents.

The Gnostic temptation has been constant in the history of the Church, and nominalism represents an entry point for this influence. This is where Evangelicalism's striving for simplicity and its rejection of practices has its roots. The evangelical inability to preserve a distinct identity in modernity is a consequence of the rejection of practices. The result has been secularization from within. To the twentieth-century American writer Flannery O'Connor—a Catholic living in a region dominated by low-church Protestants—this connection was obvious and predictable: "When the physical fact is separated from the spiritual reality, the dissolution of belief is eventually inevitable."[56]

---

54. For an evangelical critique of asceticism, see Gordon, *The Twofold Life*, 107, 143, 144, 180.

55. Jonas, *The Gnostic Religion*, 42, 44. The use of "Gnostic" as an umbrella-term for the great diversity of second and third centuries movements challenging the orthodox interpretation of Christianity has been questioned by scholars today. See for example Williams, *Rethinking "Gnosticism"* and King, *What is Gnosticism?* Recently David Brakke has argued that the term "gnostic" can be used as a designator in Ancient Christianity, but in a more limited way than has been done in traditional scholarship. It should be applied to one distinctive school of thought, and not a wide variety of groups. See Brakke, *The Gnostics*. In this article the label is used as an analytical category, related to but not exclusively tied to a specific historical context. This use is common in historical theology and theological analysis.

56. Quoted in Bieber Lake, *The Incarnational Art*, 5.

Part Two

Catholicity

Being a Free Church in Late Modernity

5

The Real Thing?

Practicing a Spirituality of Everyday Life

Tone Stangeland Kaufman

INTRODUCTION

I grew up in the Norwegian "Bible Belt," and in the public elementary school I attended we used to sing a hymn and pray the Lord's prayer in the morning, sing table grace at lunch, and pray for the blessing of the Triune God (Bless us, God the Father, bless us, God the Son, bless us, God the Holy Spirit! Amen!) before leaving the classroom to go home in the afternoon. Later on, I have reflected on how these practices might have shaped me and my fellow classmates. There really was nothing very personal, spontaneous, or enthusiastic about it, but I still believe that taking part in these practices—day in and day out—might have had an impact on us. When I pray with my children in the evening, we close with the Aaronic benediction, and I mark them with the sign of the cross on their forehead. One evening my three-year-old spontaneously put his finger on my forehead too, making the sign of the cross. It was a powerful moment, and it struck me that this simple practice might shape him and his identity. It is my hope and prayer that it will remind him that his most profound identity is neither what he possesses, nor whether or not he succeeds in a career, but rather, to whom he belongs. This little practice will hopefully be one of many that, "woven together, may form a way of life"[57] for him when growing up.

What counts as "real spirituality?" Based on an empirical study of clergy spirituality in the Church of Norway,[58] I make the case that *a spirituality of everyday life* is indeed "the real thing" both for clergy and the laity, and that it constitutes a challenge to Scandinavian Evangelical ideals of the spiritual life. I propose that categories of Christian spirituality within this context might have been narrowed by certain pietistic ideals, and that a number of spiritual practices embedded in everyday life have possibly gone unnoticed and unacknowledged. In this chapter I call for the recognition and appreciation of such invisible and often deeply embodied practices. Drawing on Cavanaugh's sacramental theology of the Eucharist and other contributions, I argue that practices such as table grace, evening prayer with children, pondering the wonders of nature, and "small talk" with God throughout the day are also "the real thing."[59] These spiritual practices are often so closely interwoven with our daily lives and habits of eating, sleeping, caring for children, and being on the go that we do not always notice them. However, they also matter.

In the Norwegian context, the spiritual tradition rooted in eighteenth century Pietism has contributed to shaping ideals for the Christian life.[60] While the revivals of the nineteenth century gave rise to a number of Free churches in Sweden, the same revivals were in Norway often channelled into so called "prayer houses" with a double identity: within the church, yet separate from it.[61] Ideals for the spiritual life held by interviewees coming from such a background may thus not be unlike those held by people coming from various Free Church backgrounds and from the evangelical tradition more generally.[62]

---

57. Bass, *Practicing Our Faith*, xi.
58. Kaufman, *A New Old Spirituality?*
59. See Cavanaugh, *Being Consumed*.

60. Since the revivals of the nineteenth century and twentieth-centuries were partly embraced by the Lutheran Church of Norway, which was a state church until 2012, pietistic and revival spiritualities have had a significant influence on a considerable number of Church of Norway pastors and lay people. This tradition has existed side by side with the "folk-church" tradition. The latter—at least to a certain extent—resembles mainline churches in the U.S.

61. Here referring to the Church of Norway.
62. For a definition of Evangelicalism, cf. Halldorf in this volume.

Data are based on twenty-one open ended qualitative interviews with ordained pastors in the Church of Norway which were strategically sampled from three different synods (dioceses), representing both ecclesiological and theological diversity in the church. The particular perspective of spirituality consists of the individual's concrete experience of being involved in practices and relationships that constitute an intentional way of life, or are directed "toward the horizon of ultimate value one perceives," to quote Sandra Schneiders.[63] In this chapter, then, *Christian* spirituality is defined as "the way in which a person experiences the relationship to God, and nurtures and expresses his or her faith with a special emphasis on Christian practice."[64] In the last decades we have seen a renewed interest in Christian practices or faith practices,[65] and I find the concept helpful for studying how a particular faith can be both nurtured and expressed.[66] I here understand Christian practice as "a cluster of activities that are both concerned with and relating to the sacred as well as addressing fundamental human needs, and that, woven together, form a way of life."[67] My understanding of

---

63. My use of the term *Christian spirituality* is inspired by Sandra Schneiders' extensive work on the subject and of her definitions, as well as by Elizabeth Drescher's critique of Schneiders' unilateral emphasis on experience, and Drescher's focus on Christian practice as key for understanding Christian spiritualty. See Schneiders, "The Study of Christian Spirituality" and Drescher, "Practicing Church."

64. As opposed to Miroslav Volf in his introduction to Christian Scharen's book, *Faith as a Way of Life*. ix–x, I do not see faith and spirituality as opposites. Christian spirituality can also be understood as the experience of lived faith, or how faith is expressed, and there are also distinct theological approaches to Christian spirituality. See for example McGinn et al., *Christian Spirituality, vol. 1;* McGinn, "The Letter and the Spirit."

65. Bass, *Practicing Our Faith;* Bass and Dykstra, *For Life Abundant;* Scharen, *Faith as a Way of Life*. Like Bass and Dykstra, I use the term "Christian practice" synonymously with "faith practice." Furthermore, these terms will not be distinguished from "spiritual practice."

66. The term "Christian practice" is an open category, and does not refer to an exhaustive list of practices. Moreover, there are several different approaches to the understanding of practices. In Bass, *The Practicing Congregation* (68) three different approaches to Christian practices are outlined; an *anthropological* (or sociological), an *ascetical*, as well as a *moral*. See this contribution for an elaboration on varying approaches to Christian practices. Furthermore, there are also numerous contributions rooted in social theory and practice theory. See for example Bourdieu, *Outline of a Theory of Practice;* For more on this, see Fahlgren, Halldorf, and Hagman in this volume.

67. This definition is inspired by Bass and Dykstra, as well as Robert Wuthnow. The latter defines the practice of spirituality in relational terms, and includes activities of both action and contemplation: "To say that spirituality is practiced means that people engage intentionally in activities that deepen their relationship to the sacred" Robert Wuthnow, *After Heaven*, 169; Savigny et al., *The Practice Turn*.

practice is thus rather inclusive, although the definition suggests important criteria for the term. Furthermore, as I will argue in the following pages, these activities can either be deeply embedded in daily life, and can thus be engaged in rather accidentally or subconsciously, or they can require a larger degree of intentionality.

The chapter proceeds as follows: I begin by introducing a spirituality of everyday life. Secondly, I present a typology of various approaches to intentional spiritual practices. Following that, I describe two of the most salient spiritual practices embedded in everyday life in my data, that is; table grace and evening prayer with children, and discuss whether or not such spiritual practices by certain interviewees are considered "the real thing," or just "a second rate practice." Finally, I make the case that these practices should be noticed and acknowledged as the real thing, as practices that truly matter for a Christian spirituality.

A SPIRITUALITY OF EVERYDAY LIFE

As I was undertaking my study of clergy spirituality, it struck me that most spiritual classics are written by representatives of a spiritual elite: an Augustine, a Julian of Norwich, a Teresa of Avila, or a Thomas Merton, who, as opposed to the interviewees in this study and most ordinary people, lived some kind of a monastic life. This means that they did not have the daily responsibility for a family. Moreover, a number of them had extraordinary spiritual experiences of various kinds. It can be contended that the clergy in my project, being employed by the church, indeed belong to a spiritual elite. However, my impression is that most of them have more in common with "the man and woman on the street," or at least with the lay people, than with Augustine or Teresa of Avila. They might rather be considered "the John and Jane Does" of the clergy. Thus their spirituality seems to be rather ordinary.

One interviewee, for example, reflected on how her spirituality had changed from revolving around activities at the margins of her everyday life to becoming more of an "everyday faith," as she put it. Her emphasis made me aware that a spirituality embedded in everyday life seemed to be of great significance also to these clergy interviewees. As I have argued extensively elsewhere,[68] I find it helpful to distinguish analytically between spiritual practices that are embedded in the everyday life, both privately and profes-

---

68. Kaufman, "Pastoral Spirituality in Everyday Life."

sionally (in ministry), and those located at the margins of everyday life. The former practices in the private sphere are part of, or are related to, the daily rhythm of living, and are often habitual and automated. Examples are table grace, evening prayer with children, "small talk" with God throughout the day, and caring for children or a chronically ill spouse. The practices located at the margin do, however, require a larger degree of intentionality. Intentional spiritual practices might include having a specific time set aside for prayer and Bible study, seeing a spiritual director, attending a silent retreat, going to confession, undertaking a pilgrimage, working actively for social and ecological justice, tithing or regularly donating money to church or to social justice causes, deliberately setting aside time for contemplative prayer, reading spiritual literature, going to conferences, etc. What is crucial, though, is that these two categories of spirituality are not opposites. Rather, they should be seen as mutually enriching. Further, practices that once required a large degree of intentionality, may also become a *habitus*. For the pastors in my study, attending worship (also on days off) is an example of a practice that is now embodied and automated. Yet, for most people in the Norwegian population, this is a highly intentional practice.[69]

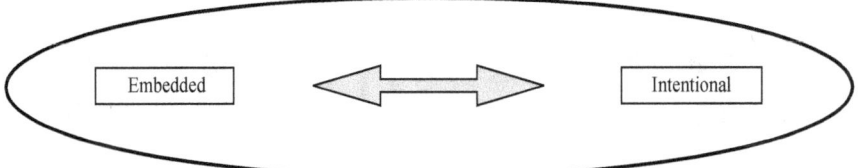

Figure 4: Embedded and Intentional Spiritual Practices as Mutually Dependent Upon and Enriching Each Other

Although both types of practices are mutually dependent on each other, I find it helpful to distinguish between them for analytical purposes. This enables one to see more clearly practices that are embedded in everyday life and that, thus, are often so automated that they become invisible. Following this section, I will introduce a typology where this distinction will be elaborated.

---

69. Monthly worship attendance in Norway is 7 percent, and those who attend more regularly are even fewer. See Botvar and Schmidt, *Religion i dagens Norge*, 17–18.

Part Two—Catholicity

A FOURFOLD TYPOLOGY OF APPROACHES TO INTENTIONAL SPIRITUAL PRACTICES

The relationship between ideals of engaging in intentional spiritual practices and the reported actual involvement in them is portrayed visually below. The horizontal axis moves from low to high ideals in relation to engagement in intentional practices, while the vertical line runs from having a low to a high degree of discipline or reported actual engagement in the practices.

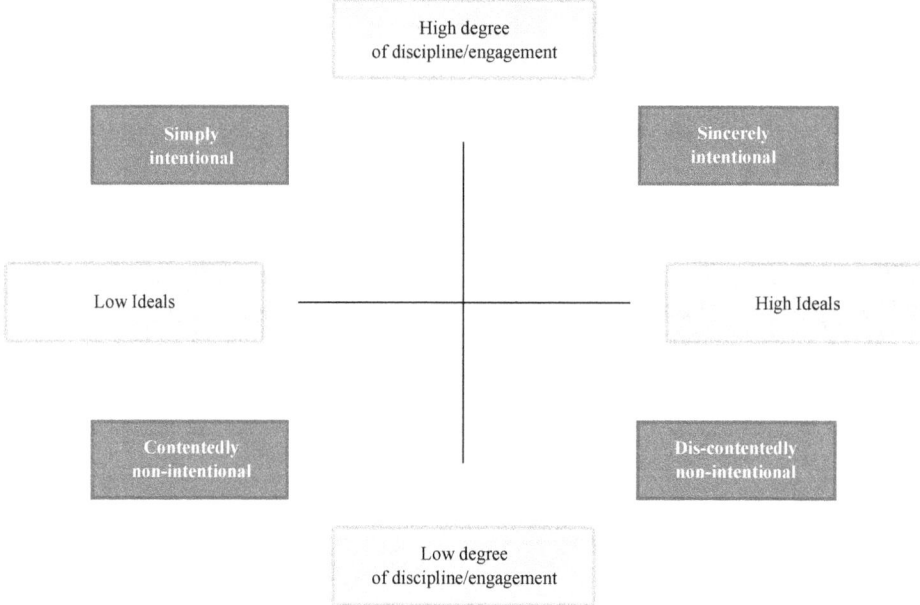

Figure 5: Four Approaches to Intentional Spiritual Practices[70]

By placing these axes in the diagram above, I end up with four cells, and hence, four main approaches to pastoral spirituality: *Contentedly non-intentional*, *Discontentedly non-intentional*, *Sincerely intentional*, and *Simply intentional*. These four approaches are *ideal types* in the Weberian sense, and are used as a heuristic tool, where one or several characteristics

---

70. I am indebted to Lisa E. Dahill for her comments during my dissertation defense in November 2011. Her suggestions contributed to improving the typology.

or practices are accentuated at the expense of the diversity and nuances in the data. Hence, they are not found empirically in pure form.[71]

Contentedly Non-intentional

The pastors with low ideals for engaging in intentional spiritual practices and a low degree of intentionality were called *Contentedly non-intentional*. They are content with partaking in the practices embedded in ministry and daily life, most often in the context of a family. Most of the pastors in this group are parents of small children, which could be the reason why intentional spiritual practices are not their focus at the moment. However, there is no doubt that their relationships to God, and their relationships to prayer in particular, are a significant part of their lives and ministries, and they do partake in practices promoting social and ecological justice. Praying "on the go," in between things, and in the midst of various situations, they experience their faith as a profound part of them, and it is very often closely related to "this *everyday faith*" (emphasis mine), as one of the interviewees, Karen, a parent of small children, puts it. She is no social justice activist, but she does find the small everyday practices to be very important: "To purchase fair trade coffee and tea and juice and such things, and that this concerns how we are to live." For her, these practices form a way of life. Furthermore, she and others experience that being parents also shapes their spirituality and ministry in a positive way. Nevertheless, the pastors of this group partake only to a small degree in spiritual practices that are *not* embedded in their ministry or family life, and if they do so, this happens rather "accidentally," or "when an opportunity presents itself," as another parent of small children, Steffen, expresses it.

Discontentedly Non-intentional

While the spiritual practices of this group actually resemble those of the previous group, the ideals and spiritual self-conception differ. The pastors who are labelled *Discontentedly non-intentional* express a sense of guilt for not living up to the ideals that have been handed down to them. Further, these interviewees tend to speak of their spiritual practices and spiritual life in far more *evaluating terms*. A number of times these pastors comment

71. For an elaboration of nuances in the data, see Kaufman, *A New Old Spirituality?*

that "they are not good at praying," or "admit that they are not very concerned about social justice." Hence, there seems to be a discrepancy between ideal and practice. Several of the participants in this group at least forget, overlook, or neglect the small continual prayer offered "on the go" when speaking of their prayer practices, and, thus, describe themselves as "poor prayers." While I interpret some interviewees as simply *underreporting* their spiritual practices, others experience *a real discrepancy* between ideal and reported practice. The latter especially pertains to practices of social justice. Although these interviewees clearly partake in spiritual practices embedded in daily life, both privately and professionally, *this is not the way they wish to attend to their spiritual life*. They fail to live up to some kind of ideal, and are, therefore, discontent about their lack of intentionality (this will be elaborated in the next main section).

A common denominator for these interviewees is that the pietistic lay movement to a certain degree is part of their spiritual background or heritage, or that they have at least spent some time in an evangelical environment. In this movement, the intentional practice of having "a quiet time," preferably in the morning, consisting of prayer and Bible study, has been a strong ideal for "the good Christian." While some of these pastors have previously had a more disciplined spiritual life, they now either struggle with this or have renegotiated their ideals. It is not clear whether they feel obliged to live up to a certain standard set by others, or whether their ideals come from within. However, their evangelical background could nonetheless be the reason why they have not managed to discover and appreciate the embedded spiritual practices actually undertaken in their daily lives, both privately and professionally.

Sincerely Intentional

Inspired by Richard Foster's two categories "sincere" and "simple,"[72] I distinguish between *Sincerely intentional* and *Simply intentional*. The interviewees who have both an unusually high degree of ideals of engaging in intentional spiritual practices and who also have the zeal and discipline to live up to them, are categorized as "Sincerely intentional." The most extreme example of this group is the one who was very concerned with having sufficient time for prayer, but who got frustrated when his children "prevented him" from having his quiet time in the morning. Thus he started

72. Foster, *Freedom of Simplicity*, 97.

getting up earlier in order to be able to pray. However, the children also got up all the earlier, and in order to "beat the kids in getting up early," he began setting his alarm at 3 a.m. However, as he laughingly noticed, this did not work in the long run, but he did manage to find other ways to carry out his ideals. Although a bit extreme, this example is still telling for this group of pastors, who might come across as highly goal oriented and zealous in attending to their spiritual lives. The pastors characterized by this sincerely intentional approach talk about "working on their spiritual lives," and have developed strategies in order to deepen their spiritual engagement, both personally and corporately. For example, they combine the more continual conversation with God throughout the day with a specific time set aside for prayer and nurturing of their relationship to God. Although this group includes pastors from various backgrounds, younger male pastors are over-represented.[73] Moreover, most of them are influenced by the pietistic and evangelical lay movements as well as from moderately charismatic movements, and more recently from the retreat movement, that is, from a tradition of contemplative spirituality.

Simply Intentional

The pastors who can be allocated to this group do not express very high ideals about how to attend to their spiritual lives, or about being engaged in practices of social justice. Yet in practice, they actually do pay attention to these issues. This could also be interpreted as a discrepancy between ideal and reported practice, although it is reversed from that of the discontentedly non-intentional group. However, it might also indicate that they are less explicit or expressive about their ideals, or at least that such outspoken ideals are not as crucial to them. These pastors seem reconciled with "the messiness of life," as Fredrik, one of the older interviewees, put it. Reflecting on his spiritual life, he says: "But it [my prayer life] is not as orderly as when I was young. [Back] then it was pious and proper. Now it is more frayed at the edges." Fredrik distinguishes between the term "pious and proper" on the one hand, and "more frayed at the edges" on the other. The term "pious" denotes a rather rigid prayer life which is a good description of himself as a younger pastor, when his spiritual life was "nice and neat." This approach is reconciled with the various experiences, phases, and the "messiness" of

---

73. This observation should not be over-interpreted, though, because having a qualitative research design, the study is not statistically representative.

life, and is thus more relaxed and flexible. Hence, it is possibly also easier for others to relate to.

The *Simply intentional* pastors are a mix as far as background is concerned. Yet I do not believe it is accidental that they, with one exception, are among the oldest participants in the sample. Furthermore, these interviewees are those who unsolicited keep bringing up issues of social justice during the interviews, and who most strongly emphasize social justice as crucial to their spirituality.[74] Typical for these pastors is a relaxed, slightly self-ironic attitude towards their own attempts at keeping up with intentional spiritual practices. As opposed to some of the bold and outspoken pastors in the category *Sincerely intentional*, these pastors are far more *modest* when sharing about their spiritual life. Hence, Cecilia, a pastor in her late 40s, only now "dares" to speak of her reading Teresa of Avila and Julian of Norwich as "spiritual reading," although she has been engaging in this practice for at least eight years. Most of those representing this approach to spirituality have not previously shared the pietistic and perhaps also legalistic ideal of having a disciplined devotional life, or they have rather radically renegotiated it. The pastors adhering to this approach are not negative to the cultivation of a certain degree of discipline. However, invitation precedes discipline. These pastors do not find duty and imperatives to be a good motivation. Yet, growing out of embedded spiritual practices and freedom, intentionality and discipline can be enriching and worth pursuing. Hence, they intentionally embed new spiritual practices in their daily life.

While some interviewees, then, are content and happy to engage in spiritual practices embedded in ministry and in everyday life in the private sphere, others have ideals of engaging in additional intentional spiritual practices as well. The interesting pattern is that all the interviewees with the latter ideals, that is, those who I have placed in the groups here termed "sincerely intentional" or "discontentedly non-intentional," either have a pietistic/evangelical or a moderately charismatic background. This same background and approach to the spiritual life also seems to constitute a dividing line for interviewees in their appreciation of embedded practices such as table grace and evening prayer with children as opposed to

---

74. They adhere to the spirituality coming from the communities of Taizé and Iona, whose songs and liturgies are rooted in a peace- and social justice movement, distinguish between this kind of spirituality and charismatic worship. The spirituality of Taizé and Iona, for example, as opposed to the latter, does not flee reality, but is rooted in everyday life with a strong emphasis on social justice.

"personal prayer" or regularly reading a devotional, as will be further explored in the following section.

"THE REAL STUFF" OR "SECOND RATE"? THE CASE OF TABLE GRACE AND EVENING PRAYER WITH CHILDREN

Evening prayer with children and table grace are two of the most salient spiritual practices undertaken by the participants in this study. Yet, since both of these practices are embedded in the daily rhythm of eating and sleeping, they are often invisible or forgotten. These practices are also strongly connected with having children and wanting to establish some family practices and habits. Hence, Karen notes that "saying grace before meals and such things" was not as natural for them before having kids:

> But of course I notice that for us, only that concerning table grace and evening prayer, that [those practices] have been brought into our lives through our kids (. . .) It has actually done something to my Christian life and my faith as well, which was not as natural for us before having kids; table grace and stuff. But with the kids we have sort of gotten table grace and evening prayer into our daily life. It is ok then (is laughing cautiously) with such simple, natural things that remind us that there is somebody to give thanks to and that there is somebody to pray to (Karen).

While these practices are salient in my data, they seem to vary in significance to the participants in the study. Karen is one of those who really appreciates this practice, as she and her family are "reminded that there is someone to give thanks to and pray to." She further acknowledges that these practices have positively influenced her faith. This statement is underlined by her being clearly emotionally moved when sharing about it in the quote above. Evening prayer with children is also a widespread spiritual practice, and for some interviewees it is practiced as a modified version of Ignatius' prayer of examen, where parent and child look back on the day together and bring it before God, the Creator. For most of them, this evening ritual that is closely related to the daily rhythm of sleep also includes a song and perhaps The Lord's Prayer.

Some of the clergy, however, fail to acknowledge or remember such kinds of practices, as they seem to be so deeply embedded in the rhythm of everyday life that they become invisible. Hence, when asked if she regularly prays with anyone else as a private person, Nina forgot the most obvious person; that is, her child. I had to specifically ask about it. Her immediate comment reads:

> Nina: Oh, yes . . . he [the son] counts then perhaps, yes.
>
> T: He counts.
>
> Nina. Yes, I do pray. . . . I do pray, when he… I mean, evening prayer with him. That's right . . . thanks. It is such a natural thing that I forget.

Here I have included her stuttering and repetitive language because I interpret it to be an expression of her reaching a new insight, or being reminded of something important. Hence, she is caught a bit off guard, which possibly influences the way she communicates. This habit or practice was so automated that she had a hard time identifying it: "It is such a natural thing that I forget." However, she expresses thanks for being reminded of it, and seems to acknowledge this as a significant practice.

While the majority of the participants highly value the embodied practices of table grace and evening prayer with children, a minority seems to regard these spiritual practices "as second-rate" practices and not "the real stuff." Annika, for instance, shares that they used to say grace before meals and pray in the evening in her family when she was growing up, but compared to the devotional practices at her friends' houses, these practices seemed insufficient:

> I am used to from my home that we sing table grace, or say grace, but [I] am not used to us reading devotionals (. . .) But I used to visit friends a lot who were much better at that [expressing their faith], and I was always sort of envious because they managed to read a devotional together, for example, and I would actually have found it very all right (. . .) Evening prayer is important, and to focus on something related to a meal, that we either say grace, sing table grace or read something. But there should be room for prayer being so ordinary that we can pray in the middle of the day—I mean, that it is not only connected to a ritual such as evening prayer, or when we're at church (Annika).

Albeit acknowledging both evening prayer and table grace as valuable practices, Annika would still prefer prayer to be something "more ordinary" so that there should be room for it all the time, and *not only in relation to rituals*. Thus, Annika seems to view rituals as something second-rate compared to other spiritual practices such as free prayer or reading devotionals. This attitude was expressed by several other pastors as well. One of them is David, who reflects on his spiritual upbringing:

> We used to sing table grace, and say [our] evening prayers. It wasn't any kind of *personal* prayer or *personal* Bible study (. . .) It wasn't really any *personal* lived life that is shared, but a kind of cultural Christian upbringing. And then I guess we went to worship regularly and went on camps in the summer and winter (. . .) No, it was maybe in a way a bit of a shy Christianity. Perhaps especially for mom, because dad, he was the one mostly responsible for reading devotionals and such things. And he was clear about us having to give thanks before meals (. . .) (David, emphasis mine).

In this quote David briefly states that they used to pray in the evening and say grace before meals (or rather sing a song of thanksgiving for the food, which is the most common way of practicing table grace in Norway). However, he then goes directly on to reflecting more extensively on what it was not. *Personal* seems to be a key word to him. Such a spirituality is seen as opposed to "a kind of cultural Christian upbringing" consisting of saying grace, evening prayer, and public worship, which he took part in growing up. He furthermore characterizes this as a "shy" kind of spirituality. He seems to think of it as "as second-rate," and not "the real stuff" of "personal prayer and Bible study."

Both David and Annika have been affiliated with rather conservative lay organizations with pietistic legacies, and this could be a possible explanation as to why they seem to rank the different kinds of spiritual practices the way they do. This spirituality characterized as "shy" and "formal" Christianity, as opposed to the "more personal or spontaneous exercise of faith," could possibly fit into the category that I have termed an embedded spirituality—that is, a spirituality with spiritual practices embedded in daily life as its crux, while it also includes public worship, liturgy, and rituals. This observation supports Joel Halldorf's claim in his chapter of this volume that evangelicals have tended to favour simplicity and spontaneity over practices.[75] Moreover, Christian backgrounds of the kind Annika and David represent seem to be the common denominator for the pastors in my study who consider their own spiritual lives or practices as insufficient (those categorized as discontentedly non-intentional). This might be one reason why spiritual practices that do not exactly fit the pietistic or

---

75. For more on this, see Halldorf in this volume.

Part Two—Catholicity

evangelical ideal of a "spiritual life" are not so easily noticed, acknowledged, or appreciated by these pastors.

MAKING A CASE FOR A SPIRITUALITY OF EVERYDAY LIFE

Elizabeth Dreyer, author of *Earth Crammed with Heaven—A Spirituality of Everyday Life* offers the concept of an asceticism of everyday life. She claims that our classic understanding of asceticism may have narrowed this category, preventing us from embracing the ascetic practices that can be found in the midst of everyday life. When my child wakes me up every other hour, I do not have to set my alarm at 3 a.m to pray, but I am invited to see the care of this child as a spiritual practice, setting my own basic needs aside in order to care for another person, as Swedish author Lena Bergström also suggests.[76] Bergström makes a Copernican inversion and challenges parents not to focus on how children prevent us from engaging in spiritual practices, but rather to ask how this particular context of being a parent offers possibilities and situations that help us mature as Christians. Everyday life, including parenthood, then, can be seen as a laboratory for the Holy Spirit. My challenge to readers with whom my findings and arguments resonate, then, would be to not only recognize and acknowledge spiritual practices that fit the pietistic, evangelical, or any other prescribed pattern, but to also notice and appreciate all the small spiritual practices that go beyond the well-known categories, and that are often embedded in everyday life. This is a call to discover "God in all things," as the Ignatian tradition expresses it.[77]

In an unpublished talk given at a Norwegian summer festival,[78] William T. Cavanaugh argues that the real divide is not between the material and the spiritual, but between the food that perishes and the food that endures, and that the way to deal with the material world is to receive it, again and again, from the hand of God:

> But I don't think that there really is such a sharp divide between the material and the spiritual. If the Word became flesh and dwelt among us, then the material world is deeply implicated in how

---

76. See also Bergström, *Att ge plats för en annan*.
77. Hughes, *God in All Things*.
78. Cavanaugh, "The Food that Perishes and the Food that Endures," at Korsvei summer camp, Seljord, Norway July 16, 2013.

God's work on earth is carried out. Rather than a contrast between spiritual and material, Jesus offers us a contrast between two kinds of food, the food that perishes and the food that endures. Jesus knows that people need real, material bread; he has in fact just fed the multitudes with real barley loaves and fish. The contrast, I think, is not between material and spiritual, but between two different ways of dealing with the material world (. . .) What, then, is the food that endures for eternal life? This is the bread of life, that Jesus identifies with himself. It is this bread that God gives in a constant flow of giving. This is the daily bread that we ask for in the Lord's Prayer, "Give us this day our daily bread." It is not just lying there as a thing to be grasped; it is only to be received, again and again, on a daily basis, from the hand of God (. . .) The Lord's Supper teaches us that every feeding is miraculous. It is not just the Lord's Supper, but every loaf of bread we consume that is provided to us by the sheer grace of God.[79]

Cavanaugh's sacramental and material understanding of the Christian life clearly links the spiritual and the material. The bread that sustains us physically is closely linked to the bread that sustains us spiritually, because in both cases the crux is to receive it from the hand of God.[80] The vision outlined in *Being Consumed* is not a call to become less, but rather more, materially minded. This approach was also prevalent in my data, as my interviewee Karen puts it: "[When saying grace], I am reminded that there is someone to give thanks and pray to." Along the same lines, Norman Wirzba claims: "To say grace or offer a benediction of thanksgiving over a meal is among the highest and most honest expressions of our humanity."[81] The same holds true for evening prayer, where one is invited to look back on the day with a contemplative gaze. Evening prayer with children is often a brief ritual, but still, it is a practice where experiences, relationships, joys, and sorrows are brought before God, the Giver of all life. Further, as Cavanaugh argues, this is a practice where child and parent are invited again and again—day in and day out—to receive the daily bread, widely understood, from the hand of God.[82]

For both Karen and other pastors in my research, Christian spirituality is, among other things, related to how and what they purchase (for

---

79. Ibid.
80. Cavanaugh, *Being Consumed*.
81. Wirzba, *Food and Faith*.
82. Cavanaugh, "The Food that Perishes and the Food that Endures," July 16, 2013.

example, fair trade, or local products), and this is again connected with "everyday faith." With this approach, nothing, really, is indifferent to our spirituality. Rather it concerns our daily lives of working and resting, eating and sleeping, caring for children and others, rejoicing and mourning, buying and selling, and partaking in the breaking of the bread and the sharing of the wine. In this chapter, then, I make the case that all of these small practices matter. They should be made more explicit, so that we become aware of, and can reflect intentionally also on the non-intentional, habitual practices of our everyday Christian life. Moreover, spirituality should not be placed in a specific religious sphere of its own. Rather, it concerns all of ordinary life, and constitutes a way of life, a way of life that, in Cavanaugh's vision, is marked by receiving and giving.[83]

CONCLUSION

I was caught by surprise with the findings of this study, as I had not expected spiritual practices embedded in everyday life to be that significant to the pastors. I was not particularly looking for this, but the explorative approach of the research helped me discover these patterns. The analytical distinction between embedded and intentional spiritual practices helped me see more clearly and acknowledge the great gifts of spiritual practices embedded in everyday life. Using the continuums from low to high ideals and from a low to a high degree of discipline of reported actual engagement in intentional spiritual practices reveals how those who have high ideals for the spiritual life, yet struggle to live up to them, may feel guilty. This might possibly be the case because they fail to see and appreciate all the practices that they are actually taking part in on a daily basis.

In this chapter, then, I argue that spiritual practices that help us receive material goods and all of life as gifts from God are not "second hand" practices, but are indeed "the real stuff." Table grace is precisely such a simple, yet significant practice. It may be regarded "an empty ritual." It may be so automated that it becomes invisible. Yet it is by no means insignificant, and should not go unnoticed, whether that be in Norwegian Pietism, in Swedish Free Church spirituality, or in American Evangelicalism. The same holds true for other everyday practices, including those that are so embedded in everyday life that we hardly notice them. One example is the Aaronic benediction and the signing of the cross on my son's forehead every evening. I

---

83. Cavanaugh, *Being Consumed*, 98–99.

believe that the practices we engage in, whether intentionally or habitually, contribute to shaping us. "Woven together, then, they form a way of life."[84]

---

84. Bass, *Practicing Our Faith*, xi.

6

The Constantinianism of the Free Church Tradition and the Promise of a New Asceticism

Patrik Hagman

In this article I will use John Howard Yoder's reasoning regarding the concept of Constantinianism to assess the drastic moral change that the Nordic Free Church tradition has undergone: from being clearly defined communities that lived according to clearly defined moral rules, today the Free churches in Finland, Sweden and Norway (Denmark being something of a special case) have developed into traditions that are morally mainstream, with representatives often keen to underline that Christians are like everyone else. I will try to show that while the "old" rule-based morality had its problems, the concept of Constantinianism allows us to tell this story in a way that complicates this "embracing of the normal." Finally, I will suggest that the ascetic tradition offers a way to regain communal distinctness without succumbing to moral rigidity.

IN THE SHADOW OF THE STATE CHURCH

In the Nordic countries when we hear Constantinianism we hear "state church," that is, we think of the Lutheran state churches. And clearly, in some sense the Nordic Lutheran churches do represent a kind of Constantinianism. John Howard Yoder defined Constantinianism as the identification of the church with the Roman Empire.[1] He went on to describe "neo-Constantinianism" as a similar alliance of church and state beyond Constantine and his context. His description of neo-Constantinianism fits the Nordic State Churches historically pretty well:

> This unity has lost the worldwide character of the epoch of Constantine, yet the fusion of church and society is maintained. We can even say it is tightened, since the wars of religion linked particular churches with particular national governments in a way which had not obtained in the Middle Ages. Now the church is servant, not of mankind at large but, of a particular society; not of the entire society, but of a particular dominating class.[2]

There are countless examples in the history of the state churches in the Nordic countries of precisely this, when they act as a servant of the particular society in which they exist, and especially the elite of that society. This kind of neo-Constantinianism (n^1C) is today increasingly a thing of the past, but when Yoder described what he called neo-neo-Constantinianism (n^2C)—the form Constantinianism takes when secularization sets in—he explicitly used Sweden (alongside the U.S.) as an example.

> [In Sweden] the churches continue to enjoy the formal support of the government but can no longer count on any important popular support. Different as these two examples are, they have in common nonetheless the fact that they represent a secularization of a Constantinian dream. In both cases it is possible that the church can continue to give her blessing to the nation and, that the church and the government, as visible institutions, mutually support one another even though it is widely recognized that it is no longer possible to speak of the mass of society as in any specific sense "Christian." In the United States the military and political loyalty of most churchmen is a sign of the continuing identity despite formal separation; in Scandinavia the church continues to support the national politics and the government continues to pay

---

1. Peter Leithart has criticized Yoder for his view of Constantine the Great and the changes that took place in his time. Leithart's book has its merits, but I cannot see that his argument in any sense fits the way Yoder talks about Constantinianism or Constantine. That is, Yoder does not at all build his argument on the kind of presuppositions that Leithart criticizes. See Leithart, *Defending Constantine*.

2. Yoder, *The Original Revolution*, 142–43.

Part Two—Catholicity

for the clergy despite the absence of many convinced Christians in the church services.[3]

Though there is a lot to be said about this characterization of the Nordic State Churches,[4] it is clear that this description fits certain aspects of the way the Lutheran churches have functioned and still function in the Nordic countries. It is also clear that there was a time when the Free churches, some more, some less, represented a conscious alternative to this way of existing as a church.[5]

Some in the Free Church tradition perhaps want to imagine the Free churches as valiant enclaves of resistance against the secular state. The reality is of course more complex. Many of the Free churches, at least in Finland and Sweden have had close ties to various political parties, and have often been more than willing to work together with the state in various questions such as education and health-care, and more recently third-world aid. And this has certainly at times been a good thing.[6]

Even though the state—neither today nor in the past—has paid any Free Church pastors, I think it is fair to say that most Free churches are perfectly willing to "bless the nation." This becomes all the more clear if we take into account Yoder's claim that what is significant about the Constantinian church is that it "has vested interest in the present order of things."[7] The Free churches today are not, generally speaking, more critical of the way society functions than people in general, and in many ways function as integrated organizations in the socio-political system the same way as other organizations of various kinds.[8]

---

3. Ibid., 143–44. Even though the ties between state and church in Sweden are still strong, since the year 2000 the state does no longer pay the clergy's salaries.

4. For a more in-depth consideration, see my *Efter folkkyrkan*.

5. For more on this, see Fahlgren in this volume.

6. A person in my own tradition, the Swedish speaking Baptists in Finland, who has been active in local politics all his life once told me that the municipality he lived in was something of a special case, since about seventy percent of the representatives came from the various Free churches or (Lutheran) revival movements in the area. It would be difficult to not see it as irresponsible for Christians not to take part in local politics in such an area.

7. Yoder, *The Original Revolution*, 66.

8. The Free churches in Scandinavia traditionally have quite varying stances on how one as a Christian should relate to society, if Christians should do political work, from the countercultural to the heavily engaged. It is an unfortunate simplification—that I nevertheless have to make use of—to speak of *one* Free Church tradition. See Halldorf, "Modernitet och katolicitet." Björn Cedersjö in his 2001 dissertation on Free Church

FROM RULE BASED MORALITY TO INTERIOR SPIRITUALITY

However, it is clear that the different Free churches at various times have clearly represented an alternative way of life compared to that of the majority in society. They used to dress differently, talk differently, perhaps avoid alcohol, TV or both, smoke less (or more!), avoid secular entertainment in most forms and so on. And while very few would have seen these things as the most important marks of their respective movements, it is clear that practices like these clearly set the people of the Free churches apart from the "world."

Today, little of this remains. We might find the importance attached to the length of women's hair and skirts in those days amusing or annoying, but these clear, bodily, communal practices did flow out of and embody the specific convictions earlier generations in the Free churches held. Indeed, and their counterparts in the Free churches of today might still hold the same convictions, though they no longer hold on to the earlier genereations' practices.

Why is this? What happened?

In his study on Free Church ethics, Björn Cedersjö traces the development in various ethical fields through three generations, the first born in the first decades of the twentieth-century and the last in the 1970s. In his material it is fairly easy to discern three stages in this development. In the first stage, strict rules are combined with various rational explanations, e.g. the ban on dancing is explained because dancing tended to be combined with heavy drinking, fighting and other immoral behavior; or cinema was forbidden because one considered the values in the films to be detrimental to people and to stand in contrast with Christian values. In the youngest generation of this study few of these rules apply anymore. It is the middle generation that is interesting. Here many of the rules still applied, at least when they were young, but the motivations people give for the rules are increasingly bizarre. For instance, it would be okay to watch a movie in the schoolhouse, whereas even to enter into the cinema would be forbidden. Cedersjö uses the image of a plague that people feared to catch.[9] Sin

---

ethics detects a marked drop in political engagement in the (then) young generation compared to their parents and grandparents. Cedersjö, *Bortom syndakatalogen*, 103–5. It seems to me that in the ten years since Cedersjö's book, there has again been a growing interest in political questions among young people in the Free churches.

9. Cedersjö, *Bortom syndakatalogen*, 97–101.

was seen as contagious, but not very concrete. It was, it seems, becoming spiritualized.

Another interesting change is the movement away from the tendency to ban things wholesale (such as the medium of cinema or the genre novels) and to an emphasis on discerning what is good and bad regarding content. In a way this is clearly a sound development, but it is striking that in practice something very different happens. The youngest generation mentions the need to discern between the good and the bad regarding comparatively "high-brow" culture, such as literature, but not regarding entertainment, which in practice seems to be considered harmless.[10] This would suggest that there is a tendency to consider areas of life where society allows a great deal of variety, such as what books one reads, to be more spiritually relevant than areas where the acceptable options are fewer, that is the aspects of life that are highly commercialized or strongly connected to the state's control of the population.

I will not dwell on the reasons for this change.[11] The result of this process is in any case that today it is very difficult to actually point out any differences between those who belong to Free churches and those who do not, beyond some shared cultural references and, of course, some beliefs. Believers might listen to Christian pop music, but it sounds more or less the same as the pop music everyone else listens to. Certainly there are some kinds of behaviors that those who have grown up in a Free church are less inclined to take part in, but these are generally behaviors that are considered problematic in main stream culture as well, such as sexual promiscuity or illegal drug use.

It is worth pointing out that the development that Cedersjö describes, and anybody who has grown up in this tradition is familiar with it, is not simply one of modifying "values" to be more similar to society in general.

---

10. Ibid., 100. I might be pushing the material a bit here—Cedersjö's presentation of the material is quite brief—but perhaps I could be so bold as to supplement the material with my own experience: when growing up my reading of certain (very serious) books was definitely considered more problematic than what I or my peers were watching on TV.

11. I do want to point out what I find to be a plausible reason for this quite dramatic change especially among Pentecostals, where there often was a dramatic change within the span of a few decades. The strict moral teaching was often combined with a strong eschatological preoccupation in the teaching and an intense conviction that Jesus would return any day. See Ibid., 300. When this teaching proved to be objectively false (Jesus did not return) it made it easier to reject the moral authority of the same preachers as well.

That clearly has taken place, but it is also a process where Christian faith is remolded so that certain aspects important to past generations no longer seem central. Entertainment, broadly speaking, has moved from being a central arena where among the oldest generation surveyed one's choices reflected one's Christian convictions and belonging to a particular community, whereas the middle generation only understood that way of thinking as blind obedience to rules or authority. For the youngest generation entertainment was considered almost irrelevant to one's faith, unless its content conflicted directly with these convictions, such as in the case of a film that portrays Jesus in a heterodox way. We can thus witness, within the span of just three generations, what William Cavanaugh calls a "migration of the Holy," where the religious focus in life moves from socially motivated common moral behavior to individual, "inner," spiritual qualities and experiences.[12]

However, if we discuss this development in terms of Constantinianism, certain aspects of it might be clarified, especially regarding the present situation of the Nordic Free Churches. True, none of the generations involved in Cedersjö's study would have made the decisions they made in a conscious attempt to gain favors from the state, but then the state is not what it used to be. Yoder did speculate about future ways Constantinianism could present itself,[13] but he did not imagine the kind of late-capitalist "withering away of the state" that we have seen in the last few decades, so his speculations in these cases are less relevant to our question.[14]

It seems, however, that the Free churches, along with other Christian churches in the Nordic countries,[15] are facing an alternative kind

---

12. See Cavanaugh has borrowed the term from Bossy, *Christianity in the West*, 153–71.

13. Yoder thought, like many scholars at the time, that secularism would marginalize Christianity a great deal further. This part of his analysis is less relevant after the "post-secular event." On this, see Hagman, "Post-Secularity and Post-Constantianism," 129–46.

14. The Nordic states, especially Finland and Sweden have since the 1980's "modified" the traditional "Nordic Welfare State" model by adapting New Public Management and neo-liberal ideology. If one today wants to describe the Nordic model as a distinct alternative, it is strictly because the policies of past decades continue to have an influence in spite of the policies of more recent governments. That is, there are still publicly funded schools and healthcare for everyone, but the rationale of this is, beside their immense popular support, increasingly construed in terms of effectiveness and national competitive advantages, rather than any vision of a good "home of the people."

15. Including not only the Lutheran churches, but also the smaller presence of

of neo-neo-neo-Constantianism from the one Yoder imagined, which acknowledges that the Caesar that Christians compromise with today is increasingly in it for the money.[16] In other words, the kind of compromises Christians do today that tend to undermine the churches' witness are less about using its cultic apparatus to provide the state with legitimacy and "glory," though that certainly still takes place, and more about the uncritical acceptance of the way of life propagated by the commercial forces and mass media.[17]

The fact that churches no longer find it necessary to question new types of technology, developments in media and entertainment, and also notions of how we dress (which need not build on gender stereotypes, though that has clearly happened in the past), is a clear sign of how the church today essentially accepts the notion of religion as pertaining only to the inner spiritual life, and a rather limited notion of morality built largely on Kantian views. It is in this sense that the changes described above appear Constantinian in character; what we see in the Free Church movements is a move away from a (more or less) counter cultural stance towards a general acceptance of the "powers that be," supremely exemplified not by the state but by the commercial forces that produce and sell those products that are no longer considered "religiously relevant" by present day Christians.

THE (RE)TURN TO PRACTICES

While this is true of all Protestant churches at least in the Nordic countries today, it creates a specific dilemma for the Free churches. As Stanley Hauerwas points out:

---

the Catholic Church, and various Orthodox churches (including growing immigrant churches).

16. I still find Hardt and Negri, *Empire*, to be the best conceptual discussion about the way states lose their power to other actors in the globalised world. Even if there is truth in the common criticism that the U.S. seems to have reverted to "old imperialism" after 9/11 rather than the type of empire Hardt and Negri describes, the analysis still holds true for smaller states like the Nordic one's. For a theological engagement with *Empire* see Hagman, "Asceticism and Empire," 39–53.

17. Incidentally, it would be possible to discuss the state's changed role in the Nordic countries *vis-a-vis* the market in terms of a kind of inverted Constantinianism, where the state increasingly finds ways to support the real power of the market in ways that are analogous with the Constantinian church's relation to the state.

For example, "voluntary church membership" was a prophetic challenge against mainstream Christianity, but once Christendom is gone the call for voluntary commitment cannot help but appear as a legitimation of the secular commitment to autonomy. In a Christendom world it took conviction to be a pagan or an Anabaptist, but given the world in which we are now living it is hard to distinguish pagans from Anabaptists.[18]

Hauerwas goes on to suggest that this is why "practices" are so important today, practices that set Christians apart and embody our convictions. As we have seen, the Free Church tradition had many such practices but they where largely abandoned in favor of a more Constantinian stance, where, if anything, the lack of visible identity markers is emphasized.[19] There seems to be among Christians today a latent imperative to style oneself according to the latest trends in clothing, culture, and technology, so as to suggest that the Christian faith in no way implies a distance to the cultural and commercial center of culture. In other words, the type of faith that aims to secure a "Christian difference" in the "inner," "spiritual" realm involves a corresponding imperative to *avoid* difference in the "outer" realm—dress-code, morality concerning alcohol, the way pop music should sound, and which TV-series one downloads from the internet.[20]

---

18. Hauerwas, *In Good Company*, 73.

19. Of course, the Free Church tradition had and has many distinctive practices that did play this role of distinguishing between the church and the "world," such as intercessory prayer, church assembly meetings, particular types of music and so on. While some of these practices remain, one could just as well make the case that so many of these types of practices no longer functioning as they once did is as much a part of the "crisis" of the Free Church as the moral practices discussed in this paper. While this is true, one could conversely ask if these particular practices lacked real staying power because the Free Church tradition always lived in a tension between shunning the world and embracing the modern. On this characteristic of the Free churches see Halldorf, *Av denna världen?*.

20. Cedersjö's account shows that there is one area where something of the traditional morality still remains strong: sexual morals. Here too a great amount of change has taken place, for instance regarding the possibility for divorce and remarriage, but there is still in the youngest generation a sense that views (and practices) regarding sexuality set believers apart. What is interesting, though, is that Cedersjö's material also seems to indicate that this is the area where change has not happened unconsciously – that is, sexual morals have been intensely discussed in these traditions from the 1960s onwards. Cedersjö, *Bortom syndakatalogen*, 65–92. It would thus seem that the fact that this area still has some kind of identity-marking character could be attributed to the conscious work put into the question. As a theologian one cannot help but find that heartwarming, even though one knows that a lot of the actual material produced by that discussion has a certain embarrassing quality to it.

Part Two—Catholicity

What Hauerwas suggests, however, is that what is arguably the most foundational of all Free Church doctrines, voluntary church membership, no longer functions in the same way it once did. Unlike what we believed, the notion that one should freely chose to follow Christ turns out not to be a timeless universal aspect of Christian truth, but a practice whose meaning is determined by the cultural situation where it is carried out, and thus dependent on all normal hermeneutical problems and principles.

It follows then that it would be critical for the Free Church tradition—and all other churches—to pursue new practices that would again function as ways to embody convictions and thus recreate the Church as a separate social body set apart from the world.[21] Obviously, reverting to the morality of our grandparents would not achieve this end, for the same reasons that voluntary church membership is no longer a challenge to mainstream culture. On the other hand, the standard liberal approach of seeking to mediate between Christianity and the current culture will by no means achieve this end either.[22]

However, today in Free churches there are other tendencies that point in a different direction. There is an increasing appreciation of the classical Christian practices such as the Eucharist and also a more liturgical mode of worship. While I wholeheartedly support this development, I don't think that it is enough to practice the Eucharist once a week and then continue to live the same way as everyone else. It is clearly possible to practice the Eucharist in a way that has little or no practical impact on the way we live and see the world and each other. Somehow the Eucharist needs to be linked to our ordinary lives.[23]

---

21. See Cavanaugh, *Migrations*, especially 46–68. There are plenty standard objections to this kind of thinking, most of which are discussed with great insight in the same book, 141–69. Cavanaugh argues that the point of depicting the church as a distinct community apart from society in general is not to argue its moral superiority, but that it follows from the Christian confession of sinfulness and the need for forgiveness which are the basis for a different way to live in community.

22. This of course is to simplify the matter quite a bit, because one could conceivably ask: "mediate between Christianity and what culture"? I.e. today's culture is pluralistic to the degree that a hybrid between, say Christianity and anarchist movements, would of course serve to create a "distinct" church set clearly apart from the cultural mainstream. Still, I think this would be an unfortunate way of putting the matter, since any concept of Christianity entering into dialogue with any other discourse "on equal terms" is likely to be built on illusions. However, as will be clear from what follows we need a way to account for the ways that church appropriates and lets itself be inspired by "secular" practices and movements.

23. For more on this, see Kaufman in this volume. William Cavanaugh has worked

Obviously, this problem is not new to the Church. As I have argued elsewhere, it is in this context we have to understand the tremendous growth of the ascetic movement in the fourth, fifth and sixth centuries AD, that is a church that is losing its distinctness due to an increasing identification between church and state.[24] This is of course what Constantinianism originally was about. I believe that we have much to learn from the early Christian ascetics about developing such practices that strive to clarify the difference between church and world, between the kingdoms and empires of this world and the Kingdom of God.[25]

Ascetic practices have three aspects: they serve to transform the personality of the ascetic in order to turn her—or the community the person is a part of—into an image of the Kingdom of God. They are thus both transformative and performative: they create an image and communicate it to the world (witness). Both of these aspects rely on the third—ascetic practices involve the body.[26] So for instance fasting in antiquity was about modifying one's passions in order to achieve more focus and control over one's life, but it was also a powerful way to communicate disapproval over the way society functioned in a culture where eating was always done in ways that reinforce the hierarchical structures of society. It is the fact that the body is involved that makes both transformation and communication possible.

Ascetic practices serve to clarify the character of the church in a way that is visible also to those that are not (yet) part of the community. Even more so than practices like baptism and Eucharist they are undertaken "before the watching world," to quote the subtitle of Yoder's book *Body Politics*.[27]

To develop new such ascetic practices, or reinterpret and modify old ones, would thus be a way for churches today to counter Constantinian

---

with this theme in several books, especially Cavanaugh, *Torture and Eucharist* and Cavanaugh, *Being Consumed*. For a Nordic attempt at something similar see Hagman, *Om kristet motstånd*.

24. Hagman, "Liturgi och asketism," 27–40.

25. See Hagman, "To Travel in One Place," 93–109. In that article I argue that Hauerwas's projects can be read as ascetical in this sense, and thus provides resources for developing ascetic practices that not only serve to make the "Christian difference" clearer, but achieves this in a way that is inherently non-violent.

26. Hagman, *The Asceticism of Isaac of Nineveh*; Hagman, "Asceticism and Empire," 39–53.

27. Yoder, *Body Politics*.

tendencies and thus strengthen the character and identity of the community. This is of course a demanding option, but that too is in line with the Christian tradition. Many such practices have already come into being and could be developed further: there is room for creativity here. I will finish this chapter with one example.

Given the world we live in, with the massive amount of information and entertainment that is available to us via media and internet on the one hand, and the ascetic focus on "leaving the world" as the primary symbol for the clear difference between church and world on the other, it seems that the way Christians use the media should probably be the most obvious example of an area where new ascetic practices would be valuable for a church looking to clarify its difference. The idea that Christians should be selective in their use of media is in some circles at least as controversial an idea as going to the movies would have been a generation or two ago. Still, there is no denying that media is an extremely important factor that influences how we envision our world, and thus potentially stands in conflict with the view of the world the Christian faith wants us to see.

The traditional ascetic approach to this problem would not be to create rules (in our sense) or to forbid certain genres or types of media. The ascetics would emphasize the need to exercise *diakrisis*, the judgment of the spirits, a practical virtue in distinguishing between the good and the bad, the useful and the harmful. To ask how this particular film, novel, or computer game affects me, my children, and my community, would from this perspective not be about censorship or control, but about responsibility and love. However, if we truly want to approach this question from an ascetical perspective, we need to focus on the bodily aspect of our media consumption—in other words, technology.

If Christians would decide to create ascetic rules (different in character from moralistic rules) regarding the use of smartphones and tablet computers—e.g., not to use them in public or when in the company of friends and family members, this would surely be a practice that fulfills the understanding of an ascetic practice presented above. Obviously, it would involve the body. But such a practice would also transform the way we are: we would be more focused on what happens where we are bodily present, less inclined to feel the need to have control over what is going on all over the world, and maybe even more committed in our personal relationships. It would also communicate this, since by now, if a person sits in a public space without a technological gadget in their hand, it is almost a bit weird.

So it would be a way to communicate a truly Christian commitment to the created physical world, over against the increasingly gnostic type of existence of late modernity, where reality is conceived as non-physical.

Last but not least, it would be costly, because we so love new things and the sense of power and freedom our technological devices give us—not to mention the satisfaction of being an elite consumer by having the latest model. Obviously, were we to follow such an ascetic rule, many of us would find that we in fact have little use for such devices at all. This rather simple example would then open up a space for existing differently in our world. It would teach us how to go against the cultural forces of our time.

I would like to add one further criterion that would be useful for the church to attend to in developing new ascetic practices. It would be good if there is a clear connection between the traditional Christian practices, such as Baptism and Eucharist and whatever new practices we develop or put into practice. The reasons for this are obvious. First, in this way we make sure that these practices actually serve to clarify a way in which Christian worship informs Christian life. Second, this will ensure that these practices have a "catholic" character—even though they can and probably should be local and contextual to be effective, it is important that it is possible to relate them to Christians living in a different part of the world or people of different denominational backgrounds. Finally, these practices will become part of the church's continual reflection on its central practices and the way it worships.

In the case of my example the connection obviously lies in the kind of community that these technologies promise and how such a community it relates to the communion of the saints. In either case it is a community with both physical and "virtual" aspects, but whereas the technological community is something we create by choosing who is and is not our friend, the church is a community that lives by welcoming. It is thus a very different stance than the one we take by excluding the bodies around us while focusing exclusively on our phone.

The notion of Constantinianism helps us understand how such practices need to be focused in order to avoid getting pulled back into the logic of our culture. Modern capitalism has an uncanny ability to transform such practices into yet another form of consumer choices and thus render them harmless. However, to create such practices in a mode that is both ascetic and catholic can make it possible for the church to, at least to a degree, become a "free" church.

7

Thinking With

The Need for Tradition in Free Church Theology

Andreas Nordlander

INTRODUCTION

While the Free churches have often had an ambiguous relation to theological tradition, many contemporary Free Church theologians desire to locate their own work in the wider Catholic tradition. Against the background of this emerging appropriation of tradition, I revisit Alasdair MacIntyre's sophisticated work on traditions of rational enquiry to bring out some of his most helpful concepts; these are then illustrated and fleshed out by briefly looking at the theological work of William Cavanaugh. Finally, I reflect on what Free Church theologians can learn from MacIntyre and Cavanaugh as they contemplate what it means to self-consciously embrace tradition, suggesting that it should involve a recognition of already being constituted by a wider and deeper history and an appreciation of the unique creative task facing Free Church theologians as they seek their own voice within the tradition.

THE AMBIGUOUS ROLE OF TRADITION IN FREE CHURCH THEOLOGY

Free Church theology, like all other kinds of theology, and indeed, like all other kinds of human thought, necessarily presupposes belonging to some sort of tradition. To say that, however, is not to say that Free Church theology self-consciously embraces its traditioned character. Indeed, the Free churches have had an ambiguous relationship to the Christian tradition, to say the least.

For instance, the ecclesiological primitivism of the Radical Reformation and its heirs tended to bracket the entire period between the New Testament writings and the modern emergence of Free churches.[1] Indeed, the very self-identity of many Free churches has been defined in opposition to the merely "human traditions" and "dead rituals" of ecclesial history.[2] Put positively, the desire to be radical has partly reflected the desire to return to the New Testament roots of the faith (from the Latin *radix*).[3] This must, moreover, be understood in the political context of early modern Europe, with its close allegiance between the emerging nation-states and different Christian confessions: the opposition to ecclesial traditions was a costly act of political defiance, and as such, deeply shaping of identity.

On the other hand, the Radical Reformation spawned its own tradition, or rather a set of variously related traditions, and did so through a process of continuing negotiations with what had gone before. Consider the continuing importance of the evangelical "saints"—Bunyan, Wesley, Whitefield, Edwards, Newton, Spurgeon, and so on—among revivalist groups. They bear witness to a sense of the importance of history within these communities.[4] This does not mean, of course, that any explicitly normative role was accorded to tradition in relation to scripture, only that it

---

1. Cf. Fahlgren, "Frikyrkligt gudstjänstliv," 190–91.
2. For more on this, see Fahlgren and Halldorf in this volume.
3. Fahlgren, "Frikyrkligt gudstjänstliv," 251.
4. The contemporary English-language use of the terms "evangelical"—which is a transdenominational designation—has a wider extension than "Free Church," not least including a large segment of churches tracing their origin to the magisterial reformers. But the borders are extremely porous here: Many of the Free churches would identify themselves as evangelical, and the spirituality of Evangelicalism is very closely related to the history of the Free churches. In the Swedish context, "evangelical" is increasingly used as a self-designation among the Free churches (though, it seems, less so among those Lutherans who otherwise share evangelical sensibilities).

de facto shaped the identity of the Free churches. One must distinguish between *theories* of the role of tradition and the *actual* role of tradition.

The debate about the relation between scripture and tradition, in the context of Reformation polemics, brought out increasingly polarized statements. The Protestants insisted on *sola scriptura*, the primacy of the Bible over tradition, being in all theological matters the so called *norma normans non normata*. Against this stood the Council of Trent and its articulation of a two-source theory of revelation—scripture *and* tradition. Nonetheless, as the influential evangelical theologian Alister McGrath points out, the magisterial reformers were also highly appreciative of the early Christian tradition in so far as it witnessed to a genuine struggle to understand the biblical texts. Luther could even go so far as to describe his purpose as a return to "the Bible and Augustine."[5] The radical reformers, however, tended to be more radical in their insistence on the scripture principle. In practice, however, the overwhelming majority of churches stemming from the Radical Reformation accepted the main creeds of the early church, even as they, in contrast to the Lutheran and Reformed traditions, were suspicious of writing their own denominational confessions, since such confessions operate precisely as traditions in the original sense, namely as guides for the interpretation of scripture.[6] The assumption of the self-explanatory power of the Bible is thus at its strongest among the Free Church heirs of the Radical Reformation. Even so, a "canon within the canon" has emerged here as everywhere, as could arguably be seen in the evangelical emphasis on personal conversion, or in the Pentecostal foregrounding of Luke-Acts against the Lutheran and Calvinist foregrounding of the Pauline writings, to name but two examples.[7] Once more, one must distinguish between *theorizing* the formative role of tradition and the *de facto* formative role of tradition.

The Free Church, then, has clearly been marked by an ambiguous relation to tradition. There are, however, many signs that Free Church theologians—theologians rooted in Free Church denominations—are becoming more aware and accepting of the positive role of tradition, following in this respect the general trend among Protestant theologians, who as a rule are much more affirmative of tradition than their forebears.[8] The reasons for

---

5. McGrath, *A Scientific Theology*, 43–44.
6. For more on this, see Fahlgren in this volume.
7. Cf. Dayton, *Theological Roots of Pentecostalism*, 23–26.
8. Williams, "Tradition." See also Boersma, *Heavenly Participation*, chapter 7; and Williams, *Evangelicals and Tradition*. Another sign of the shift is the publication of major

this are no doubt varied and complex. One important factor in the return to tradition is a shift in the philosophical landscape, where the notion of a self-sufficient, neutral, and rational subject has become increasingly difficult to accept—often described as a shift from modern to postmodern sensibilities.[9] My purpose here, however, is not to rehearse this history, its causes and consequences, benign or otherwise. Rather, I would like to approach the question of tradition from a more philosophical angle: What is tradition? How does it work? And what does it mean for a theologian to *self-consciously* take up a place within the historical trajectory of Christian reflection? This means that I am going to focus on the intellectual side—on theological reflection—even though I fully agree that since traditions are always socially embodied there are no sharp distinctions between thought and praxis, they are always dialectically related.

I will turn first to Alasdair MacIntyre and his development of a sophisticated notion of tradition-constituted enquiry, or tradition-specific rationality, because his approach has something to teach us about thinking theologically with and within a specific tradition; I will then move on to reflect on William Cavanaugh's work as a model in this regard, before ending with some reflections on the retrieval of tradition in Free Church theology.

MACINTYRE AND THE CONCEPT OF TRADITION

The Dynamic of Tradition

MacIntyre has developed a dynamic—that is to say, non-static—concept of tradition, in many of his writings. Here I will draw mainly on *After Virtue* and *Whose Justice? Which Rationality?*[10] His main concern is to discuss Western ethical traditions, and how they have developed rival understandings of such things as the virtues, justice, and rationality. But he also ad-

---

book series on this theme from evangelical publishers, such as the *Ancient Christian Commentary* and the *Reformation Commentary on Scripture*, both from InterVarsity Press, and *Evangelical Ressourcement: Ancient Sources for the Church's Future*, from Baker. In Sweden, this appreciative attitude toward tradition is increasingly seen in the work of Free Church theologians such as Sune Fahlgren and Roland Spjuth, and also in the writings of church leaders and pastors such as Ulf Ekman and Peter Halldorf.

9. Philosopher James K. A. Smith, for instance, makes an explicit connection between postmodernity and the retrieval of theological tradition in *Who's Afraid of Postmodernism?* The same is true of theologian Robert Webber in his much-cited book *Ancient-Future Faith*.

10. MacIntyre, *After Virtue*; MacIntyre, *Whose Justice?*

vances a more general account of the indispensability of tradition for human thinking, where tradition is broadly conceived so as to include theory and practices, institutions and so on, if we are to have access at all to rational enquiry.[11] His concept of tradition has certain affinities with Thomas Kuhn's notion of a *paradigm*, Hans Georg Gadamer's idea of a *horizon*, Charles Taylor's *social imaginary*, John Milbank's concept of a *muthos*, or even with the somewhat misleading notion of a *worldview*.[12] Tradition is, in short, the framework that allows us a fundamental take on the world—intellectually, affectively, practically and so on. As such, it is always operative before being explicitly thematized by the subject. In other words, we discover belonging to it after the fact, if at all.

MacIntyre's originality, however, lies in trying to spell out how traditions evolve over time, while nonetheless retaining continuity as one and the same tradition. This dynamic understanding of tradition is reflected in his definition of the concept: "A living tradition is an historically extended, socially embodied argument."[13] And later, in *Whose Justice?*, he expands on this and says, "a tradition is an argument extended through time in which certain fundamental agreements are defined and redefined in terms of two kinds of conflicts: those with critics and enemies external to the tradition (…) and those internal, interpretative debates through which the meaning and rationale of the fundamental agreements come to be expressed and by whose progress a tradition is constituted."[14]

This is an important corrective to the common understanding of tradition as a reactionary force, a repetition of the past, a guardian of what has been—an understanding that may owe more to Burke's political philosophy than to Christian thought. And again this is where MacIntyre advances an original thesis in relation not only to Burke, but also to later philosophers of science, such as Polanyi, Kuhn and Feyerabend, who all take tradition to be essentially conservative.[15] But for MacIntyre, who is inspired here by a theological rather than a philosophical understanding of tradition—he acknowledges the inspiration of John Henry Newman—the very point of

---

11. MacIntyre, *Whose Justice?* 367.

12. Kuhn, *The Structure of Scientific Revolutions*; Gadamer, *Wahrheit und Methode*; Taylor, *A Secular Age*; Milbank, *Theology and Social Theory*.

13. MacIntyre, *After Virtue*, 222.

14. MacIntyre, *Whose Justice?* 12.

15. See the discussion in MacIntyre, "Epistemological Crisis."

tradition is to be able to account for the progress of rational enquiry (or in theological terms, for the legitimate development of doctrine).[16]

The main point, then, is this: We must insist on the *dynamic character* of tradition against the criticism of tradition as merely a nostalgic return to this or that, as if there could ever be a return to the past. The directionality of the living is forward. In theology, this critique is particularly frustrating when it assumes that arguing from out of the Christian tradition is simply wanting to defend the *status quo*! An accusation that really means: You do not want to think at all; you just want to passively take over a set of opinions and to be relieved of the task of thinking yourself. But this is a quintessentially modern critique of tradition-constituted thinking that fails to take into account its tradition-constitutive dimension, that is to say tradition as an on-going argument. Says MacIntyre: "to be an adherent of a tradition is always to enact some further stage in the development of one's tradition."[17] This conceptual pair—tradition-constituted and tradition-constitutive thinking—I think is a very useful way of describing this dynamic. While it is true that the primary condition of possibility for rational thought must be pre-given to me, which is to say that my intellectual possibilities are constituted precisely in belonging to a tradition, this very pre-givenness affords me a certain constitutive power to develop fresh trajectories of intellectual enquiry. Passivity and activity necessarily go together, reception and production. What MacIntyre is saying, then, is that "tradition" names this continuous dialectic between the past and the present.

The Stages of Development: Crisis and Awareness

So, if traditions are dynamic and evolving entities, how can we describe this process? Zooming in considerably from his more general reflections on the dynamics of tradition, MacIntyre has developed a schema or typology intended to pick out the salient features of the development of a tradition from its initial stages toward maturity:[18]

1. The origin of tradition is the contingent beliefs, institutions, and practices of some particular community, which constitute for them a

---

16. MacIntyre, *Whose Justice?*, 353–54. G. K. Chesterton made similar claims with respect to the orthodox Christian tradition in his book *Orthodoxy*.

17. MacIntyre, *Whose Justice?* 11.

18. Ibid., chapter 18.

given. This simply amounts to a recognition of the immemorial historicity of human existence, a recognition that renders futile all modern attempts to construct foundationalist epistemologies.

2. Then, in the second stage, tensions, problems, incoherencies make themselves known in various ways. This could be a result of external pressure from other traditions, to be sure, but it could also be generated within the community and recognized by its own standards of rationality.

3. The problems laid bare in the second stage then prompt a systematic reflection on the beliefs, institutions, and practices of the community, and their reformulation such that what is in fact a tradition of thought proper begins to develop. At this stage theorizing has become important.

4. The fourth stage is reached when the participants of the tradition look back on its previous stages and recognize development: We understand better now than we did before! The beliefs, institutions, and practices now cease to be givens and are explicitly thematized.

5. Finally, there arises the need to reflect on and try to understand what one has actually been doing in developing a tradition of enquiry— that is, to try to understand the operations of tradition-constituted and tradition-constitutive thinking as such. In short, a kind of meta-reflection emerges within the tradition.

6. Quite apart from the more normal operations of the development of a tradition—stages 1 to 5—MacIntyre adds a last important stage toward maturity. This is when a tradition encounters an "epistemological crisis," that is, when, by its own standards, it ceases to make progress, when its trusted methods yield nothing, when old certainties begin to crumble. In order to survive such a crisis a more radical conceptual invention or theoretical discovery is needed, though its continuity with the previous history of the tradition must also be clear—novelty without continuity means rupture, not development.[19]

While it is always wise to take schematizations such as these with a pinch of salt, and especially not to expect any exact instantiation of them in

---

19. Interestingly, MacIntyre's own examples of successfully meeting the challenge of crisis are the theological doctrine of the trinity as formulated in the fourth century, and Bohr's theory of the internal structure of the atom in modern physics.

real life, I do believe MacIntyre's different stages pinpoint important dimensions in the development of a tradition. It seems, moreover, that the schema should not be understood primarily as a linear history, but rather as a perpetual dialectic in which all living traditions engage. Hence, all traditions continually risk falling into incoherency or even a state of crisis, which will prompt renewed reflection of a more or less radical kind, and which will in turn shape the meta-reflection on traditional enquiry as such. There is of course always the possibility that a tradition will not be able to sustain itself in the face of crisis and will die out—as happened, for instance, with the old Nordic religion, or with the gods of ancient Greece—moving, as it were, from living tradition to intellectual relic. In fact, on MacIntyre's account no one can claim, in Hegelian fashion, to have finally articulated the full truth, or to have reached the end of history. While a claim to truth must certainly be made, it is always possible that future developments will show that one's grasp of it was inadequate. A point with which theologians—seeking, after all, knowledge of God—should be thoroughly familiar.

In the next section I will use William Cavanaugh's work as an illustration of how a contemporary theologian may be read through the lens of some of MacIntyre's main concepts, trying to flesh out what has so far been rather abstractly presented, before returning to the retrieval of tradition among Free Church theologians.[20]

WILLIAM CAVANAUGH: MODELLING THEOLOGY AS EMBODIED ARGUMENT

To understand the dynamic interaction between past and present in the Christian tradition we need models, and William Cavanaugh is, I think, among those contemporary theologians who do this best. One reason for this is the way in which his work is grounded in the concrete realities of human life and death in this place and at this time. In fact, more than most other theologians his on-going conversation with and within the Catholic tradition takes place against the background of extremely serious contemporary political and social issues. Let me give two examples of this approach; they both illustrate, I think, the idea of tradition as an on-going socially embodied argument about the meaning of the tradition itself. That

---

20. To be sure, MacIntyre does flesh out his argument in rich historical narratives, but they are of less interest in this context, concerned as we are with appropriating his scheme as a model for contemporary theology.

is to say, they illustrate a form of theological thinking that is clearly both tradition-constituted and tradition-constitutive.

The first example is the book *Torture and Eucharist: Theology, Politics, and the Body of Christ*, which is an analysis of Chile under the Pinochet regime, and in particular the use of torture and its consequences, and of the response of the Catholic Church, which changed dramatically over time.[21] Here Cavanaugh enters a debate internal to the Church about how its political role should be understood and enacted, and describes a deeply problematic and incoherent situation. As the book demonstrates there is no possibility of simply repeating the Christian tradition in this context, for that tradition is not sufficiently clear or unified to know how to deal with the atrocities of the Pinochet regime. Clearly, the Catholic bishops who were inspired by Jacques Maritain's New Christendom, which advocated a concern with the soul of society and not with its bodies, were bearers of tradition in this way of thinking. But their resources were inadequate when it came to dealing with the situation they faced, and so they had to begin to practice another way of being church, which is to say that they had to retrieve tradition differently. In this particular context it took the form of a renewed appreciation of the church precisely as *body* and of the centrality of the Eucharist in its way of life. Tradition is not just waiting for us to be passively repeated, but it requires the arduous work of carrying something forward so as to develop it in response to current needs. As MacIntyre says, "to be an adherent of a tradition is always to enact some further stage in the development of one's tradition."[22] It seems to me that the process of the Catholic Church under the Pinochet regime that Cavanaugh describes and analyses so well illustrates what MacIntyre has in mind when he speaks of the dynamics of tradition as an on-going socially embodied argument.

Let me take one more example from Cavanaugh's work: from the rather recent, small and tightly argued book *Being Consumed: Economics and Christian Desire*.[23] In brief, Cavanaugh here sketches a broadly Augustinian view of the world and of human beings in particular as a rival alternative to late capitalist consumerism. He argues, for instance, that as long as freedom is defined merely as absence of external constraints, as long as it is not essentially related to a vision of the goal of human life and flourishing, so-called freedom always reduces to power play. But if human

---

21. Cavanaugh, *Torture and Eucharist*.
22. MacIntyre, *Whose Justice?*, 13.
23. Cavanaugh, *Being Consumed*.

beings, as primarily creatures of desire, are instead made free as their desire is rightly ordered to things that are more intrinsically valuable—such as community—then the possibility of a theological critique of consumerism, detachment, unbalanced globalization, and so on opens up and becomes persuasive.

This, I believe, could also be understood along the lines of the Christian theological tradition as an extended argument. Here it is not so much a question of an internal argument over the meaning of basic convictions; Cavanaugh rather turns to theological tradition to engage those external to that tradition. But even so, it is not a mere repetition of previous thought, a merely passive arguing for the *status quo*. Far from it! The point, once more, is rather to enter into a conversation with the Christian tradition in order to develop it in response to current needs.

So, I think these are ways in which Cavanaugh's work models how doing theology from within the trajectory of Christian tradition is also a creative undertaking, where understanding unfolds in something like an argument. And this argument is always carried out both with the polyphonous voices internal to the tradition, in response to the needs of the current situation, and in dialogue with external voices arguing for a different take on the world.

THE FREE CHURCHES AND THE RETRIEVAL OF TRADITION

Against the background of MacIntyre's analysis of traditions of enquiry and Cavanaugh's embodied illustration of the dynamics of Christian tradition, what can Free Church theology learn as it contemplates what it means to self-consciously embrace tradition?

Many Free Church theologians, who know their postmodern theory—and perhaps their MacIntyre too—accept and believe that all thinking is thinking with, that it is tradition-constituted. They understand that they themselves belong to the Free Church tradition in all its variety, but many also feel that the resources of this tradition are now inadequate: too shallow, too modern, too unaware of its own formative role precisely as tradition. This could perhaps be construed along the lines of MacIntyre's second stage, or even as a moment of crisis for Free Church theology: a crisis of knowledge, of legitimacy, of courage. Such a situation, as we have seen, results in systematic theoretical reflection. It is in the process of making one's own—perhaps previously unthematized—traditional resources explicit that many begin to sense the insufficiency of those resources in the face of a new situation, and consequently begin to look in the direction of the wider and deeper Catholic tradition. At least this would be one way of understanding the ongoing appropriation of tradition among Free Church theologians suggested above.

But what does it mean to think theologically with tradition? What is involved in this relocation and appropriation? In answer to that question, I want to suggest that at least two closely related issues should be at the forefront: We need to ask, first, what the wider Catholic tradition has already bequeathed to us in virtue of our formation in one tradition within the great tradition. That is, the Free Church tradition needs to be relocated within the wider tradition, such that the root system of our theology may grow both wider and deeper. But second, we need to consider what it is that we bring with us, uniquely, to that wider tradition, and the way in which that wider tradition must therefore be rendered with a creative difference. In MacIntyre's terms, we should carefully consider both the way in which we are constituted and the way in which we are constituting, always finding ourselves in the midst of that destabilizing but ever creative dialectic called tradition. Let us discuss these in turn.

What is involved in appropriating a tradition? Following MacIntyre, we would have to say that traditions are not simply taken up; rather we always find ourselves already "one of the bearers of a tradition."[24] Cavanaugh also writes about this in *Being Consumed*, though in a slightly different context, ,where he says that "to make tradition the subject of choice (. . .) is to kill it as a tradition, any claim a cultural or religious tradition might make on the individual is threatened by the overriding imperative of choice."[25] The point is a solid one: You do not shop for a theological tradition like you shop for a pair of new shoes. For this would only defeat the very purpose and function of tradition, reducing it to the naked choice of a de-historicized subject. However, neither are we simply stuck with our traditions or loss of traditions. Rather, something else, something more complex, is at work here. MacIntyre is less helpful in this theological context, for we are not now discussing entirely rival traditions as such, where one leaves the one for the other, but traditions nested within each other. The case of Free Church theology must be something like discovering already belonging to

---

24. MacIntyre, *After Virtue*, 221.
25. Cavanaugh, *Being Consumed*, 68.

or being nourished by a tradition that we had previously neglected or even rejected. And this, moreover, in the multidimensional way of discovering both one's theological formation in the Free Church as *tradition*, and discovering the ways in which that very tradition is nested in the wider tradition of the church—or more pointedly still, discovering that the wider tradition is made up precisely of an ongoing conversation wherein the Free Church already participates with its distinct voice.

In this light, and recalling MacIntyre's typology of stages, contemporary Free Church theology could perhaps also be read as being at that crucial fifth stage, where critical reflection upon how tradition operates becomes a pressing concern. Free Church theology, it seems to me, is looking back with fresh eyes over the course of history—its own as well as that of the wider tradition—and asking what it is that has been going on. A kind of meta-reflection on theological tradition from the point of view of the Free Church is emerging.

With this we are already at the second point mentioned above, which consists of finding one's own voice. The question is: What do Free Church theological voices contribute to the wider and deeper tradition of historical Christian faith? To ask such questions became necessary once we began to understand that our theological work is not just constituted *by* tradition, but is also constitutive *of* tradition. Against this background it would be strange indeed for Free Church theologians to begin to see themselves as bearers of the wider Catholic tradition, if their formation within the Free Church did not color the voice with which they come to speak in that wider tradition. The point is a simple but profound one: tradition is the dialectic of receptivity and production, such that for Free Church theologians to fully embrace it would mean to embrace both elements—the depth of roots and the freedom of creativity. Anything less than this, it seems to me, would be to retreat to a comforting conservatism and not accept the responsibility of bearing forward. After all, as Nicholas Adams observes, "tradition is not a thing. It is people giving gifts to their children."[26]

What is, finally, the crisis of Free Church theology, motivating its rapprochement to the wider Catholic tradition? Is the crisis perhaps to be located at the very being of theology itself—the internal recognition that the Free churches need good theology in order to thrive in contemporary society? Could it even be that Free Church theologians are not so much looking for a tradition to adopt, as for a tradition to adopt them? That we

---

26. Adams, "Reasoning in Tradition."

are searching, not so much for a tradition to claim as our own, but for a tradition that would make a claim on us! And might this not be in part because our native Free Church tradition has been so ambivalent in its claim on us as theologians? And so with the self-conscious embrace of the traditioned character of theological reflection comes a much needed and long desired confirmation: You are a theologian and that is quite all right! More than that, there is good work to be done.

If Free Church theology is indeed responding to something like a theological crisis on more than one level by beginning to reflect more seriously on the traditional character of theology, and to theorize tradition more deeply, then some of the themes briefly discussed above could be very helpful if carefully considered. Especially the central point that the dynamics of tradition is what allows us a certain creative space with respect to what has gone before, as described by MacIntyre and exemplified by Cavanaugh. And that this creative space—contrary to what the discourse of modernity would have us believe—is not narrowed down the deeper we are grounded in historical Christian faith. It is rather enlarged. Indeed, I would argue that the depth of one's rootedness within a particular tradition is measured by the creative potential for development one is able to perceive within it. As MacIntyre says, in a precise formulation that well encapsulates the argument I have been trying to make with regard to the need for tradition in Free Church theology: "An adequate sense of tradition manifests itself in a grasp of those future possibilities which the past has made available to the present."[27]

---

27. MacIntyre, *After Virtue*, 223.

Part Three

Lutheran Responses

8

We Are All Moderns

Swedish Free Church and Folk Church Ecclesiologies as Kindred Spirits

Jan Eckerdal

INTRODUCTION

The term *Folk Church* has had a massive impact on the ecclesiological discussion within the Church of Sweden over the last 100 years. It has become one of the most significant concepts in many of the theological self-descriptions in the Church of Sweden. But what this term actually means is disputed. One fairly common way of positioning the Folk Church is to describe it as something that primarily developed in polemic tension with the ecclesiologies expressed by the growing Free churches during the first decades of the twentieth-century. While the Free churches emphasized the community of believers as a basic embodiment of the church, the Folk Church theologians regarded that as a too exclusive and therefore excluding vision. According to the folk church perspective, such a view underplayed the fact that God's grace is offered as a possibility to everybody, regardless of lifestyle or (lack of) piety. Therefore, so the story is often told, the Folk

Part Three—Lutheran Responses

Church and the Free Church ecclesiologies ended up representing fundamentally opposed opinions.

Even though there is some truth in this way of positioning the two in opposite ends of a spectrum, it is also a description that may conceal other important aspects. In the light of a sacramental understanding of the church as a Eucharistic body—in this article articulated with the help of William T. Cavanaugh—a different picture emerges. From this perspective the Swedish Folk Church versus Free Church debate partly seems to be limited by a language which expresses an implicit demand for univocity, for example in its understanding of what it means to embody the church. This univocal understanding meant that such a thing as the qualification of the church as the body of Christ was difficult to handle since it was easily perceived as a univocal identification between the empirical church and Christ, rather than a sacramentally charged analogy.

EINAR BILLING AND THE FREE CHURCHES

The most influential representative of the Swedish folk church ecclesiology is the theologian and bishop Einar Billing (1871–1939).[1] Even though there were a number of other theologians involved in the development of the folk church ecclesiology Billing has gained a special status and his name has become almost synonymous with folk church theology. In the Swedish theological conversation, Billing's book *Den svenska folkkyrkan* (The Swedish Folk Church) is often referred to as the central articulation of the Swedish Folk Church ecclesiology.[2]

Given Billing's central role, it is interesting to note that the opposition between the Free churches and the Folk Church, which is so often assumed, does not fully correspond with Billing's position. In the internal ecclesiological discussions within the Church of Sweden, Einar Billing stressed that the Church of Sweden must acknowledge that many of the accusations from the Free churches contained a justified critique of the State Church. In one important respect Billing's Folk Church ecclesiology actually made common cause with the Free churches: they both wanted to find an alternative to state church ideology. For pragmatic reasons Billing wanted to keep the state church system for the time being. But he stressed that if it would come

---

1. Einar Billing was professor of theology in Uppsala 1909–1920 and bishop of the diocese of Västerås, 1920–1939.

2. Billing, *Den svenska folkkyrkan*.

to a situation where the state church system would jeopardize the Christian integrity of the church, it must not hesitate to sever the bonds with the state. Therefore he wanted the Church of Sweden to have an ecclesiological foundation that was not dependent on being a state church.[3]

The main problem with the state church ideology is, according to Billing, that it is based on a kind of universality that is not theologically accurate.[4] The state church lends its universality from the nation-state, which means that it is a universality that is enforced within its own territory by structural means of power, a structure where the church is one function, among others, of the state. It was important for Billing to point out the specific theological problem with such a universality, since he himself at the same time was eager to emphasize that a faithful Christian church must contain a certain universality. The church must reflect the universality of God's grace. Christ died and was raised for the whole of humankind, and this universality must also make some kind of imprint in the way that the church is organized. But this is a universality that cannot be forced on anybody, since the grace of God is an offer, not a form of coercion. And therefore, in Billing's Folk Church theology, the kind of universality that the Swedish State Church partly represented is considered as ecclesiologically inaccurate.

For these reasons Billing worked hard in the 1920s to convince the governing body of the Church of Sweden to open up an unconditional possibility for Swedish citizens to leave the Church of Sweden (something that would take until 1952 before it was implemented in Swedish law).[5] In Billing's opinion, since a proper Folk Church, is not governed by the universality of the nation-state, but by the universality of the grace of God, there must be a possibility to opt out. Thus, on this point Billing does in some sense resemble the principle that the Mennonite theologian John Howard Yoder later described as "the freedom of unbelief."[6] But in Billing's thinking the principle is motivated by the sort of universality that characterises the Folk Church. (It can however be noted that Billing's theological critique does not touch upon the obvious objection to state church universality;

---

3. Billing, *Kyrka och stat i vårt land*, 36, 52.

4. Ibid., 75.

5. For an analysis of Billing's and others work on this matter within the Church of Sweden, see Thidevall, *Kampen om folkkyrkan*.

6. Yoder, *The Royal Priesthood*, 109.

Part Three—Lutheran Responses

namely that it is strictly limited by the national borders. It is a Swedish "universality!").

To Billing the Folk Church is "the forgiveness of sins to the people of Sweden."[7] The duty of the church is to administer God's offer of forgiveness and reconciliation, by the sacramental means of grace and by the preaching of the Word of God. But how this offer is received is not a question that should be ecclesiologically regulated at all, since such a regulation inevitably will make the loving and universal grace of God conditional. And this is linked to the question of what Billing actually did find problematic with the Free Church ecclesiologies of the time.

From Billing's perspective the problem with the Free Church alternative to state church ideology is that it too often becomes what he, using an expression with implicit negative connotations, calls *föreningskyrklighet* (that is, church as an association of people who confess a personal faith and share some kind of similar spiritual experiences). The theological mistake that *föreningskyrklighet* makes is, according to Billing, that it takes its ecclesiological point of departure from a secondary aspect of the true Christian church, namely the personal faith of those people of whom the "association" consists. The Folk Church on the other hand, Billing says, starts with the first principle, which is the grace of God. The principle of God's grace is primary in the sense that it always exists before and independent of any human response.[8]

Therefore, the personal faith and the spiritual life within the community of believers must be a secondary aspect of the church. Billing agrees that it is a desirable aspect—a spiritually devoted core community can be an important tool in making the Folk Church parish a vital place. But in Billing's vision of the Folk Church this core community must always perceive itself as a secondary and non-essential feature of the Folk Church.[9] Otherwise it will, perhaps unwittingly, sooner or later end up expressing an exclusivistic ecclesiology. The core community is always a community of fellow sinners. But when it claims to be the prime embodiment of the

---

7. Billing, *Vår kallelse*, 7.

8. Billing, *Den svenska folkkyrkan*, 125.

9. This is, for example, a recurring theme in Billing's book *De heligas gemenskap*. When he discusses the value of more closely connected Christian communities, he repeatedly stresses that this is a very difficult topic that needs to be handled with great caution in order not to let the position of the community overshadow other and more important aspects of the church—especially the forgiveness of sins. Billing, *De heligas gemenskap*.

church, the almost unavoidable risk is, according to Billing, that this status will encourage the community of believers to misinterpret their own belonging as something that distances themselves from their fellow sinners in the world. They will become a church, which regards itself as a pure community of believers and therefore wants to live separate from the people of the world, people who for example are to be found in the State Church.

This is not, in Billing's opinion, because people in the Free Church communities have a special predisposition for sectarianism, but rather an aspect of a temptation that all communities of people struggle with. Billing writes: "It is odd how close to us frail humans the temptation is to—as long as we are on the inside—close doors that should be kept open, and to feel a certain pleasure in belonging to an exclusive circle."[10]

In short, Billing's answer to why the Folk Church is preferable to *"föreningskyrkan"* is that the Folk Church offers a more efficient structural antidote to the always present human temptation to exclude others and to put limits on God's love.

FOLK CHURCH AND FREE CHURCH CONFRONTATION

Billing's perception of *föreningskyrklighet* is of course not an unbiased account: it is colored by his theological context. Billing is one of the Swedish theologians associated with the so-called Young Church Movement. The Young Church Movement was a revival movement within the Church of Sweden, which emerged during the first decades of the twentieth-century, not least within the Christian student organization in Uppsala (UKSF). UKSF became, among other things, a context where encounters between different theological traditions took place and Billing's statements on *"föreningskyrklighet"* were partly formed by some of these encounters.

An event that in particular seems to have had a decisive influence on the young church theologians' perception of Free Church ecclesiologies was a debate that UKSF arranged in March 1912. The theme of the discussion was "The Folk Church and the Free Church Concept of the Congregation."[11] P. P. Waldenström, one of the founding figures of the Swedish Covenant Church, participated in this discussion. Waldenström refered to the attempts by him and other "believing students" in Uppsala to

10. Billing, *Kyrka och stat i vårt land*, 26.
11. The contributions to the discussion is published in the book *Folkkyrkan och den frikyrkliga församlingsprincipen*.

form a separate Eucharistic community as a reaction to what they viewed as indiscriminate Eucharistic practices in the state church.[12] Waldenström described how, at the Eucharist, he and his friends would stick together as a group when they approached the altar, in order to fill up the entire altar rail. In that way they received the bread and wine, as Waldenström puts it, "as a communion of the faithful and not together with all sorts of people."[13] Waldenström motivates this separation from other communicants by referring to Luther's catechesis: "The catechesis states, that Holy Communion is instituted for the Disciples of Christ, which means that they ought to separate themselves from the world."[14]

This and other similar statements were interpreted by the Young Church theologians as rather non-ambiguous ecclesiological claims to identify the pure and true Christian church in Sweden with the Free Church communities of believers. Waldenström himself denies that the Free Church communities actually regarded themselves as pure churches in this sense.[15] But he underlines with colorful examples that they are much purer than the State Church and "as far as it is possible we are bound to keep the congregation pure."[16] So, while not wanting to affirm the accusation of creating pure Christian communities, he still claims his is the purer church. And he does so with rhetoric that nevertheless invites the interpretation that the identification with the pure Christian church is univocal (something that probably partly is evoked by the polemic tension of the discussion). When all the failures of the Christian church tend to be expressed as the failures and sins of the other church (in this case the State Church), it allows for an identification of those who are not linked with this fallen church as the true embodiment of the pure Christian church.

DISEMBODIED FOLK CHURCH

Thus, from Billing's Folk Church point of view Waldenström represents a Free Church theology that nurtures an ecclesiological exclusivism. And if such exclusivistic communities also get the theological status of being the embodiment of the true church—the body of Christ—to Billing that is,

12. Ibid., 34.
13. Ibid.
14. Ibid.
15. Ibid., 37.
16. Ibid.

ultimately an ecclesiological misrepresentation of God's pre-existing and universal grace.

However, when Billing addresses this perceived univocal identification with the true Christian church, he does not make any suggestions on what a more accurate embodiment of the church might look like. Instead he simply denies the theological significance of visible social embodiment. Again, to Billing the universality of the true church is based on the universality of the pre-existing grace of God, not in the active reception of God's grace expressed in embodied responses. In other words, Billing criticizes the Free Church communities of believers for expressing a too univocal identification with the true Christian church. But he deals with the problem by an equally univocal denial of the community of believers as an embodiment of the church altogether.[17] Through Billing's strong emphasis on the pre-existing grace of God, his ecclesiology becomes, as it turns out, disembodied. The Folk Church consists of the administration of God's grace, through the preaching of the Word of God and the offering of the sacraments, but not the embodied reception of this grace in a Christian community.

This disembodied tendency of course has consequences when Billing puts his theology into practice. Billing can on the one hand make rather bold claims in favour of the universality of the Folk Church, not least with reference to the parochial system.[18] At the border of one parish another parish starts, which gives the Folk Church a universal reach and not only among the community of believers.[19] But since his universal ecclesiology does not suggest how the church is socially embodied in the world, this is nevertheless a universal ecclesiological vision that hardly becomes a political challenge to any other social embodiments.

This is, for example, evident in Billing's response to the fact that the Swedish Folk Church theology partly integrated nationalistic motives as a central component of its theology.[20] This was a tendency that Billing repeatedly expressed concerns about, especially in his later works, not least with the development in the German Folk Church in the 1930s as a worrying

17. I discuss the disembodied character of Billing's ecclesiology in more length in Jan Eckerdal *Folkkyrkans kropp*.

18. Billing, *Den svenska folkyrkan*, 118–46.

19. Again, it is a universality which only exists within the borders of the Swedish nation.

20. For an analysis of the nationalistic tendency of Swedish folk church theology, see Blückert, *The Church as Nation*.

example.[21] But since Billing's theology in itself does not include an explicit vision of the social embodiment of the church, it does not contain sufficient tools for pointing out the problematic aspects of a church that takes on a nationalistic embodiment. Thus, even though Billing did not fully approve of this tendency, his theology nevertheless turned out to be quite suitable for those who worked for a harmonization between church and nation.[22]

A possible way of understanding the reasons why Billing's ecclesiology ends up with a disembodied tendency could be summarized like this: the historical church is always a mixed body, consisting of sinners and saints, governed by righteous and unrighteous motives and structures. But such a tension is difficult to maintain theologically in a context where there is an implicit demand for univocal identification. Could it be that for Billing there were no available resources for imagining an embodiment of the church that could contain this tension? Therefore Billing, with some fatal consequences, chose to leave embodiment outside his ecclesiology.

MODERN ECCLESIOLOGIES

Seen from this point of view the Swedish Free Church versus Folk Church debate in the beginning of the twentieth-century appears as something very much shaped by its modern context. In all their differences they both appear as modern ecclesiologies. Not least in the sense that they both seem to accept a language that presupposes univocal identification, for example in matters concerning the embodiment of the church. When Waldenström claims that the community of believers embodies the church, this is interpreted as a univocal and absolute identification with the heavenly church, which leads to the discussion whether the Free Church community is as pure as this claim would suggest.

The inclination towards univocity is often described as one of the most typical features of modern thought.[23] Characterized in this way, a significant focus in modernity is to find univocal knowledge and express it in equally univocal language in order to make the world more transparent. In the terminology of theologian William C. Placher this predisposition for univocal language is, when adopted in theological thought, often turned

21. These concerns are most sharply expressed in Billing, *Kyrka och stat i vårt land*.
22. Eckerdal, *Folkkyrkans kropp*, 138–42.
23. Placher, *The Domestication of Transcendence*, 27–36, 71–76; For more on this, see Halldorf in this volume.

into a "domestication of transcendence." According to Placher such domestication has haunted modern conceptualizations of God.[24] When God is univocally defined, God's strangeness, his complete otherness, is erased. When human concepts are used with an inherent claim to be able to speak about God in a univocal way, God is reduced to an idol, an enlarged image of ourselves. The result is a radical deviation from the Christian theology of creation. The biblical creation narrative of course tells the story the other way round; human beings are made in the image of God.

This underlying univocal understanding is, for example, shown in the Folk Church theologians' reactions when the faith communities of the Free churches claimed to be true embodiments of the church. In accordance with a univocal worldview, this was interpreted as a claim for complete identification between the faith community and the true and pure heavenly church, a claim that the folk church theologians found unacceptable. According to them this would diminish the church of Christ, which cannot be exhausted into an empirical community of people. Their interpretation was reinforced by the fact that Free Church representatives, on the other hand, gave little clues as to why an embodiment of the church does not have to come with inherent claims for univocal identification.

However, this did not lead the Folk Church theologians into a discussion on what an alternative and more faithful theology of embodiment would look like. The discussion is locked in a troublesome either-or: Either the church is a complete embodiment of the pure church (the Free Church perspective), or it is not at all an embodiment (folk church perspective). The question is never asked, for example, if it is possible to describe the church as the body of Christ without an inherent absolute identification between Christ and church. Instead, especially in Billing's case, the Folk Church theology in a sense accepted the underlying univocal identification, with the result that it found questions of embodiment unacceptable and left it outside its ecclesiology. The shared univocal pre-understanding of what it means to embody the church seems to have cramped the possibility of imagining embodiment otherwise. This is one of the most bothersome weaknesses of the Swedish Folk Church theology, since the lack of theological reflection on embodiment makes it harder to recognize and theologically evaluate how the concrete church actually is embodied in its day-to-day life.

---

24. Placher, *The Domestic of Transcendence,* See also Long, *Speaking of God,* 15.

Part Three—Lutheran Responses

THE BODY OF CHRIST

The sacramental understanding of the church as a Eucharistic body, the body of Christ, challenges both the univocal identification of the community of believers with the pure church and its univocal rejection. Within a sacramentally loaded framework it is possible to understand the analogy of the church as the body of Christ as precisely an analogy, one with an analogical capacity to contain both similarities and differences in relationship to Christ. That also suggests a theological imaginary that reaches beyond the static polarization that characterizes the options at hand when the Swedish Free Church versus folk church debate emerged.

When, for example, William T. Cavanaugh discusses what he labels as "The Sinfulness and Visibility of the Church," this sacramental ecclesiological imaginary opens up for a more dynamic ecclesiological embodiment. Cavanaugh's accentuation of the church as a Eucharistic body situates the discussion within the liturgical practice of the Eucharist. Cavanaugh:

> The church is not Christ, but the sacramental presence of Christ on earth (. . .). The church is the body of Christ, but not because of its obedience to Christ, which is so often lacking. The claim that holiness is one of the marks of the church is not a moral claim, but a claim that God has elected the church to be both body and bride of Christ. Divine election does not erase the sin of the church, but neither does the sin negate divine election (. . .) What the church makes visible to the world is the whole dynamic drama of sin and salvation, not only the end result of a humanity purified and unified.[25]

According to Cavanaugh, the position of the church as the body of Christ is not something that the church has deserved because of the way the people of God are representing Christ in the world, but because God has elected the church. Of course this does not make the sins of the church less sinful. But through the liturgical practices, these sins are situated within a larger drama, where they are neither denied nor allowed to get the final word, but are instead made visible, judged, and forgiven.

Cavanaugh's Body of Christ ecclesiology is based on a potential that the Eucharistic understanding of the church opens, where the church becomes what it is by taking part of a liturgical drama. In this drama the church as a community can be sacramentally identified with the body of

---

25. Cavanaugh, *Migrations*, 162.

Christ, but without the consequence that Christ thereby becomes univocally identified, and limited by, this embodiment. In the terminology of Einar Billing: within this larger sacramental drama it is possible to recognize the community of believers as a proper embodiment of the received grace of God, without the risk that this will also mean that the grace of God is exhausted within the boundaries of the community and thereby domesticated by it. The eternal grace of God—the pre-existing grace that Billing is so concerned to preserve—is still always greater.

The vision of the church as a Eucharistic body allows for the possibility of an embodiment that is, not a univocal identification with Christ, but is nevertheless a true embodiment. This way of analogically situating the church as an empirical community within Christ also puts the Swedish ecclesiologies discussed in this article in a different light. The sacramentally loaded analogy of the Church as the body of Christ opens up a theological imaginary that seems not to have been an available resource in the Swedish theological conversation in the beginning of the twentieth-century.

This raises a question for both Swedish Free Church and Folk Church traditions: what does it mean that one of the most decisive and formative periods in our ecclesiological heritages, is situated in a time, where such sacramental perspectives were absent from the discussion?

9

What's So Great about Being Different?

A Folk Church Response to Exceptionalism

Jonas Ideström

A MULTICULTURAL EUCHARIST

It's a Sunday. About thirty people are gathered to worship in a church in central Flemingsberg, a suburb of Stockholm. The parish is part of the Evangelical Lutheran Church of Sweden. The neighborhood has several of the characteristics of socially marginalized areas of Swedish cities: a diversity of ethnic and national heritages among the inhabitants and a fairly high level of unemployment.[1]

The congregation gathered in the church consists to a large extent of people who live in the neighborhood. Some were born in Sweden and are members of Church of Sweden, while others have their roots in the Middle East, and still others come from countries in sub-Saharan Africa. Some of them belong to other denominations, such as the Roman Catholic or the Syrian Orthodox Church.

---

1. See Sernhede et al., *Youth, Otherness and the Plural City*.

Jonas Ideström—*What's So Great about Being Different?*

In the Eucharistic prayer the minister, dressed in alb and stole, breaks the bread and reads: "The bread which we break is a sharing in the body of Christ." And the congregation responds: "Though we are many, we are one body, for we all share in one bread."[2]

The congregation forms a half-circle in front of the altar and receives the body and blood of Christ distributed by a minister and a lay person. After prayer and a hymn, about half of the congregation meets for coffee and tea in another room in the church building.

THE RISK OF ECCLESIOLOGICAL EXCEPTIONALISM

In the liturgy of the Eucharist, an expression of the body of Christ becomes visible in a particular room and place and, according to William T. Cavanaugh, a different kind of space is created.[3] This way of interpreting the Eucharist is a cornerstone of much of Cavanaugh's work. It presupposes an understanding that various narratives and social practices form the social and political world in which we live our live.[4] The practices we participate in and the narratives we embrace embody different ends and therefore they are never morally or theologically innocent. By using the Eucharist as a hermeneutical tool, Cavanaugh engages in critical and constructive analysis of issues such as torture, nationalism, and the liberal market economy. As his work shows, this is in many ways a fruitful approach to practical and prophetic ecclesiology.[5]

In this article I focus on the theopolitical implications of the Eucharist as they are embodied in the practical life a local church.[6] For an understanding of the theopolitical implications of the Eucharist I point to the significance of the close ecclesial context in which the liturgy is celebrated. My argument can be read in relation to an ongoing ecclesiological discussion on the future of the Nordic Folk Churches. As the symbolic contract

---

2. This liturgical practice is part of the High Mass liturgy according to Church of Sweden's Service Book.

3. Cavanaugh, *Theopolitical Imagination*, 92.

4. Ibid., 1–7; Ideström, *Lokal kyrklig identitet*, 65–72.

5. For the concept "practical and prophetic ecclesiology" see Healy, *Church, World and the Christian Life*.

6. I find the concept "theopolitical" useful since it indicates that theology (and therefore, of course, ecclesiology as well) is political per se since it has to do with how we live our lives in relation to God, one another, and creation. See Cavanaugh, *Theopolitical Imagination*.

between church and society has been re-written and the role of the old state church has fundamentally changed, the need for reimagining the identity of the church has become inevitable.[7] This need is expressed in various ways in the life of the church and in formal ecclesiological reflections. At different levels in the Church of Sweden there is a clear trend towards what can be described as "brand marketing" of the church. More money and time is spent on information and marketing to make the church "visible" in the public square. One example is the work on a logo for the Church of Sweden. The ambition has been to make the Church of Sweden recognizable as an organization, and today most parishes use this logo. Without neglecting the need for a church to find useful and effective methods of communication, there are strong ends in the marketing paradigms and practices that are ecclesiologically significant and problematic. The endeavor to make the sender distinct and recognizable, thereby gaining market shares in the ongoing struggle for attention, contributes to the formation of an ecclesial self-understanding that highlights differences and demarcations—to find one's "Unique Selling Point." It is often said within the church, "We need to find out who and what we are before we can engage in dialogue with others." This kind of statement has clear connotations of the marketing paradigm in its emphasis on distinction and difference. In the ongoing ecclesiological reflections, the need to articulate difference is expressed in other ways as well. If much of Folk Church ecclesiology more or less presupposes strong links between church and nation or church and state, then more voices are heard which emphasize the need to understand the church as being different from the world. Without a doubt such critical perspectives are needed and, as I see it, Cavanaugh's work has important insights to contribute with regards to this,[8] but there are pitfalls to be aware of when entering this ecclesiological territory.[9] The concern that this article feeds into is that if the church defines and sees itself as being fundamentally different from the context in which it acts and lives—a position I define as ecclesiological exceptionalism—it runs the risk of losing its potential to be truly exceptional.

---

7. Sigurdson, "Return of the body," 125.

8. Swedish theologian Jan Eckerdal gives a constructive and important example of this when using Cavanaugh's work in a study of Einar Billing's—one of the most influential Folk Church theologians—ecclesiology. See Eckerdal, *Folkkyrkans kropp* or Eckerdal in this volume

9. My focus is rather on these pitfalls than on any theologian or work in particular.

JONAS IDESTRÖM—*What's So Great about Being Different?*

It is where bread is broken and the cup is shared that questions concerning difference in relation to the Eucharist eventually need to be reflected upon and evaluated. Therefore the argument here is based on material from extensive fieldwork in the local church in Flemingsberg during 2005-2006.[10] I do not argue for a "Folk Church ecclesiology" in preference to some other kind of ecclesiology. I do not find it particularly fruitful to pitch blueprint ecclesiologies against one another. Ecclesiology becomes interesting, vibrant and necessary when faced with the problems, joys and wounds of our life together and no church tradition is immune to tendencies towards exceptionalism.[11] Yet this article can be read as a Folk Church response to tendencies towards exceptionalism in the sense that the local church that I have observed describes and sees itself as a Folk Church.

My ecclesiological approach is inspired by work developed within the network of Ecclesiology and Ethnography.[12] British theologian Paul Fiddes, one distinct voice within the network, argues that scripture and doctrine are significant expressions of the voice of God in the life of the church, though not in the sense of applied theory in the context of the local church. Fiddes argues for a dialogical understanding of how meaning and truth are revealed in the church.

> God communicates God's own self through actions, relationships, and symbols in daily life, though this self-offering is fully expressed only in the person of Jesus. So we cannot simply impose a set of revealed truths on a situation.[13]

Neither doctrine, nor scripture, nor social theory can be applied as revealed truths in ecclesial practice. It is only through the process of a dialogical and interpretative process that meaning and truth can be revealed.

It is based on such an understanding that I step into the rich and somewhat messy reality of the life of the local church. In the ethnographic material generated there I focus on elements that provide constructive contributions to reflections on the theopolitical aspects of the Eucharist. As my study shows, there are plenty of challenges facing the Church of Sweden

10. The fieldstudy is presented in Ideström, *Lokal kyrklig identitet*.

11. McClintock Fulkerson makes a good argument as to why relevant theology comes out of a wound and how this understanding can be related to empirical ecclesiology. McClintock Fulkerson, "Interpreting a situation," 136-44.

12. See Ward, *Perspectives on Ecclesiology and Ethnography* and Scharen, *Explorations in Ecclesiology and Ethnography*.

13. Fiddes, "Ecclesiology and Ethnography," 19.

in Flemingsberg, but, as Cavanaugh has argued elsewhere, God can draw straight out of crooked lines. The creative Spirit of God has been—and is—at work through the life and history of the Church of Sweden as well, and therefore there is something to be learned from its life and practices. In the life of the local church in Flemingsberg I see patterns in an implicit ecclesiology that I find constructive with regard to issues concerning difference and the theopolitical implications of the Eucharist.

CASE STUDY: THE CELEBRATION OF THE EUCHARIST IN FLEMINGSBERG

Before I return to the celebration of the Eucharist in Flemingsberg, I need to say something about the wider ecclesial context. Since the Reformation the ties between the government and what was eventually given the name "Church of Sweden," have been close. The formal relations between church and state were changed in the year 2000, but seventy percent of the population still remain members of the Church of Sweden, though few participate in the life of the church on a regular basis.[14] In the parish of Flemingsberg forty percent (13,000) of the inhabitants were members of the Church of Sweden in 2005 and on an average Sunday thirty to fifty people celebrated the liturgy. The parish of Flemingsberg has a rather large number of employees,[15] and in the local parish council there are representatives from political parties who also participate in the decision-making bodies of the civil local government. Ministers, deacons, and musicians from the parish work at the University hospital and at the remand prison within the geographical borders of the parish and in my study it became clear that the employees and the members of the parish council shaped the practical identity of the local church to a large extent.[16]

Church as in and for the Place

Let us now return to Flemingsberg and the local church. The church building, where the Eucharist is celebrated, is clearly visible in the centre of the

---

14. For an introduction to the history and contemporary situation of the Nordic Folk Churches see Ryman, *Nordic Folk Churches*.

15. There were fourteen employees in 2005.

16. In my study I point to some of the challenges that this raises in relation to interpretations of the mission and vocation of the church.

neighbourhood surrounded on three sides by tall blocks of flats. The architecture resembles the shopping centre and public library next to it. This material participation in the neighbourhood clearly mirrors how firmly rooted the local church is in the life of the geographical parish.[17] Representatives of the parish often emphasize that they are a church *in* and *for* Flemingsberg. There is a strong sense of solidarity with the place, its history and people.

One reason for this is the long history of geographically determined parishes in the Church of Sweden. Most of its parishes can be described as "churches of place with strong local connections," to borrow a description from a report from the Church of England.[18] In the report this local "rootedness" is described in a way that is, also applicable to the church in Flemingsberg.

> This local rootedness is often very longstanding, encouraging a commitment to people that is, tolerant of slow progress and assigns importance to particular relationships and the needs of specific people and groups.[19]

This commitment to a particular place and its people is also expressed in the Church Order for the Church of Sweden, where it is made clear that the parish has a responsibility with regards to everyone living in, working in or visiting the parish.[20] I observed how the sense of solidarity with Flemingsberg has shaped relations between the local communities and the church. Ministers in the local church could describe themselves as ambassadors for Flemingsberg, trying to fight a widespread stigmatised view of Flemingsberg as an area full of problems.[21] As one of the ministers described how she talks about the parish when meeting people from other parts of the country:

> They often have questions, based on their preconceptions, as to whether it's dangerous here, and then it's up to me to describe

---

17. For an extended discussion on the theopolitical implications of buildings and ecclesial practices in a suburban context see Widmark, "Space, Materiality and the Politics of Leaving."
18. *Faithful Cities*, 3.
19. Ibid.
20. *Kyrkoordning för Svenska kyrkan*, chapter 2 § 1. http://www.svenskakyrkan.se/default.aspx?id=637938, August 26, 2013.
21. Idestrõm, *Lokal kyrklig identitet*, 225–27.

Part Three—Lutheran Responses

positive things in the parish, the potential, and that we do a lot of work on reaching out in our parish.[22]

Representatives of the local church also saw it as part of their mission to try to "build bridges" between "congregations within the parish."[23] This vocation was based on a view of Flemingsberg as being clearly segregated. In a formal document, where the local church describes the social life of the geographical parish, they take the reader on a walk through these different areas. The imagined walk makes it clear that material borders such as roads and train tracks manifest strong social demarcations between different areas. A residential area described as mainly "Swedish" is separated by the train tracks from the area where the church building is situated, which is described as "international." And this "international" residential area is also clearly separated from an area with institutions, such as a hospital and a college. Or as one of the employees described it: "It is multicultural (. . .) and there are two parts, as it were: a nice side with the hospital and the students and a side where people live."[24] This understanding of the geographical parish as being segregated and separated into different social areas, with little or no interaction between them, was deeply rooted among representatives of the parish.

I found it interesting to see that even though the local church was not an obvious object of identification for most inhabitants, which is the case in many rural parishes in Sweden, it still had a well-developed network of relationships with other institutions and organizations in Flemingsberg: schools, day-care homes, hospitals, service homes, and social authorities. These networks were maintained by ongoing encounters between people and were to a large extent shaped by trust and solidarity. One example was a social worker who, in cooperation with the deacons, used the facilities in the church building for an activity with a group of men in the neighborhood. But this solidarity with the place and its inhabitants also implied holding people and authorities up to criticism. For example, the deacons, who had good relationships with social workers in the area, also assisted

22. Ibid., 221.

23. In Swedish *"församling"* is used both for parish and congregation. An interesting observation in the field study was that the term was used in a way that made it difficult to know whether people were referring to the congregation or the geographical territory of the parish. Ibid., 118–21. In this article I use *the local church* and *the parish* interchangeably. I will make it clear when I refer to "parish" as a geographical territory.

24. Ibid., 228.

individuals in getting help from the local authorities. In that work they were sometimes sharply critical of the way people were treated by the local authorities. As one of the deacons said:

> When it comes to the crunch for the individual then you have (...) prophetic diaconal work and to stand on the side of the weak (...) and we don't have the same system of norms as the local authorities' social services need to follow. Then you can raise hell because you don't have the same norms.[25]

The norms to which the deacon refers relate to liturgical life in the parish:

> Sundays and Wednesdays [the days when they celebrate the service and Eucharist] are somehow the cornerstones of our day-to-day work. I feel that it is in the service that I fulfill my mission, somehow, and then to go out and do something and reconnect that to the service. And then we often have activities in relation to a service it becomes less divided, somehow, and it's also an example of how we work. It's our way of thinking.[26]

Another example is the regular ecumenical prayer sessions at the remand prison in Flemingsberg. I participated in a prayer session led by a pastor from a Baptist church and a musician from the Church of Sweden in a room kept for prayer and meditation (the only room without bars in the windows). In the prayer session the six men who participated were invited to light candles during the intercession. All of them did. After the prayer the candles had to be put out, but instead of leaving them there the musician brought them to the church building in Flemingsberg where they were lit in the Eucharistic liturgy. This was a way for the local church to demonstrate that the men at the remand prison also shared in the communion of the local church.[27]

In my analysis I could conclude that the work of the local church embodied values that involved standing up for individuals and taking responsibility for the local neighbourhood. These values resulted in, and were shaped by, well-developed relationships with individuals, institutions, and organizations, and yet they left room for a critical and prophetic vocation. Together with social practices, these values were clearly related to and

25. Ibid., 217.
26. Ibid., 179. From focus group interview with the deacons.
27. Ibid., 181–82.

intertwined with liturgical life, including the Eucharist, in the parish. My overall analysis of the practical identity of the local church showed that a significant identity structure was thus formed in relation to the liturgical life of the parish.[28]

A Eucharistic Politics

A second significant element that shaped the ecclesial context in which the Eucharist was celebrated is the role of narratives in the Gospels as moral and ethical guidelines. As with the example of the deacons just mentioned, I saw examples of how work in the local church was understood and interpreted in relation to the work of Jesus.

I experienced a sense of walking in the landscape of the Gospels when walking the streets of Flemingsberg. Several times, references to what Jesus did were used to call into question tendencies to segregation or exclusion of people. The critical edge was turned both against politics in society and against the life and practices of the church.

An interesting example of this is a piece written by the vicar printed in an information leaflet distributed within the geographical parish. In a short text she argues against the politics of a nationalistic political party, the Sweden Democrats (SD), who were running for seats in the upcoming elections in the Church of Sweden.[29] She starts by stating that the Church of Sweden has a long tradition of being a democratic Folk Church and then continues:

> As Christians we have an even longer tradition of defending a view of human beings as having equal value regardless of heritage, sex, sexual orientation or religious affiliation. That view, which is based on what Jesus said and did, is something we defend even more. We practise it in every service we celebrate.

She argues that all groups involved in the decision-making bodies of the Church of Sweden, except the SD, "want to follow Jesus in this."

---

28. Ibid., 175–204.

29. This was a burning issue in the elections in September 2013 as well. A summer speech given by Jimmie Åkesson, the SD leader, is posted on the party's national website. In the speech he focuses heavily on the upcoming elections in Church of Sweden. He is concerned about tendencies that he sees, which suggest that Church of Sweden is becoming "less Swedish." Åkesson, "Jimmie Åkessons talmanus sommartal 2013-08-24 Sölvesborg," https://sverigedemokraterna.se/?p=12749, August 27, 2013.

According to the SD it is by cutting off contact with Muslims, not supporting immigrants and people seeking asylum, and denying homosexuals the right to live in secure relationships, that security is preserved and traditions are defended. What the SD says no to is to a large extent what we are proud of in the parish of Flemingsberg.

What this shows is that Jesus is often seen as a role model and what he did provides a foundation for the values and norms guiding the work of the parish. The interpretation of Jesus as role model in this line of reasoning also reflects a clear pattern in the ongoing reflections among representatives of the local church. There is an emphasis on seeing human beings as having equal value and thereby it is a goal to articulate what is common rather than what is different. This quest was also supported with reference to the creation story and the conviction that all human beings are created in the image of God.

There was an ongoing dialogue in the local church about the narratives of the Gospels in relation to theopolitical issues. Even though texts from the Old Testament and the Epistles were read in the liturgy, the focus in sermons and pastoral reflections was clearly on Gospel narratives. Next to this emphasis on human beings as having equal value regardless of heritage and identity, an understanding of the identity of the church in relation to the cross was fundamental. The cross was not only primarily seen as a sign of victory but of an ongoing struggle for humanity and the church. This focus on the cross clearly reflects a tradition where the Passion narrative and the agony of Good Friday have influenced spirituality to a great extent. Living in dialogue with the Gospel narratives means both walking towards the cross and away from the empty tomb and the witnesses to the risen Lord.

When I interpret the thick and complex picture of the practical identity of the local church I see an implicit ecclesiology, an understanding of what it is to be a church in relation to the divine economy, which is dynamic. On the one hand the church can be perceived as a social body that makes Christ, who is already present, visible in the local community. On the other hand there are things that point to an understanding of Christ being present through the church. Christ is understood to be "present in the world where a fundamental relational pattern of the incarnation liberates people to commune with one another and with God," and this is understood to be embodied in a special way in the liturgy.[30]

30. Ibid., 280–81.

Part Three—Lutheran Responses

Rowan Williams describes this well when he reflects on the identity of the church in relation to the resurrection narratives in the Gospels. He points to the theme of otherness in those narratives, "the unrecognisability of the risen Jesus."[31] "[H]e is not what they have thought Him to be, and thus they must 'learn to know' Him afresh, from the beginning."[32] Williams argues that this says something fundamental about the identity of the church.

> The Church may be Christ's "Body," the place of His presence; but it is entered precisely by the ritual encounter with His death and resurrection, by the "turning around" which stops us struggling to interpret His story in light of ours and presses us to interpret ourselves in the light of the Easter event.[33]

So celebrating the Eucharist gives the church a solid identity yet refuses the church to finalize it and constantly reminds the church that "this identity only exists in an endless responsiveness to new encounters with Him."[34] Christ is both friend and stranger and the path to resurrection runs through Gethsemane, the cross and the grave. On this path any ambitions to control the body of Christ are also crucified. Walking towards the cross means walking towards the politics of God, forcing the church to see the whole world as God's world and all human beings as one body in God.

As Cavanaugh argues, the Christian aspiration to wholeness and unity is central to any reflections on the identity of the church.[35] It is firmly based in the biblical stories of creation and fall that make clear "that human sin is not the way it is meant to be, nor indeed the way that it really is."[36] Cavanaugh reminds us of Augustine's argument that the earth is not divided by nature "into different earthly cities or nations" but only as a result of sin, and in contrast the city of God is the universal reality. "Christ (. . .) is the one who gathers the many into himself."[37] Therefore, Cavanaugh concludes, "the task of the church is to interrupt the violent tragedy of the earthly city

---

31. Williams, *Resurrection*, 75.
32. Ibid.
33. Ibid., 76.
34. Ibid.
35. Cavanaugh, "Separation and Wholeness," 8.
36. Cavanaugh, *Migrations*, 61.
37. Ibid.

with the comedy of redemption, to build the city of God, beside which the earthly city appears to be not a city at all."[38]

Church as a Space of Hope

It is in relation to this task that I interpret what I observed in Flemingsberg and the theopolitical aspects of the Eucharist. In the detailed descriptions of the local church that were generated from what I observed, I sense how solidarity with the place, the ongoing sharing of a common life in the neighbourhood, and the cross-centred dialogue with the Gospel and the Eucharist made it possible for the local church to engage in a prophetic dialogue with people and organizations in the area.[39] Such a dialogue is always conducted at a place and in a space among people. In Flemingsberg I saw how the local church, through its social practices, participated in the production of what I define as spaces of hope: both social spaces, in and through which the prophetic dialogue can be conducted, and ecclesial spaces, in which the church can be true to its vocation to work for wholeness and unity of creation and humanity.

Of course there are elements in the local church that stand in the way of producing such spaces. Spaces of hope are not strong and powerful ecclesial centres that the church can control, but rather fragile spaces filled with a hope that points to God, the foundation of true hope.

In the material from Flemingsberg I see how these fragile spaces are related to the creation of space in the celebration of the Eucharist. Together they are weaved into a thick and complex fabric through which the theopolitical significance of the Eucharist has to be understood and interpreted. Against ethnographic ecclesiological accounts of the breaking and sharing of bread and wine, like the one I have referred to here, one can conclude that the sacramental reality of the Eucharist is never embodied in a social and ecclesial vacuum. Its potential for producing spaces that "interrupt the violent tragedy of the earthly city" is therefore always dependent on a wider ecclesial context than the actual liturgy while at the same time, in the language of Gordon Lathrop, the actual liturgy can work as a necessary venue for a holy dialogue.[40]

---

38. Ibid., 63.
39. The concept is used in Bevans and Schroeder, *Constants in Context*.
40. Lathrop, *Holy People*.

Part Three—Lutheran Responses

CONCLUSION: NOT DIFFERENCE BUT WITNESS

Based on this interpretation of what I observed in Flemingsberg, and in dialogue with Cavanaugh and Williams, I find it necessary to argue that the church is not primarily called to be different, but to witness to the One who is wholly different. This might seem to be splitting hairs, and in a way it is, but in the end it might make a big difference. The potential to interrupt the violent tragedy of the earthly city is achieved by participating in the delicate art of weaving the fabrics of trust, solidarity, and fellowship. We all know how easily these fabrics can be torn apart and how costly it is to repair them. It is in relation to this art and vocation that the theological self-understanding operating in those responsible for ecclesial practices and witnessing is of such great importance. In the descriptions of the local church in Flemingsberg I see patterns in an approach that I find constructive and relevant. It is an approach that on the one hand is based on a desire to articulate what is common and shared with everyone within the geographical territory—an ecclesial self-understanding that does not articulate difference. On the other hand, it is an approach that is, firmly anchored in the Eucharist and the Gospel narratives. As long as the bread is shared, as long as Christ is proclaimed, and as long as people pray together and for one another, the emphasis on common human values and the quest for a church that is, for everyone within the geographical territory does not lead to a hollow or arrogant universalism. It is rather in this dialogue that the potential for contributing to spaces of hope in an environment of segregation and separation has its roots.

It is by being such a witness that the church can challenge politics that are based on articulating differences. In other words, the real challenge for the church in tribal times is to participate in God's calling to all of humanity to become one body. The church is called to be a witness of what is truly common and in doing that it might also be truly exceptional.

Part Four

"Love Your Neighbor"

10

Eucharistic Identity in Modernity

William T. Cavanaugh

The chairman of the Danish parliament Erling Olsen once said that "the very idea of the social welfare state is the secularized idea of 'love your neighbor' in Christianity."[1] In this essay, I want to take this idea seriously. I have been a critic of the state as such, and I have often contrasted the modern state with the church and with the generation of Christian forms of social life. It would be a mistake, however, to regard the state as something wholly alien to Christianity, to regard some of the more unhealthy pathologies of the modern state as something "they" did to "us."[2] The fact is that the modern state as it arose in Europe and North America from the late medieval period onward was constructed by Christians in a Christian context, often using Christian tools. The rise of the state represents the final victory of civil over ecclesiastical power in a long struggle dating back to Constantine's conversion, but this victory is inadequately described as a simple grab for power. It is also understandable in part as an attempt to institutionalize the Gospel and extend it more completely into all aspects of European life. This recognition helps us better to understand the history

---

1. Erling Olsen, quoted in Peter Lodberg and Björn Ryman, "Church and Society," 101.

2. I have been taken to task by Brad Anderson for underplaying the extent to which American nationalism is a construction of American Christians and Christianity, drawing on biblical themes. See Anderson, *Chosen Nation*, 1–35.

Part Four—"Love Your Neighbor"

and dynamics of the modern state, and it also helps us to appreciate what is good about the state, from a Christian point of view. I will nevertheless argue that the modern state is not the fulfillment of the Gospel, but a falling short—and sometimes a distortion—of a truer Christian sociality that can be located in the Eucharist as the Christian social practice *par excellence*.

I will begin by describing the rise of modernity and the modern state as a series of effects of well-intentioned attempts to clarify and defend authentic Christian doctrine and practice, especially with regard to the Eucharist. I will then comment on the modern welfare and warfare states and suggest ways that Eucharistic theology and practice can inform a more faithful Christian social witness.

TRUE BODIES

In my work I have argued that Christians need to take a fresh look at the Eucharist as an important source of social and political engagement, and not assume that our participation in the modern state is simply natural, inevitable, and the only way for Christians to act for the common good. This message strikes many Christians as strange, for we have learned to make a sharp division between the religious realm—to which the Eucharist clearly seems to belong—and the social and political realms, over which the state presides. The idea that the Eucharist is inherently social and therefore foundational for Christian social life does not abide by the separation of sacred and secular to which we have become accustomed in modernity. But the roots of the separation of the Eucharist from its connection to Christian social life do not lie in modernity. The tale begins much earlier, in the eleventh century.

The Eucharist, of course, takes the form of a meal, a communal gathering into what Paul referred to as the Body of Christ; we eat the Body of Christ and are thereby incorporated into this Body along with other people. The act of individual consumption is turned inside out, for the individual person does not simply take Christ into herself but is taken up into Christ's larger, communal body, of which persons are not individual parts but interdependent appendages and organs, in Paul's famous vision in 1 Corinthians 12. The early church understood the Eucharist this way, and so referred to the church gathered as the *corpus verum*, the true body of Christ, and the Eucharistic elements on the altar as the *corpus mysticum*, the mystical body. Here "mystical" did not denote "less than real" but, as Henri de Lubac puts it, "more of an action than a thing."[3] For both the patristic era and the early medieval church, the Eucharist was "communion," the "sacrament of conjunction, alliance, unification."[4] The Eucharist was what restored penitents to full communion with their fellows.[5]

The story of how this began to change, as de Lubac uncovered it, is now well known. Beginning in the eleventh century, the terms *verum* and *mysticum* became inverted, so that the focus shifted from the communal gathering of people to the elements on the altar as the "true" body of Christ. Eucharistic piety in the later Middle Ages would be increasingly focused on veneration of the host, as in the Corpus Christi feasts inaugurated in the thirteenth century, and the encounter of the individual with Christ in the elements. The story as told this way is, of course, oversimplified. Late medieval Eucharistic piety on the eve of the Reformation was still the glue of the social order in many places, as Eamon Duffy's work makes plain.[6] As Laurence Hemming and Susan Parsons point out, the true fetishization of either the elements or the community would have to await modernity and the invention of a subject-object dualism.[7] We should add that Eucharistic sociality in the medieval period was never idyllic; the medieval social body was constructed of rigid hierarchies that were far from Paul's ideal, and those excluded from full participation in the social body, especially Jews, were oppressed. Nevertheless, the shift that de Lubac describes is consonant with a relative deemphasis on the Eucharist as social action and the church as the communal body that resulted from this action. It is consonant as well with an interiorization of piety in the late medieval period in which Charles Taylor locates the seeds of secularization. It is important to note, however, that the shift de Lubac describes is the result of the eleventh century controversy sparked by Berengar of Tours. In response to Berengar's apparent spiritualization of the Eucharist and denial of material change in the elements, emphasis on the action of the Eucharist was replaced by language of substance, and the distinction between the sacramental and

3. de Lubac, *Corpus Mysticum*, 49.

4. Ibid., 17.

5. Ibid., 19.

6. Duffy describes the situation in late medieval England in these terms: "The Host, then, was far more than the object of individual devotion, a means of forgiveness and sanctification: it was the source of human community." Duffy, *The Stripping of the Altars*, 93.

7. Hemming and Frank Parsons, "Editors' Preface" in de Lubac, *Corpus Mysticum*, xiv.

ecclesial bodies of Christ was emphasized.[8] The shift, in other words, was an effect of the attempt to protect the doctrine of the Eucharist from diminishment—specifically, the threat of reduction of the Eucharist to something merely immanent.

Almost simultaneous with the Berengar controversy in the eleventh century was the controversy over lay investiture that, by severing links between the civil and ecclesiastical authorities, would have an enormous long-term influence on the development of the modern state. Again, the church under Pope Gregory VII had to react to the takeover of ecclesiastical appointments by civil authorities; the church could not allow appointments of bishops and abbots to be controlled by lay rulers. In reacting, however, the delicate balance between civil and ecclesiastical authorities which had seesawed throughout the early Middle Ages was ruptured, with serious consequences. Before the investiture controversy, priests and kings were understood as corresponding to the dual natures of Christ, divine and human. Kings no less than popes were called vicars of Christ, and kings exercised a liturgical function within the church. After the investiture controversy, however, kings began to claim their authority directly from God without the mediation of the church. They were said to be vicar or image of God. As Ernst Kantorowicz writes, "as opposed to the earlier 'liturgical' kingship, the late-mediaeval kingship by 'divine right' was modeled after the Father in Heaven rather than after the Son on the Altar."[9] While the *corpus verum* of Christ was increasingly confined to the altar, kings appropriated Christian symbolism, including the concept of the *corpus mysticum* which was used to describe the way that the people belonged to the king's body.[10] At the same time, the Popes tried to strip kings of church-conferred dignities, as in the decree of Pope Innocent III declaring that royal anointments did not confer the Holy Spirit. As Kantorowicz comments, "As so often, the Roman Pontiff appears here as the chief promoter of precisely that 'secularism' which in other respects the Holy See tended to fight."[11] What Kantorowicz means by "secularism" here needs to be understood precisely as the distancing of the church from the sphere of civil governance, not yet the marginalization of God from the public realm. The lay investiture controversy and the controversy over Berengar are not usually seen as related,

---

8. de Lubac, *Corpus Mysticum*, 154, 162, 213.
9. Kantorowicz, *The King's Two Bodies*, 93.
10. Ibid., 197.
11. Ibid., 320–21.

but they are: both illustrate the possibility that the defense of Christ's body will come at the expense of the confinement of Christ's body.

The Eucharistic controversies of the Reformation also played a role in the rise of the modern state and modernity more generally. Ulrich Zwingli's attacks on both the mass and the doctrine of transubstantiation were intended to eliminate the notion that the Eucharist had magical powers that could be used to benefit individuals and their dead relatives. In late medieval Catholic practice (if not official teaching) attending mass was thought to ward off premature death, and those who died could be liberated from purgatory by a certain number of masses said on their behalf.[12] The social dynamism of the Eucharist had been reduced in practice in many places to a trafficking in divine favors. Zwingli's idea that the "is" in "This is my body" really means "signifies"—and his corresponding distinction between spirit and flesh—was meant to require personal, interior commitment on the part of the Christian believer instead of reliance on external rituals to effect change. The denial of Christ's bodily presence in the Eucharist, however, had the effect of reinforcing the modern spatial dichotomy between God and the natural world, and between the spiritual and the material. As historian Brad Gregory has recently argued in his provocative book *The Unintended Reformation: How a Religious Revolution Secularized Society*, "A 'spiritual' presence that is, *contrasted* with a real presence presupposes an either-or dichotomy between a crypto-spatial God and the natural world that precludes divine immanence in its desire to preserve divine transcendence."[13] The Zwinglian view of the Eucharist is the corollary of proto-modern metaphysical univocity, in which God is seen as sharing being with creatures, and therefore competing for "space" with creatures. The older view saw God as totally other, as not a being in the universe, and therefore able to be omnipresent in creation because not competing on the same level for space. As Gregory says, "The denial of the possibility of Christ's real presence in the Eucharist, by contrast, ironically implies that the 'spiritual' presence of God is *itself* being conceived in spatial or quasi-spatial terms—which is why, in order to be kept pure, it must be kept separate from and uncontaminated by the materiality of the 'mere bread.'"[14]

---

12. See Clark, *Eucharistic Sacrifice*.

13. Gregory, *The Unintended Reformation*, 42–43.

14. Ibid., 43. For more on Gregory and the significance of metaphysical univocity, see Halldorf in this volume.

Part Four—"Love Your Neighbor"

Although Martin Luther preserved the idea of the real presence of Christ in the Eucharistic elements in his arguments against Zwingli, his theology of the Eucharist also tended toward individualism and the subject-object dualism that marks the modern era. In his efforts to reform the practice of the mass as a work, Luther rejected the notion that the Eucharist is something in which the Christian actively participates; it is rather something that we can only receive. In his *Treatise on the New Testament*, Luther writes "[I]n the mass we give nothing to Christ, but only receive from him; unless they are willing to call this a good work, that a person sits still and permits himself to be benefited, given food and drink, clothed and healed, helped and redeemed."[15] The individual is then meant to go out and give to others, but to eliminate the circulation of merits amongst Christians living and dead, Luther says that the Eucharist, because it depends on interior faith, directly benefits only the individual with faith: "every one takes and receives of it for himself only, in proportion as he believes and trusts (. . .) no one can observe or hear mass for another, but each one for himself alone. For there is nothing there but a taking and receiving."[16] As John Bossy notes, individualism was not the reformers' intention. Nevertheless,

> [A] sense of fatality, of results achieved which were the opposite of those intended, hangs over their efforts: as if the current of social and cultural evolution which was carrying them forward was at the same time pushing them aside into shallow waters. In the Lutheran case the ambition to restore a communal eucharist resulted in a practice of communion as individualist and asocial as that of the Counter-Reformation.[17]

As the mention of the Counter-Reformation indicates, the problem was a Catholic one as well as a Protestant one. In Bossy's words, "The history of the Eucharist after the Reformation is more than a history of the misfortune of reformers. More or less everybody was affected by the heresy which loomed at the further end of the Christianity of the spirit: that the union to be sought was with that other spirit, God, not with that tiresome incarnation your neighbour."[18]

---

15. Luther, *Luther's Works, vol. 35*, 93.

16. Ibid., 94. I treat this question at much greater length in my article "Eucharistic Sacrifice and the Social Imagination," 585–605.

17. Bossy, "The Mass as a Social Institution," 60.

18. Bossy, *Christianity in the West*, 141.

THE CORRUPTION OF THE BEST IS THE WORST

The story I have been telling so far is a drastically abbreviated history of how Christian communal life, as crystallized in the Eucharist, changed through a series of moves intended to defend its centrality to Christian life, and changed in such a way as to make modernity possible. The story cannot be told fully without telling the story of the rise of capitalism and the gradual accruing of power to civil authorities in the late Middle Ages that became the sovereign territorial state. I do not wish to give the impression that changes in Eucharistic theology and practice were all cause and no effect. But I want to take seriously the reality that modernity arose out of Christendom, for better and for worse, and not simply over against Christendom or Christianity. I want to take seriously the insights of Charles Taylor and others that in some crucial respects modernity is not simply the overthrowing of the Christian yoke, but an attempt to extend and universalize the Gospel.

Charles Taylor's widely-acclaimed book *A Secular Age* makes the case in rich detail that the secularization of the modern West cannot be understood as the "subtraction" of God from a previously existing God/nature dualism, but rather as the unintended result of a series of mutations within Christian belief and practice that created such dualisms to begin with.[19] Taylor traces this process to late medieval attempts to overcome the two-tiered medieval system whereby a higher level of righteousness and conformity to the counsels of perfection was expected of monks and the clergy—especially the "religious" as opposed to "secular" clergy –than of the laity. The laity, according to Taylor's account, inhabited an enchanted social world permeated by communal ritual that later reformers would denigrate as superstitious and magical. Well before the Reformation, Taylor sees what he calls, generically, "reform," the attempt to bring ordinary Christians to a more interiorized and personally committed faith. The popularity of the *devotio moderna* and Thomas à Kempis's *Imitation of Christ* in the fourteenth century illustrates this movement toward interior dialogue and a more intensely personal prayer life.[20] The movement toward a more individualized practice of Eucharistic devotion fits well into Taylor's narrative. The focus on interiority played a role in the rise of the modern subject/object dualism, as well as the new spatial distinction between God and world that would

---

19. Taylor, *A Secular Age*, 22.
20. Ibid., 70.

influence the rise of science. The attack on "dead ritual" and merely exterior forms of Christian practice, when coupled with an emphasis on the interior spiritual life, would in time lead to the disenchantment of the world. According to Taylor, the Reformation unleashed a sustained theological attack on the "white magic" of the church, that is, sacramentality, treating any object in the world as charged with God's presence, because God cannot be confined in things, and God's power cannot be manipulated by priests and other mere human beings. It is not that the magisterial reformers denied the power of the sacraments altogether. Calvin, for example, thought that we are really fed by Christ's grace in the Eucharist. "But what he can't admit," writes Taylor, "is that God could have released something of his saving efficacy out there into the world, at the mercy of human action, because that is the cost of really sanctifying creatures like us which are bodily, social, historical (. . .). So we disenchant the world; we reject the sacramentals; all the elements of 'magic' in the old religion."[21] This type of disenchantment, meant to protect God from the world, would eventually lead to a world in which God was unnecessary.

The rise of the state plays an important role in this narrative, because Taylor sees the rise of a disciplinary society as one of the key building blocks of secularity. In the earlier Augustinian view, government was seen as necessary to restrain vice, not inculcate virtue. But accompanying the new emphasis on personally committed faith was a movement by early modern elites to use government to make virtuous, well-behaved, civilized subjects. Princes saw the advantages of the creation of docile subjects for extending their own control, but Taylor argues that many were sincerely motivated by an impulse to extend the reach of the Gospel to every corner of everyday life by extending it to every corner of the individual's conscience. This happens in both Protestant and Catholic kingdoms; Calvin's Geneva would have its analogues in Jesuit activity in Bohemia, Bavaria, and wherever the new confessional boxes were vigorously promoted and employed. What appears to be the very opposite of secularization, Taylor shows, is in fact a deep precursor to modern secular culture, in both its absorption of ecclesiastical powers by the state, and the corollary aspiration of a direct relationship between a centralized state power and the rights- and duties-bearing individual.[22] The individual would become increasingly disembedded both from an enchanted cosmos and from local forms of belonging outside of

---

21. Ibid., 79.
22. See Taylor's chapter "The Rise of the Disciplinary Society" in ibid., 90–145.

which the self was formerly unable to conceive of itself. Free subjects whose interiority was open only to God would become the abstract individuals who are conceived (fictionally) as creating a state by freely contracting to protect each other's rights.[23]

Taylor is right to trace the roots of the fading of the Eucharist and the sacraments more generally from the public, communal life of European Christians to the Protestant and Catholic Reformations and the rise of the modern state. Taylor describes this process as part of the disenchantment of the modern world, which in early modernity is not yet the fading of Christianity from public life, but rather *Entzauberung*, in Max Weber's term, usually translated "disenchantment," the diminishment of *Zauber*, or magic, which would prepare the way for the exit of Christianity from public relevance. According to Taylor, the modern self differs from its precursors by being "buffered" from material reality and social life. A premodern, "porous" self who suffered from melancholy was firmly in its grip; "black bile" was not the cause of melancholy, but simply *was* melancholy. Buffered selves, by contrast, adopt a mind/body dualism, such that learning that certain chemicals in the brain cause depression allows the modern self to take some distance from the malady.[24] The buffered self is no longer in the grip of ghosts and spirits and demons that were simply part of the world for the medieval Christian. The buffered self is further distanced from the social context she finds herself in. Whereas the premodern self was embedded in social ritual and could not conceive of the self outside that context, the buffered self as a sovereign individual is generally required to actively choose an identity.[25] One is not simply a Christian by birth into a Christian order, but must actively choose whether to be a Christian, Buddhist, agnostic, etc. This "optionality," Taylor thinks, is what distinguishes the modern age from all previous ages.

Taylor's overall account, I think, is convincing, but I depart from him on one crucial point: I do not think that the changes he describes are adequately conveyed by the term "disenchantment." There is no question that people describe their experiences in this way; demons and fairies belong to the past. But the way that people actually behave, it seems to me, indicates that people continue to relate both to the material world and to the social

---

23. This is a rather drastically abbreviated summary of Taylor's argument in ibid., 146–211.

24. Ibid., 37–38, 131.

25. Ibid., 148–50.

Part Four—"Love Your Neighbor"

world in ways that are deeply enchanted, that is, given over to powers beyond the control of the self. With regard to the material world, it is true that Westerners tend to reduce causation to the brute machinations of the inert physical world. Among Christians, even Catholics these days tend to see the sacraments as symbolic, such that what is altered in the Eucharistic celebration is not the elements on the altar but the inner disposition of the worshiper. If one observes the same Catholics shopping at IKEA, on the other hand, I think it is inadequate to describe their relationship to the material world as buffered in Taylor's sense. Karl Marx was right; in a capitalist society, commodities are fetishized. The further we travel into a consumerist society, the more that marketing saturates the image systems of our culture, the harder it is to argue that we live in a disenchanted world. In a society in which information and behavior is organized around the central goal of the acquisition of consumer items, commodities are deeply imbued with magic. Eugene McCarraher's work on the enchantments of Mammon demonstrates persuasively, I think, that sacramentality did not die in the West, but was rather largely displaced into consumer capitalism.[26] We still behave as though the material world were deeply penetrated by the sacred, but now that reality is no longer mediated by the sacraments of the church but by our pursuit of what Brad Gregory calls "the goods life," that is, the search for meaning in material things.

Taylor's account of disenchantment and disembedding in social life is also questionable. It is true that the acids of modernity have produced a distance between the individual and the organic social groups that stand between the individual and the state. But the rise of nationalism in the nineteenth and twentieth centuries is hard to square with the narrative of disenchantment and buffering that Taylor tells. Once the modern state had been constructed, it became necessary to promote nationalism as a kind of glue that would bind the individual to the collective. Taylor recognizes the role of patriotic ritual in the modern state, but thinks it is of a fundamentally different character from social rituals like the Eucharist in the medieval period:

> Of course, we go on having rituals—we salute the flag, we sing the national anthem, we solemnly rededicate ourselves to the

---

26. "Far from being an unambiguous agent of disenchanted secularity, capitalism might be best understood as a perverse regime of the sacred, an order of things bearing powerful and unmistakable traces of enchantment." McCarraher, "The Enchantments of Mammon," 430.

cause—but the efficacy here is inner; we are, in the best case, "transformed" psychologically; we come out feeling more dedicated (...) The "symbol" now invokes in the sense that it awakens the thought of the meaning in us. We are no longer dealing with a real presence. We can now speak of an act as "only symbolic."[27]

It may indeed be the case that people describe such actions as "only symbolic." They may regard the flag as only a piece of cloth, and the national anthem as only a song. What matters, however, is not their description of their own inner experiences, but what they do with their bodies, especially during wartime. If someone is willing to kill for flag and country, then it is manifestly not the case that, as Taylor puts it, "the efficacy here is inner." It is more accurate to say that sacramentality has migrated from the church to the nation-state, and the real presence has moved from the Eucharist to the flag. The danger in misdescribing modernity as disenchanted is not merely academic but political. Describing patriotic rituals as "only symbolic" has the political effect of shielding nationalism from scrutiny. It allows a Christian to avoid seeing the potential conflicts between his allegiance to Christ and his allegiance to the nation. Christians can verbally affirm the real presence of Christ in the Eucharist and affirm that patriotic ritual is "only symbolic" *precisely so that* their actual behavior can affirm the opposite.

Nationalism is alive and well in the United States but faded in Europe in the latter part of the twentieth century. Though national feeling is not absent from the contemporary welfare state, the emphasis is not on collective self-assertion but on providing for the self-realization of the individual. In Sweden, the welfare state is founded on what Lars Trägårdh has called "the Swedish theory of love" which "posits that all forms of dependency corrupt true love. Only mutual autonomy can guarantee authenticity and honesty in human relationships."[28] According to Trägårdh and Henrik Berggren, Swedish social policy is marked by the moral imperative to liberate the individual from all forms of subordination and dependency: "the poor from charity, the workers from their employers, wives from their husbands, children from parents (and vice versa when parents have become elderly)."[29] The price of such liberation is dependency on the state; as Berggren and Trägårdh note "the powers given to the state to emancipate the individual

---

27. Taylor, "Western Secularity," 51.
28. Berggren and Trägårdh, "Pippi Longstocking," 12–13.
29. Ibid., 13.

make that same individual powerless against the state."[30] The power of the state has grown in order to check the power of intermediate bodies like unions and the family. The result is a society characterized, according to Berggren and Trägårdh, by both the assertion of individual autonomy and a conformist social order.

Despite the common stereotype of Swedes as socialists and Americans as individualistic cowboys, Berggren and Trägårdh argue that Sweden is much more consistent in its embrace of individualism. Whereas in the United States the value of protecting families and intermediate associations against interference from the state is sometimes recognized, Sweden tends to protect children's rights over against the interference of parents. This is institutionalized in policies regarding adoption, divorce, day care, taxation, student loans, and other provisions that cut the family out from mediating the relationship between state and individual.[31] The long suspicion of and resistance to religious free schools in Sweden is likewise based on the notion that parents have a limited right to impose their beliefs on their children. These policies make Sweden and the rest of Scandinavia, in Berggren's and Trägårdh's words, "the least family-oriented and most individualized societies on the face of the earth."[32] We should note that, in this sense, the welfare state is the mirror image of libertarianism; both seek to liberate the individual from personal dependence on others.

Again, however, this ideology was not simply imposed from the top-down by social engineering, and it was not anti-Christian in its original inspiration. Berggren and Trägårdh argue that individualism and egalitarianism are deeply-rooted in Lutheran yeoman culture, which has a long history of self-reliance and resistance to the aristocracy.[33] Whatever the particulars of Swedish social history, it is not difficult to see the influence of Christianity in the impulse to make sure that each person is respected and taken care of. As the quote from Erling Olsen with which I started this chapter has it, the welfare state is simply the attempt to institutionalize the Gospel imperative to love your neighbor as yourself.

30. Ibid., 15.

31. Ibid., 16–22. An example of this dynamic in another context is the 2012 German court decision outlawing the circumcision of children, because it alters their bodies without their informed consent; "German court outlaws religious circumcision," http://www.theglobeandmail.com/news/world/german-court-outlaws-religious-circumcision/article4371222/. The decision was eventually overruled by the German parliament.

32. Berggren and Trägårdh, "Pippi Longstocking," 19.

33. Ibid., 13–14.

William T. Cavanaugh—*Eucharistic Identity in Modernity*

The unfairly neglected thinker Ivan Illich has made the case that the modern era is best understood not as the rejection of Christianity but its perversion. *Corruptio optimi quae est pessima*: the corruption of the best is the worst. What is best about Christianity is the absolutely unprecedented incarnation of God in particular human flesh. God's enfleshment in Christ extends outward from Christ to all humanity through the body of Christ, the church that is gathered into Christ's body by the consumption of Christ's body in the Eucharist. For Illich, the parable of the Good Samaritan illustrates the new kind of relationship that is made possible by the enfleshment of God. The Samaritan acts out of a spontaneous freedom, not from obedience to a generalizable rule. Rather than obey the normal *ethos* of attending only to those belonging to one's own *ethnos*, one's own people, the Samaritan recognizes the wounded Jew as his neighbor. What is most important about this episode for Illich is that the Samaritan was not responding to some categorical imperative for the treatment of others. He was responding to a concrete, embodied human being, moved by what Luther called a *jammer* in his gut. It was not in obedience to an *ought* that the Samaritan acted, but in response to a call from another human being's fleshly need. It was intended to venture a relatedness to the other person, a relatedness that could only be established if the Jew could recognize the action as gratuitous, not obligatory.[34]

For Illich, the Good Samaritan is not merely an individual exemplar. He serves as a sign of what Jesus wants the church to become: a network of personal relations that crosses human-made boundaries but does not obliterate differences.[35] This body of people, the church, is a "skein of relations,"[36] not a grouping of people around certain shared characteristics. It is furthermore not a mere human invention but the extension of the Incarnation, the enfleshment of God which changed everything. In Illich's words

> I believe, as I hope you do, in a God who is enfleshed, and who has given the Samaritan, as a being drowned in carnality, the possibility of creating a relationship by which an unknown, chance encounter becomes for him the reason for his existence, as he

---

34. Illich, *The Rivers North of the Future*, 206–7, 222.

35. Ibid., 197–99. According to Illich, in the Good Samaritan parable Jesus disrupts the Greek idea of friendship, in which one could only be friends with one's social equals. For Jesus, one can be friends with anyone one chooses to befriend; ibid., 147.

36. This phrase is Charles Taylor's, from the Foreword to Illich's book, p. xii.

Part Four—"Love Your Neighbor"

> becomes the reason for the other's survival—not just in a physical sense, but a deeper sense, as a human being. This is not a spiritual relationship. This is not a fantasy. This is not merely a ritual act which generates a myth. This is an act which prolongs the Incarnation. Just as God became flesh and in the flesh relates to each one of us, so you are capable of relating in the flesh, as one who says ego, and when he says ego, points to an experience which is entirely sensual, incarnate, and this-worldly, to that other man who has been beaten up.[37]

The Eucharist is the action by which the Spirit gathers this community; it prolongs the Incarnation by making the body of Christ through people sharing and eating Christ's flesh.[38] According to Illich's teacher Gerhart Ladner, the possibility in history of making community outside the community into which one was born was established by the Eucharistic celebrations of the early Christians.[39]

For Illich, modernity is best understood as a process of disembodiment, one of the trajectories of which he also traces back to Berengar.[40] Disembodiment comes in the distancing of personal relations and spontaneity via the institutionalization of care for others in the modern state.[41] "Take away the fleshly, bodily, carnal, dense, humoural experience of self, and therefore of the Thou, from the story of the Samaritan and you have a nice liberal fantasy, which is something horrible. You have the basis on which one might feel responsible for bombing the neighbour for his own good."[42] One thinks here of Paul Ramsey's defense of the just war tradition by using the parable of the Good Samaritan:

> It was a work of charity for the Good Samaritan to give help to the man who fell among thieves. But one step more, it may have been a work of charity for the innkeeper to hold himself ready

---

37. Ibid., 207.
38. Ibid., 142–43.
39. Ibid., 216–17.
40. Ibid., 208. Illich finds it remarkable that no one, it seems, in a thousand years of Christian life before Berengar had a problem with eating the flesh of Christ, but it suddenly became a problem in the eleventh century. The fact that "How can this be Christ's flesh when it looks so much like bread?" only became a problem in the High Middle Ages suggests the beginning of a process of disembodiment, according to Illich.
41. "Western democratic ideas are an attempt to institutionalize an 'ought' which by its very nature is a personal, intimate, and individual vocation." Ibid., 191.
42. Ibid., 207.

> to receive beaten and wounded men, and for him to conduct his business so that he was solvent enough to extend credit to the Good Samaritan. By another step it would have been a work of charity, and not of justice alone, to maintain and serve in a police patrol on the Jericho road to prevent such things from happening. By yet another step, it might well be a work of charity to resist, by force of arms, any external aggression against the social order that maintains the police patrol along the road to Jericho. This means that, where the enforcement of an ordered community is not effectively present, it may be a work of justice and a work of social charity to resort to other available and effective means of resisting injustice: what do you think Jesus would have made the Samaritan do if he had come upon the scene while the robbers were still at their fell work?[43]

Ramsey illustrates here the step-by-step process from which one moves from love of one's enemy to the justification of war.

Ramsey recognizes that "this is no proper way to interpret a parable of Jesus," but he does consider the step-by-step process he describes as exhibiting the perfectly justifiable process by which a social ethic emerged from the revelation of Jesus.[44] The process, in other words, is not merely one of secularization in the sense of the marginalization of Christian ideals. Illich argues that it is rather the corruption of Christian ideals. Christ has expanded the scope of love beyond one's own *ethnos*, but this results in an impulse to universalize, generalize, and institutionalize that eventually ends in a disembodied, rule-bound ethic and the abstract legalism that characterizes the modern state.[45] This legalism Illich traces back to the centralization of the church bureaucracy in the High Middle Ages, the institution of compulsory confession, and the institutionalization of Christian charity. Illich does not simply reject all institutions, but he pleads for a stronger resistance to their depersonalizing effects. He never renounced his Catholic priesthood and believed that the church was Christ's body, but he also recognized that the risk of incarnation was precisely that God would get mixed up in a fallen world.[46] When Christian charity is secularized, in

---

43. Ramsey, *The Essential Paul Ramsey*, 62.

44. Ibid., 62. The implication, of course, is that Jesus himself did not have a social ethic.

45. Ibid., 144–45.

46. Ibid., 179.

the precise sense of its transfer from church to civil control, the risk that the Spirit of Jesus will be disembodied and lost is magnified.

THE EUCHARIST AND THE STATE

The welfare state can be understood as the attempt to institutionalize care and respect for the individual other, regardless of his or her belonging to any other community, the respect for the other as human being. The goal of the welfare state is independence. The Good Samaritan story, on the other hand, illustrates a care that is personal and interdependent. The Samaritan recognizes that his own life is found in the wounded Jew to whom he attends. The welfare state liberates the individual from dependence upon others by creating a direct relationship of dependence between the individual and the state. The individual relates to the state as spokes on a wheel; as one departs from the center, individuals get increasingly distant from each other. Just as in Michel Foucault's image of the Panopticon, individuals relate to the center but this very relationship cuts them off from one another. The result I think can best be understood as a distortion of a Eucharistic body. If we follow the trajectory of the various mutations of the Eucharist and social bodies that I have traced here, we can see that care for the other regardless of her or his *ethnos* has been transmuted into the creation of the other as generic individual. Because the individual has been rendered interchangeable and generic—as in John Rawls' famous image of the individual standing behind a "veil of ignorance"—the modern project becomes to liberate individuals from each other. This is not, however, a return to the autonomous individual in the state of nature; a body of sorts is created, the nation-state, onto which new kinds of identity and belonging are projected. The relationship of the individual to the center means both that international forms of belonging are truncated, and that local forms of belonging are superseded.

What would an authentic Eucharistic sociality look like in today's world? Let me say first that there can be no thought of turning back the clock, a romanticism for the medieval period that was in fact riven with static social hierarchies. We can tell no simple Fall narrative of a Golden Age that was. Nor can we hope to smash the state in some grand revolutionary gesture without inviting a worse violence than that of the status quo we rightly decry. What we can do is to turn to what is at the heart of Christian sociality, our call into the Body of Christ, and build communities that offer the world a more personalized practice of social life. Here our guide can be Matthew 25, where the encounter with the one who suffers is an encounter not with a generic other but with Christ himself. Our guide is also I Corinthians 12, where the encounter with Christ incorporates us into a new sociality. We meet Christ in the individual other only to be pulled into the Other's own body, which is none other than the Body of Christ. Independence is seen for what it is: it is not only undesirable, it is a myth, an untruth. We belong to one another because we belong to Christ. We share the same feet and hands, the same nervous system, such that when one suffers, all suffer together, and when one rejoices, all rejoice together. Diversity is not therefore diminished, but is rather promoted, for it is precisely our differences that make us indispensable to one another. The hand cannot say to the foot "I have no need of you" precisely because the hand is not a foot, and the hands need feet to do the walking. This is the kind of body that the Eucharist calls us into. We eat Christ and are thereby eaten by Christ, incorporated into His body with people who may not even know that they too are members of Christ's body.

This last point needs to be underscored. All are members or potential members of the cosmic Christ. The body of Christ is only fully realized eschatologically; the borders of the body are not coterminous with the borders of the institutional church. The church *in via* is full of the world and is never sure of its own boundaries. The Eucharist is not primarily about the peripheries of the church but rather its center. Indeed, the spatial language is misleading. State and Eucharist are not separate spaces but different enacted stories about the ends of human life. The danger of the state is not simply that it will accrue too much power vis-à-vis the church, but that the story it will tell about human sociality is that the best we can do is to be independent of one another.

In the most recent U.S. presidential election (2012), one of the two Catholic candidates for vice-president—Paul Ryan—put forth a vision of a greatly reduced welfare state, while leaving the military intact. Although Ryan occasionally cited the Catholic social teaching on subsidiarity to add legitimacy to his plan, his main intellectual inspiration appears to have been Ayn Rand, the radical libertarian whose "objectivist" philosophy strived for an absolute independence of each individual from the state and from each other.[47] Ryan's budget plan was rightly critiqued by the U.S. Conference of

---

47. In 2005, Ryan said "[T]he reason I got involved in public service, by and large, if I had to credit one thinker, one person, it would be Ayn Rand. And the fight we are in here, make no mistake about it, is a fight of individualism versus collectivism." He frequently

Part Four—"Love Your Neighbor"

Catholic Bishops for failing to protect the poor, to share sacrifice across social classes, and to consider cuts to military spending.[48] Feeding the hungry is a good. Government food stamp programs help people who need help. What the bishops need to say more clearly is that food stamps and similar programs are a lesser good than direct personal care of people for one another. Shared sacrifice should begin at the local level—in the churches especially—as they reach out at a personal level to people who suffer. Addressing social problems begins with getting our story right. Our ultimate goal is not to be independent from one another, but neither is it for an impersonal bureaucracy to take care of those who are vulnerable. Our goal is to be members of one another, to suffer and rejoice together. Government aid is a safety net; it is not the Kingdom of God.

The story I have told of the Eucharist and the state is not merely a history lesson. If Christ lives then the Eucharist is still the beating heart of our social existence, the truest way we know of relating to one another. The church can no longer impose its discipline on society, thanks be to God. The modern state has liberated the church from the means of coercion, and has imposed a kind of formal equality of individuals that has done away with static social hierarchies. It has institutionalized, imperfectly, the care for others. These we can celebrate as goods, and as in some ways the outworking of the Gospel. But the Gospel is corrupted if all we can hope for is independence from one another and, ultimately, from God. The best we Christians can do in response is to build personal forms of community that enact the Body of Christ, here and now, and invite others to taste and see.

---

gave copies of Rand's writings to his staffers and urged them to read them. During the 2012 election campaign, however, Ryan attempted to distance himself from Rand and tried to emphasize the Catholic nature of his thought. When asked about Rand, Ryan said "I reject her philosophy. It's an atheist philosophy. It reduces human interactions down to mere contracts and it is antithetical to my worldview. If somebody is going to try to paste a person's view on epistemology to me, then give me Thomas Aquinas." Few found his late appeal to Aquinas convincing. See Jane Mayer, "Ayn Rand Joins the Ticket," *The New Yorker*, August 11, 2012.

48. United States Conference of Catholic Bishops, "Federal Budget Choices Must Protect Poor, Vulnerable People, Says U.S. Bishops' Conference," April 17, 2012. Ninety faculty members of Georgetown University also wrote an open letter to Ryan, stating "In short, your budget appears to reflect the values of your favorite philosopher, Ayn Rand, rather than the Gospel of Jesus Christ." The letter can be found at https://docs.google.com/document/d/1JRLM7Jh9PnrxptafWYENXdAmxnXd4gQJMYTu3H4TFHA/edit?pli=1.

Bibliography

Åberg, Bengt. *Individualitet och Universalitet hos Waldemar Rudin*. Stockholm: Verbum, 1968.
Adams, Nicholas. "Reasoning in Tradition." In *The Blackwell Companion to Christian Ethics*, edited by Stanley Hauerwas and Samuel Wells, 209–221. Oxford: Blackwell Publishing, 2004.
Ahrén, Per-Olov. *Nattvardsgudstjänsten i Svenska Missionsförbundet*. Stockholm: Gummessons bokförlag, 1966.
Åkesson, Jimmie. "Jimmie Åkessons talmanus sommartal 2013-08-24 Sölvesborg," https://sverigedemokraterna.se/?p=12749.
Ambjörnsson, Ronny. *Den skötsamme arbetaren: idéer och ideal i ett norrländskt sågverkssamhälle 1880–1930*. Stockholm: Carlsson, 1998.
Ambjörnsson, Ronny, and Ralph Carrigan. *The Honest and Diligent Worker*. Stockholm: HLS (Högsk. för lärarutbilning), 1991.
Anderson, Benedict. *Imagined Communities: Reflections on the Origin and Spread of Nationalism*. London: Verso, 1983.
Anderson, Braden P. *Chosen Nation: Scripture, Theopolitics, and the Project of National Identity*. Eugene, OR: Cascade Books, 2012.
Anheier, Helmut and Lester M. Salamon. "The Nonprofit Sector in Comparative Perspective." In *The Nonprofit Sector: A Research Handbook*, 2nd ed., edited by Walter W. Powell and Richard Steinberg, 89–114. New Haven: Yale University Press, 2006.
Aurelius Haettner, Eva. "The Language of Desire and Feelings is the Language of Truth." No pages. Online: http://nordicwomensliterature.net/article/language-desire-and-feelings-language-truth.
Balmer, Randall. *The Making of Evangelicalism*. Waco: Baylor University Press, 2010.
Bass, Diana Butler. *The Practicing Congregation: Imagining a New Old Church*. Herndon, VA: Alban Institute, 2004.
Bass, Dorothy C. *Practicing Our Faith: A Way of Life for a Searching People*. San Francisco, CA: Jossey-Bass, 1997.
Bass, Dorothy C., and Craig R. Dykstra. *For Life Abundant: Practical Theology, Theological Education, and Christian Ministry*. Grand Rapids: Eerdmans, 2008.
Bebbington, David. *The Dominance of Evangelicalism: The Age of Spurgeon and Moody*. Downers Grove, IL: InterVarsity, 2005.
———. *Evangelicalism in Modern Britain: A History from the 1730s to the 1980s*. London: Routledge, 2000.
Beck, Ulrich. *The Risk Society: Towards a New Modernity*. London: Sage, 1992.
Bell, Daniel M. *Liberation Theology after the End of History: The Refusal to Cease Suffering*. London: Routledge, 2001.

Bibliography

Berggren, Henrik. *Seklets ungdom: retorik, politik och modernitet 1900–1939*. Stockholm: Tiden, 1995.

Berggren, Henrik, and Lars Trägårdh. *Är svensken människa? Gemenskap och oberoende i det moderna Sverige*. Stockholm: Norstedts, 2006.

———. "Pippi Longstocking: The Autonomous Child and the Moral Logic of the Swedish Welfare State." In *Swedish Modernism: Architecture, Consumption and the Welfare State*, edited by Helena Matsson and Sven-Olov Wallenstein, 10–23. London: Black Dog, 2010.

Bergström, Lena. *Att ge plats för en annan: Om andlighet, föräldraskap och vardagsliv*. Örebro: Cordia, 2002.

Bevans, Stephen B., and Roger P. Schroeder. *Constants in Context: A Theology of Mission for Today*. Maryknoll, NY: Orbis, 2004.

Bexell, Oloph. *Sveriges kyrkohistoria, vol. 7: Folkväckelsens och kyrkoförnyelsens tid*. Stockholm: Verbum, 2003.

Bieber Lake, Christina. *The Incarnational Art of Flannery O'Connor*. Macon, GA: Mercer University Press, 2005.

Billing, Einar. *De heligas gemenskap*. Uppsala: Sveriges kristliga studentrörelse, 1911.

———. *Den svenska folkkyrkan*. Stockholm: Sveriges kristliga studentrörelses förlag, 1930.

———. *Kyrka och stat i vårt land i detta nu*. Stockholm: Sveriges kristliga studentrörelses bokförlag, 1942.

———. *Vår kallelse*. Stockholm: Sveriges kristliga studentrörelses bokförlag, 1956 (1909).

Blückert, Kjell. "Att erövra folket: Folkhem och folkkyrka som metaforer för hegemoni." In *Mångkulturalitet och folkligt samarbete*, edited by Krister Ståhlberg, 89–98. København: Nordisk Ministerråd, 2001.

———. *The Church as Nation: A Study in Ecclesiology and Nationhood*. Frankfurt am Main: Lang, 2000.

Boersma, Hans. *Heavenly Participation: The Weaving of a Sacramental Tapestry*. Grand Rapids: Eerdmans, 2011.

Boëthius, Ulf. *När Nick Carter drevs på flykten: kampen mot "smutslitteraturen" i Sverige 1908–1909*. Stockholm: Gidlund, 1989.

Bossy, John. *Christianity in the West 1400–1700*. Oxford: Oxford University Press, 1985.

———. "The Mass as a Social Institution, 1200–1700." *Past and Present* 100 (1983) 29–61.

Botvar, Pål Ketil, and Ulla Schmidt. *Religion i dagens Norge: Mellom sekularisering og sakralisering*. Oslo: Universitetsforlaget, 2010.

Bourdieu, Pierre. *Outline of a Theory of Practice*. Cambridge: Cambridge University Press, 1977.

Bradley, David. "Family Laws and Welfare States." In *The Nordic Model of Marriage and the Welfare State*, edited by Kari Melby et al. Copenhagen: Nordic Council of Ministers, 2000.

Brakke, David. *The Gnostics: Myth, Ritual, and Diversity in Early Christianity*. Cambridge: Harvard University Press, 2012.

Branch, Lori. *Rituals of Spontaneity: Sentiment and Secularism from Free Prayer to Wordsworth*. Waco: Baylor University Press, 2006.

Brauer, Jerald C. "Conversion: From Puritanism to Revivalism." *The Journal of Religion* 58:3 (1978) 227–243.

Carlsson, Carl-Gustav. *Människan, samhället och Gud: grunddrag i Lewi Pethrus kristendomsuppfattning*. Lund: Lund University Press, 1990.

Bibliography

Cavanaugh, William T. *Being Consumed: Economics and Christian Desire*. Grand Rapids: Eerdmans, 2008.

———. "Eucharistic Sacrifice and the Social Imagination in Early Modern Europe," *Journal of Medieval and Early Modern Studies* 31:3 (2001) 585–605.

———. "The Food that Perishes and the Food that Endures." Lecture given at Korsvei summer camp, Seljord, Norway, July 16, 2013.

———. "Killing for the Telephone Company: Why the Nation-state Is Not the Keeper of the Common Good." *Modern Theology* 20:2 (2004) 243–74.

———. *Migrations of the Holy: God, State, and the Political Meaning of the Church*. Grand Rapids: Eerdmans, 2011.

———. "Separation and Wholeness: Notes on the Unsettling Political Presence of the Body of Christ." In *For the Sake of the World. Swedish Ecclesiology in Dialogue with William T. Cavanaugh*, edited by Jonas Ideström, 7–31. Eugene, OR: Pickwick Publications, 2010.

———. *Theopolitical Imagination: Discovering the Liturgy as a Political Act in an Age of Global Consumerism*. New York: T. & T. Clark, 2002.

———. *Torture and Eucharist: Theology, Politics, and the Body of Christ*. Oxford: Blackwell, 1998.

Cedersjö, Björn. *Bortom syndakatalogen: En studie av svensk frikyrklig etik från 1930-talet till 1990-talet*. Lund Studies in Ethics and Theology 10. Örebro: Libris, 2001.

Chesterton, G. K. *Orthodoxy*. London: Lane, 1909.

Childs, Marquis. *Sweden: The Middle Way*. New Haven: Yale University Press, 1936.

Chilo. "ÖM:s 12 riksläger—en mäktig högtid." *Missionsbaneret*, July 1, 1943.

Claesson, Urban. *Folkhemmets kyrka: Harald Hallén och folkkyrkans genombrott: En studie av socialdemokrati, kyrka och nationsbygge med särskild hänsyn till perioden 1905–1933*. Uppsala : Uppsala University, 2004.

Clark, Francis. *Eucharistic Sacrifice and the Reformation*. 2nd ed. Oxford: Blackwell, 1967.

Cross, Richard. "'Where Angels Fear to Tread': Duns Scotus and Radical Orthodoxy." *Antonianum* 76 (2001) 7–41.

Cross, Whitney R. *The Burned-over District: The Social and Intellectual History of Enthusiastic Religion in Western New York, 1800–1850*. Ithaca: Cornell University Press, 1950.

Curtis, Heather D. *Faith in the Great Physician: Suffering and Divine Healing in American Culture, 1860–1900*. Baltimore: Johns Hopkins University Press, 2007.

Dahlqvist, Hans. "Folkhemsbegreppet: Rudolf Kjellén vs. Per-Albin Hansson." *Historisk Tidsskrift* 122 (2002) 446–463.

Dayton, Donald. *Discovering an Evangelical Heritage*. New York: Harper & Row, 1976.

———. *Theological Roots of Pentecostalism*. 2nd ed. Peabody, MA: Hendrickson, 2000.

Deminger, Sigfrid. *Kejsarens pengar och Guds: En debattbok om de ekonomiska relationerna mellan trossamfunden och staten*. Örebro: Libris, 1971.

———. "Sätt in statsbidraget i dess rätta sammahang." 9 December, 1971.

Drescher, Elizabeth. "Practicing Church: Vernacular Ecclesiologies in Late Medieval England." PhD diss., Graduate Theological Union, 2008.

Dreyer, Elisabeth. *Earth Crammed with Heaven: A Spirituality of Everyday life*. New York: Paulist, 1994.

Duffy, Eamon. *The Stripping of the Altars: Traditional Religion in England 1400–1580*. 2nd ed. New Haven: Yale University Press, 2005.

Bibliography

Eckerdal, Jan. *Folkkyrkans kropp: Einar Billings ecklesiologi i postsekulär belysning.* Skellefteå: Artos, 2012.

Edwards, Jonathan. *A Treatise Concerning Religious Affections.* Philadelphia: James Crissy, 1821.

Ellis, Christopher J. *Gathering: A Theology and Spirituality of Worship in the Free Church Tradition.* London: SCM, 2004.

En Jesu vän. "Till unga nyomvända." *Missionsbaneret,* March 9, 1939.

Ericson, Eric A. "Gud ledde denna vecka." *Missionsbaneret,* July 25, 1935.

Ericson, Per. "Varningsord om Kejsarens pengar och Guds." *Svenska Dagbladet,* February 9, 2004.

F. G. "Ungdomshögtid i Örnsköldsvik." *Missionsbaneret,* August 26, 1943.

Fahlgren, Sune. "Baptismens spiritualitet—speglad i gudsdtjänstlivet: Svenskt perspektiv." In *Samfund i förändring: baptistisk identitet i Norden under ett och ett halvt sekel,* edited by David Lagergren, 104–14. Tro & liv Skriftserie. Stockholm: Tro & liv, 1997.

———. "Frikyrkligt gudstjänstliv." In *I Enhetens Tecken: Gudsjänsttraditioner och Gudstjänstens förnyelse i svenska kyrkor och samfund,* edited by Sune Fahlgren and Rune Klingert, 179–92. Örebro: Bokförlaget Libris, 1994.

———. *Predikantskap och församling: Sex fallstudier av en ecklesial baspraktik inom svensk frikyrklighet fram till 1960-talet.* Örebro: Libris bokhandel, 2006.

Faithful Cities: A Call for Celebration, Vision and Justice. Peterborough: Methodist Publishing House, 2006.

Fiddes, Paul. "Ecclesiology and Ethnography: Two Disciplines, Two Worlds?" In *Perspectives on Ecclesiology and Ethnography,* edited by Pete Ward, 13–35. Grand Rapids: Eerdmans, 2012.

Finney, Charles G. *Lectures on Revivals of Religion.* London: Fleming H. Revell, 1940

Folkkyrkan och den frikyrkliga församlingsprincipen: Diskussion å Uppsala kristliga studentförbund den 6 mars 1912. Uppsala: Lindblad, 1912.

Foster, Richard J. *Freedom of Simplicity.* San Francisco: Harper & Row, 1981.

Foucault, Michel. *Discipline and Punish: The Birth of the Prison.* New York: Vintage, 1995.

Frykman, Jonas. *Dansbaneeländet: ungdomen, populärkulturen och opinionen.* Stockholm: Natur och kultur, 1988.

———. *Modärna tider: vision och vardag i folkhemmet.* Malmö: Liber Förlag, 1985.

Gadamer, Hans-Georg. *Wahrheit und Methode: Grundzüge einer philosophischen Hermenutik.* Tübingen: J. C. B. Mohr, 1990.

"German Court Outlaws Religious Circumcision," *The Globe and Mail,* June 26, 2012, http://www.theglobeandmail.com/news/world/german-court-outlaws-religious-circumcision/article4371222/.

Gordon, A. J. *The Twofold Life: Or, Christ's Work for Us and Christ's Work in Us.* London: Hodder & Stoughton, 1889.

Goss, Kristin A. "Civil Society and Civic Engagement: Towards a Multi-Level Theory of Policy Feedbacks." *Journal of Civil Society* 6:2 (2010) 119–43.

Gregory, Brad S. *The Unintended Reformation: How a Religious Revolution Secularized Society.* Cambridge: Harvard University Press, 2012.

Grell, Ole Peter. *The Scandinavian Reformation: From Evangelical Movement to Institutionalisation of Reform.* Cambridge: Cambridge University Press, 1995.

Gundry, Stanley N. *Love them In: The Life and Theology of D. L. Moody.* Chicago: Moody, 1999.

Bibliography

Gustafson, David M. *D. L. Moody and Swedes: Shaping Evangelical Identity among Swedish Mission Friends 1867–1899*. Linköping: Linköping University Press, 2008.

Gustafson, Emil. *Bref till nyomvända*. Kräcklinge: Betlehemsstjärnans, 1898.

———. *En konungs brud*. Kräklinge: Betlehemsstjärnans, 1898.

———. *Jag fann honom icke*. Kräcklinge: Betlehemsstjärnans, 1890.

Götestam, Freddy. "Det integrerar oss inte i statsapparaten." *Missionsbaneret*, October 28, 1971.

Hagman, Patrik. "Asceticism and Empire: Asceticism as Body-Politics in Isaac of Nineveh and Hardt & Negri." *Studia Theologica* 65:1 (2011) 39–53.

———. *The Asceticism of Isaac of Nineveh*. Oxford: Oxford University Press, 2010.

———. *Efter folkkyrkan: En teologi om kyrkan i det efterkristna samhället*. Skellefteå: Artos, 2013.

———. "Liturgi och asketism som motståndsyttringar i den tidiga kyrkan." In *Flumen Saxosum Sonans: Studia in Honorem Gunnar av Hällström*, edited by Marjo Ahlqvist et al., 27–40. Åbo: Åbo Akademis förlag, 2010.

———. *Om kristet motstånd*. Skellefteå: Artos, 2011.

———. "Post-Secularity and Post-Constantianism: The Case of the Evangelical Lutheran Church in Finland." In *Crisis and Change: Religion, Ethics and Theology Under Late Modern Conditions*, edited by Tage Kurtén and Jan-Olav Henriksen, 129–46. Newcastle Upon Tyne: Cambridge Scholars, 2012.

———. "To Travel in One Place: Openings for a New Asceticism in the Theology of Stanley Hauerwas." *Political Theology* 13:1 (2012) 93–109.

Hajnal, John. "European Marriage Pattern in Perspective." In *Population in History: Essays in Historical Demography*, edited by V. D. Glass and D. E. Eversley. London: Arnold, 1965.

Halldorf, Joel. *Av denna världen?: Emil Gustafson, moderniteten och den evangelikala väckelsen*. Skrifter utgivna av Svenska kyrkohistoriska föreningen. II, Ny Följd. Vol. 67. Skellefteå: Artos, 2012.

———. "Lewi Pethrus and the Creation of a Christian Counterculture." *Pneuma* 32:3 (2010) 354–68.

———. "Modernitet och katolicitet." *NOD: Forum för tro, kultur och samhälle* 9:2 (2012) 29–33.

Hallingberg, Gunnar. *Läsarna: 1800-talets folkväckelse och det moderna genombrottet*. Stockholm: Atlantis, 2010.

Hardt, Michael, and Antonio Negri. *Empire*. Cambridge: Harvard University Press, 2000.

Hauerwas, Stanley. *In Good Company: The Church as Polis*. Notre Dame, Ind.: University of Notre Dame Press, 1995.

Healy, Nicholas M. *Church, World and the Christian Life: Practical-Prophetic Ecclesiology*. Cambridge: Cambridge University Press, 2000.

"Helgelseförbundets kvartalsmöte." *Trons Segrar* 4 (1893) 127.

Hindmarsh, Bruce. *The Evangelical Conversion Narrative: Spiritual Autobiography in Early Modern England*. Oxford: Oxford University Press, 2005.

Hirdman, Yvonne. *Att lägga livet tillrätta: studier i svensk folkhemspolitik*. Maktutredningens publikationer. Stockholm: Carlsson, 1989.

Holmes, Stephen R. *Baptist Theology*. London: T. & T. Clark, 2012.

Hughes, Gerard W. *God in All Things: The Sequel to God of Surprises*. London: Hodder & Stoughton, 2003.

Huntford, Roland. *The New Totalitarians*. New York: Stein and Day, 1972.

Bibliography

Ideström, Jonas. *Lokal kyrklig identitet: En studie av implicit ecklesiologi med exemplet Svenska kyrkan i Flemingsberg*. Skellefteå: Artos, 2009.

Illich, Ivan. *The Rivers North of the Future: The Testament of Ivan Illich*. Edited by David Cayley. Toronto: Anansi, 2005.

Inglehart, Ronald, and Christian Welzel. *Modernization, Cultural Change, and Democracy: The Human Development Sequence*. Cambridge: Cambridge University Press, 2005.

Jacobsen, Douglas. *The World's Christians: Who They Are, Where They Are, and How They Got There*. Chichester: Wiley-Blackwell, 2011.

Janzon, Göran. *"Den andra omvändelsen": från svensk mission till afrikanska samfund på Örebromissionens arbetsfält i Centralafrika 1914–1962*. Örebro: Libris, 2008.

Jonas, Hans. *The Gnostic Religion: The Message of the Alien God and the Beginnings of Christianity*. Boston: Beacon, 1963.

Kant, Immanuel. *Werke VI*. Frankfurt am Main: Insel, 1964.

Kantorowicz, Ernst. *The King's Two Bodies: A Study in Medieval Political Theology*. Princeton: Princeton University Press, 1957.

Kaufman, Tone Stangeland. *A New Old Spirituality? A Qualitative Study of Clergy Spirituality in the Church of Norway*. Oslo: MF Norwegian School of Theology, 2011.

———. "Pastoral Spirituality in Everyday Life, in Ministry, and Beyond: Three Locations for a Pastoral Spirituality." *Journal of Religious Leadership* 12:2 (2013) 81–105.

Kennerberg, Owe. *Innanför eller utanför: En studie av församlingstukten i nio svenska frikyrkoförsamlingar*. Örebro: Libris, 1996.

King, Karen L. *What Is Gnosticism?* Cambridge: Harvard University Press, 2003.

Klinenberg, Eric. *Going Solo: The Extraordinary Rise and Surprising appeal of Living Alone*. New York: Penguin, 2012.

Kuhn, Thomas. *The Structure of Scientific Revolutions*. 3rd ed. Chicago: University of Chicago Press, 1996.

Kyrkoordning för Svenska kyrkan (Church Order, Church of Sweden). http://www.svenskakyrkan.se/default.aspx?id=637938.

Larsson, Mats. *De "riktigt kristna," deras "wänner" och "motståndare": en lokal- och frikyrkohistorisk studie av Askers baptistförsamlings identitet och mentalitet, 1858–1887*. Linköping: Linköping University Electronic Press, 2007.

Lasch, Christopher. *The Culture of Narcissism: American Life in an Age of Diminishing Expectations*. London: Abacus, 1982.

Lathrop, Gordon. *Holy People: A Liturgical Ecclesiology*. Minneapolis: Augsburg Fortress, 1999.

Leithart, Peter J. *Defending Constantine: The Twilight of an Empire and the Dawn of Christendom*. Downers Grove, IL: IVP Academic, 2010.

Lm, C.Th. "En tanke från Gud." *Missionsbaneret*, May 17, 1939.

Lockyer, Herbert. *All the Parables of the Bible*. Grand Rapids: Zondervan, 1988.

Lodberg, Peter, and Björn Ryman. "Church and Society." In *Nordic Folk Churches: A Contemporary Church History*, 99–121. Grand Rapids: Eerdmans, 2005.

Long, Stephen D. *Speaking of God: Theology, Language and Truth*. Grand Rapids: Eerdmans, 2009.

Louth, Andrew. *The Origins of the Christian Mystical Tradition: From Plato to Denys*. 2nd ed. Oxford: Oxford University Press, 2007.

Lubac, Henri de. *Corpus Mysticum: The Eucharist and the Church in the Middle Ages*. Notre Dame: University of Notre Dame Press, 2007.

Bibliography

Lumsden, James. *Sweden, Its Religious State and Prospects, With some Notices of the Revivals and Persecutions, which are at Present Taking Place in that Country.* London, 1855.

Luther, Martin. *A Treatise on the New Testament, that is, the Holy Mass.* Translated by Jeremiah J. Schindel. In vol. 35 of *Luther's Works*, edited by E. Theodore Bachmann. Philadelphia: Fortress, 1960.

MacIntyre, Alasdair. *After Virtue: A Study in Moral Theory.* 2nd ed. Notre Dame: Notre Dame University Press, 1984.

———. "Epistemological Crisis, Dramatic Narrative, and the Philosophy of Science." In *The Tasks of Philosophy: Selected Essays, Volume 1.* Cambridge: Cambridge University Press, 2006.

———. *Whose Justice? Which Rationality?* Notre Dame: Notre Dame University Press, 1988.

Maddox, Randy. *Responsible Grace: John Wesley's Practical Theology.* Nashville: Abingdon, 1994.

Magnusson, John. "Den troende ungdomen och de andliga livsfrågorna." *Missionsbaneret*, July 15, 1937.

Mauritz. "Juniorläger och midsommarkonferens för ungdom i Strömsholmstrakten." *Missionsbaneret*, July 16, 1942.

Mayer, Jane. "Ayn Rand Joins the Ticket." *The New Yorker*, August 11, 2012, http://www.newyorker.com/online/blogs/newsdesk/2012/08/paul-ryan-and-ayn-rand.html.

McCarraher, Eugene. "The Enchantments of Mammon: Notes Toward a Theological History of Capitalism." *Modern Theology* 21:3 (2005) 429–61.

McClintock Fulkerson, Mary. "Interpreting a Situation." In *Perspectives on Ecclesiology and Ethnography*, edited by Pete Ward, 124–44. Grand Rapids: Eerdmans, 2012.

McGinn, Bernard. "The Letter and the Spirit: Spirituality as an Academic Discipline." In *Minding the Spirit*, edited by Elizabeth A Dreyer, and Mark S. Burrows, 25–41. Baltimore: Johns Hopkins University Press, 2005.

McGinn, Bernard, John Meyendorff, and Jean Leclercq, eds. *Christian Spirituality: Origins to the Twelfth Century.* World Spirituality 16. London: Routledge & Kegan Paul, 1985.

McGrath, Alister. *A Scientific Theology: Nature.* London: T. & T. Clark, 2002.

Michelson, Rulle. "Junior och ungdomsläger i Målsta." *Missionsbaneret*, August 22, 1940.

Milbank, John. *Theology and Social Theory: Beyond Secular Reason.* 2nd ed. Oxford: Blackwell, 2006.

———. *The Word Made Strange: Theology, Language, Culture.* Cambridge: Blackwell, 1997.

Mitterrauer, Michael. *Ungdomstidens sociala historia.* Göteborg: Röda bokförlaget, 1998.

Murray, Andrew. *Holy in Christ.* London: James Nisbet, 1887.

Myrdal, Alva, and Gunnar Myrdal. *Kris i befolkningsfrågan.* Stockholm: Bonnier, 1934.

Netz, Nils. "Med blicken mot framtiden—ungdomsfrågor." *Missionsbaneret*, January 18, 1945.

Nilsson, Jan Olof. *Alva Myrdal: en virvel i den moderna strömmen.* Stockholm: B. Östlings bokförlag Symposion, 1994.

Noll, Mark. *The Rise of Evangelicalism: The Age of Edwards, Whitefield, and the Wesleys.* Downers Grove, IL: InterVarsity, 2003.

Olson, Hans-Erik. *Staten och ungdomens fritid: Kontroll eller autonomi?* Lund: Arkiv, 1992.

"Open Letter to Rep. Paul Ryan." https://docs.google.com/document/d/1JRLM7Jh9PnrxptafWYENXdAmxnXd4gQJMYTu3H4TFHA/edit?pli=1.

Bibliography

Pethrus, Lewi. *Samlade skrifter*. Vol. 5. Stockholm: Filadelfia, 1958.

———. *Samlade skrifter*. Vol. 6. Stockholm: Filadelfia, 1958.

Pickstock, Cathrine. "Duns Scotus: His Historical and Contemporary Significance." *Modern Theology* 21:4 (2005) 543–74.

Placher, William. C. *The Domestication of Transcendence: How Modern Thinking about God Went Wrong*. Louisville: Westminster John Knox, 1996.

Popenoe, David. *Disturbing the Nest: Family Change and Decline in Modern Societies*. New York: A. de Gruyter, 1988.

Putnam, Robert D. *Bowling Alone: The Collapse and Revival of American Community*. New York: Simon & Schuster, 2000.

Qvarsebo, Jonas. "Swedish Progressive School Politics and the Disciplinary Regime of the School, 1946–1962: A Genealogical Perspective." *Paedagogica Historica: International Journal of the History of Education* 49:2 (2012) 217–35.

Ragné, Ragnar. "Östersundslägret." *Missionsbaneret*, July 13, 1939.

———. "Vadstenalägret." *Missionsbaneret*, July 26, 1945.

Ramsey, Paul. *The Essential Paul Ramsey: A Collection*. Edited by William Werpehowski and Steven D. Crocco. New Haven: Yale University Press, 1994.

Randall, Ian. *What a Friend We Have in Jesus: The Evangelical Tradition*. London: Darton, Longman and Todd, 2005.

Red. "Är det synd att gå på bio?" *Missionsbaneret*, February 19, 1959.

———. "Domen över ungdomen." *Missionsbaneret*, August 13, 1942.

———. "Ungdomsarbetet III." *Missionsbaneret*, July 4, 1935.

Riesman, David. *The Lonely Crowd: A Study of the Changing American Character*. New Haven: Yale University Press, 1950.

Roberts, Michael. *Essays in Swedish History*. London: Weindenfeld and Nicolson, 1976.

Robertson, Darrel M. *The Chicago Revival, 1876: Society and Revivalism in a 19th Century City*. Metuchen, NJ: Scarecrow, 1989.

Rothstein, Bo. "Att administrera välfärdsstaten: Några lärdomar från Gustav Möller." *Arkiv för studier i arbetarrörelsens historia* 36/37 (1987) 68–84.

Ryle, John Charles. *A Call to Prayer*. New York: American Tract Society, 186–

Ryman, Björn. *Nordic Folk Churches: A Contemporary Church History*. Grand Rapids: Eerdmans, 2005.

Scharen, Christian B. *Explorations in Ecclesiology and Ethnography*. Grand Rapids: Eerdmans, 2012.

———. *Fatih as a Way of Life: A Vision for Pastoral Leadership*. Grand Rapids: Eerdmans, 2008.

Schatzki, Theodore R., Karin Knorr Cetina, and Eike von Savigny, eds. *The Practice Turn in Contemporary Theory*. London: Routledge, 2001.

Schneiders, Sandra M. "The Study of Christian Spirituality." *Studies in Christian Spirituality* 8 (1998) 38–57.

Sellerfors, Sven. "Några nyfrälsta ungdomars vittnesbörd." *Missionbaneret*. July 14, 1938.

Sergo. "Biografbesöket." *Missionsbaneret*, May 17, 1939.

Sernhede, Ove, et al. *Youth, Otherness and the Plural City: Modes of Belonging and Social Life*. Göteborg: Daidalos, 2005.

Sigurdson, Ola. "The Return of the Body: Re-imagining the Ecclesiology of Church of Sweden." In *For the Sake of the World. Swedish Ecclesiology in Dialogue with William T. Cavanaugh*, edited by Jonas Ideström, 125–45. Eugene, OR: Pickwick, 2010.

Bibliography

Smith, Christian, and Melinda Lundquist Denton. *Soul Searching: The Religious and Spiritual Lives of American Teenagers*. New York: Oxford University Press, 2010.

Smith, James K. A. *Who's Afraid of Postmodernism? Taking Derrida, Lyotard, and Foucault to Church*. Grand Rapids: Baker Academic, 2006.

Sollerman, Erik. "Den andliga utvecklingen i barn- och ungdomstid." *Missionsbaneret*, February 1, 1945.

———. "Trygghet i farornas värld." *Missionsbaneret*, July 12, 1945.

Sollerman, Josef. "De ungas plats i församlingen." *Missionsbaneret*, September 10, 1936.

SOU 1946:68. *Betänkande och förslag angående det fria och frivilliga folkbildningsarbetet del I, Allmänt folkbildningsarbete*.

Steane, Edward. *The Religious Condition of Christendom. 3rd Part*. London: Office of the Evangelical Alliance, 1859.

Sweeney, Douglas A. *The American Evangelical Story. A History of the Movement*. Grand Rapids: Baker Academic, 2005.

Taylor, Charles. *A Secular Age*. Cambridge: Harvard University Press, 2007.

———. *The Ethics of Authenticity*. Cambridge: Harvard University Press, 2003.

———. *The Sources of the Self: The Making of Modern Identity*. Cambridge: Harvard University Press, 1989.

———. "Western Secularity." In *Rethinking Secularism*, edited by Craig Calhoun et al. New York: Oxford University Press, 2011.

Thidevall, Sven. *Kampen om folkkyrkan: ett folkkyrkligt reformprograms öden 1928-1932*. Stockholm: Verbum, 2000.

Troeltsch, Ernst. *The Social Teaching of the Christian Churches*. London: George Allen & Unwin, 1950.

Trägårdh, Lars. "The 'Civil Society' Debate in Sweden: The Welfare State Challenged." In *State and Civil Society in Northern Europe: The Swedish Model Reconsidered*, edited by Lars Trägårdh, 9-36. New York: Berghahn, 2007.

———. "Democratic Governance and the Creation of Social Capital in Sweden: The Discreet Charm of Governmental Commissions." In *State and Civil Society in Northern Europe: The Swedish Model Reconsidered*, edited by Lars Trägårdh, 254-70. New York: Berghahn, 2007.

———. "The Historical Incubators of Trust in Sweden: From the Rule of Blood to the Rule of Law." In *Trust and Organization: Confidence across Borders*, edited by M. Reuter, F. Wijkström, and Bengt Kristensson Uggla, 181-204. London: Palgrave Macmillan, 2013.

———. "Rethinking the Nordic Welfare State Through a Neo-Hegelian Theory of State and Civil Society." *Journal of Political Ideologies* 15:3 (2010) 227-39.

———. "Rethinking the Position of Civil Society in the Nordic Social Contract: Social Trust and Radical Individualism." In *Nordic Civil Society at a Cross-Roads: Transforming the Popular Movement Tradition*, edited by Filip Wijkström and Annette Zimmer, 313-33. Baden-Baden: Nomos, 2011.

———. "Statist Individualism: On the Culturality of the Nordic Welfare State." In *The Cultural Construction of Norden*, edited by Bo Stråth and Øystein Sørensen, 253-85. Oslo: Scandinavian University Press, 1997.

Ungdomsvårdskommitténs betänkande I, med utredning och förslag angående psykisk barna- och ungdomsvård. Statens offentliga utredningar, 1944:30. Stockholm: Nordiska bokh. i distr., 1944.

Bibliography

Ungdomsvårdskommitténs betänkande II, med utredning och förslag angående stöd åt ungdomens föreningsliv. Statens offentliga utredningar, 1944:31. Stockholm: Nordiska bokh. i distr., 1944.
Ungdomsvårdskommitténs betänkande III, ungdomen och nöjeslivet. Statens offentliga utredningar, 1945:22. Stockholm: Nordiska bokh. i distr., 1945.
United States Conference of Catholic Bishops. "Federal Budget Choices Must Protect Poor, Vulnerable People, Says U.S. Bishops' Conference." April 17, 2012, http://www.usccb.org/news/2012/12-063.cfm.
Volf, Miroslav, and Dorothy C. Bass. *Practicing Theology: Beliefs and Practices in Christian Life*. Grand Rapids: Eerdmans, 2002.
Wacker, Grant. *Heaven Below: Early Pentecostals and American Culture*. Cambridge: Harvard University Press, 2003.
Walan, Bror. *Församlingstanken i Svenska missionsförbundet: en studie i den nyevangeliska rörelsens sprängning och Svenska missionsförbundets utveckling till o. 1890*. Stockholm: Gummesson, 1964.
Wallman Lundåsen, Susanne, and Lars Trägårdh. "Social Trust and Religion in Sweden: Theological Belief Verus Social Organization." In *Religion and civil society in Europe*, edited by Joep De Hart et al., 109–24. New York: Springer, 2013.
Ward, Graham. *The Politics of Discipleship: Becoming Postmaterial Citizens*. Grand Rapids: Baker Academic, 2009.
Ward, Pete. *Perspectives on Ecclesiology and Ethnography*. Grand Rapids: Eerdmans, 2012.
Ward, W. R. *Early Evangelicalism: A Global Intellectual History, 1670–1789*. Cambridge: Cambridge University Press, 2006.
Webber, Robert. *Ancient-Future Faith: Rethinking Evangelicalism for a Postmodern World*. Grand Rapids: Baker Academic, 1999.
Wenell, Fredrik. "Religion som politisk resurs: frikyrkorna i enhetsstatens skugga." In *Civilsamhället klämt mellan stat och kapital: välfärd, mångfald, framtid*, edited by Lars Trägårdh, et al. Stockholm: SNS förlag, 2013.
Westin, Gunnar. *Den kristna friförsamlingen genom tiderna: Martyrer och frihetskämpar*. Stockholm: Westerbergs, 1955.
Widmark, Henrik. "Space, Materiality and the Politics of Leaving: Church of Sweden and Rosengård's Social Segregation." In *For the Sake of the World: Swedish Ecclesiology in Dialogue with William T. Cavanaugh*, edited by Jonas Ideström, 49–64. Eugene, OR: Pickwick, 2010.
Williams, Anna. "Tradition." In *The Oxford Handbook of Systematic Theology*, edited by Kathryn Tanner et al. Oxford: Oxford University Press, 2009.
Williams, D. H. *Evangelicals and Tradition: The Formative Influence of the Early Church*. Grand Rapids: Baker Academic, 2005.
———. *Retrieving the Tradition and Renewing Evangelicalism*. Grand Rapids: Eerdmans, 1999.
Williams, Michael A. *Rethinking "Gnosticism": An Argument for Dismantling a Dubious Category*. Princeton: Princeton University Press, 1996.
Williams, Rowan. *Resurrection: Interpreting the Easter Gospel*. London: Darton, Longman and Todd, 2002.
Wirzba, Norman. *Food and Faith: A Theology of Eating*. Cambridge: Cambridge University Press, 2011.
Wuthnow, Robert. *After Heaven: Spirituality in America since the 1950s*. Berkeley: University of California Press, 1998.

Bibliography

Yoder, John Howard. *Body Politics: Five Practices of the Christian Community before the Watching World.* Nashville: Discipleship Resources, 1992.

———. *The Original Revolution: Essays on Christian Pacifism.* Scottdale, PA: Herald, 1972.

———. *The Royal Priesthood: Essays Ecclesiological and Ecumenical.* Grand Rapids: Eerdmans, 1994.

www.ingramcontent.com/pod-product-compliance
Lightning Source LLC
Chambersburg PA
CBHW051743230426
43670CB00012B/2136